European Culture and Society
General Editor: Jeremy Black

Published

Lesley Hall *Sex, Gender & Social Change in Britain since 1880*
Keith D. Lilley *Urban Life in the Middle Ages: 1000–1450*
Jerzy Lukowski *The European Nobility in the Eighteenth Century*
Neil MacMaster *Racism in Europe, 1870–2000*
Noël O'Sullivan *European Political Thought since 1945*
W. M. Spellman *European Political Thought 1600–1700*
Gary K. Waite *Heresy, Magic and Witchcraft in Early Modern Europe*
Diana Webb *Medieval European Pilgrimage, c. 700–c. 1500*

European Culture and Society Series
Series Standing Order
ISBN 0–333–74440–3
(outside North America only)

You can receive future titles in this series as they are published by placing a standing order. Please contact your bookseller or, in case of difficulty, write to us at the address below with your name and address, the title of the series and the ISBN quoted above.

Customer Services Department, Macmillan Distribution Ltd
Houndmills, Basingstoke, Hampshire RG21 6XS, England

EUROPEAN POLITICAL THOUGHT SINCE 1945

Noël O'Sullivan

palgrave
macmillan

First published 2004 by
PALGRAVE MACMILLAN
Houndmills, Basingstoke, Hampshire RG21 6XS and
175 Fifth Avenue, New York, N.Y. 10010
Companies and representatives throughout the world

PALGRAVE MACMILLAN is the global academic imprint of the Palgrave
Macmillan division of St. Martin's Press, LLC and of Palgrave Macmillan Ltd.
Macmillan® is a registered trademark in the United States, United Kingdom
and other countries. Palgrave is a registered trademark in the European
Union and other countries.

ISBN 0–333–65559–1 hardback
ISBN 0–333–65560–5 paperback

This book is printed on paper suitable for recycling and made from fully
managed and sustained forest sources.

A catalogue record for this book is available from the British Library.

A catalog record for this book is available from the Library of Congress.

10   9   8   7   6   5   4   3   2   1
13 12 11 10 09 08 07 06 05 04

Printed in China

In memoriam

MC
EK
MO

and for WW
Doctores sapientissimi

Contents

Acknowledgements   x

Preface   xi

1 The Postwar Agenda   **1**
The Limited State and the Problem
  of Moral Foundations   2
The Welfare State and the Problem of Growing
  Executive Power   7
From Social and Cultural Homogeneity to Radical
  Pluralism   10
The End of Eurocentric History and the Search
  for a European Political Identity   12
The Problem of Amnesia   16
Conclusion   19

2 British Political Thought since 1945:
The Limitations of Pragmatism   **20**
The British Left   23
Liberal and Conservative Visions of the
  Free Society   28
The Quest for a Rational Consensus   41
The Quest for a Non-Rationalist Consensus   43
Identity Politics: The Search for a Radical
  Pluralist Consensus   45
Multicultural Political Theory   48
Beyond Identity Politics: Republican Theory   54
The Politics of the Third Way   56

The Constitutional Issue, the Problem of British Identity
    and the European Union   58
Conclusion   62

3 **From Revolutionary Idealism to Political Moderation:
   The French Search for an Accommodation with
   Liberal Democracy since 1945**   **63**
   Radical Political Thought   64
   Towards a Non-Revolutionary Political Discourse   72
   Voices of Political Moderation   79
   Alain de Benoist and the Nouvelle Droite   85
   Towards a New French Liberalism?   86
   Conclusion   93

4 **Nationalism, Democracy and Unification in
   Postwar German Political Thought**   **95**
   The Allied Plans for a New German Identity   95
   Conservative Critics of the Federal Republic:
       Cultural Alienation and Political Impotence   97
   The Radical Critique of the New Democracy   105
   The Quest for a Moderate Consensus: Legal Rights,
       the Social Market Ideal and 'Constitutional
       Patriotism'   107
   Responses to Unification   116
   The Berlin Republic   123
   Conclusion   125

5 **In the Shadow of *The Prince*: Italian Political
   Thought since Liberation**   **126**
   The Failure of Postwar Crocean Liberalism   128
   The Identity Crisis of the Radical Left   131
   Antonio Negri and the New Left   135
   Conservative Responses to Postwar Italian Democracy   137
   Constitutionalism, Social Democracy and
       'Democratic Realism'   140
   The Extreme Right   144
   Postmodern Pluralism   146
   The New Italian Republic   149
   Conclusion   152

6 Political Thought in East-Central Europe:
   From Empires to the European Union   **155**
   The Critique of Totalitarianism   157
   Alternatives to Totalitarianism   167
   The Velvet Revolutions of 1989 and the Problem
      of Transition   174
   Conclusion   175

7 Towards a New Post-Democratic Agenda?   **178**
   The Nature of European Political Identity   181

Notes   190

Bibliography   218

Index   232

Acknowledgements

This is a rash enterprise, taken on in the face of a vast literature. For making it more manageable I am indebted to assistance from Roland Axtmann, Andrea Baumeister, Michael Burgess, Peter Glazer, Jack Hayward, the late Paul Hirst, Massimo la Torre and Colin Tyler, all of whom read and commented on drafts of various parts. Responsibility for what I made of things remains of course my own.

I owe an especially profound debt to conversations with Bhikhu Parekh. Our differences of opinion do not in any way reduce my indebtedness to him.

Terka Acton, the publisher at Palgrave, and Sonya Barker, the Assistant Editor, were always encouraging, especially at times when I thought I was losing my way.

Oxford University Press granted permission for me to rework some material previously published by them as part of Chapter 2. Likewise, Blackwell Publishing Ltd granted permission for me to rework material in an article on 'European Political Identity' published in the *Journal of Applied Philosophy*, vol. 27, no. 3, 2000 which I incorporated in the final chapter.

I could not have completed the book without teaching-leave awards from the British Academy and the Arts and Humanities Research Board, and matching periods of leave granted by Hull University. It is a pleasure to be able to record my gratitude to these institutions.

Preface

This book aims to be more than just a series of accounts of the highly disparate views of a large number of very different thinkers in different European countries about a vast range of social and political issues. Its approach is thematic, in the sense that it attempts to discern an overall unity in the complex course of European political thought since 1945. This unity does not consist in a set of common ideas or values which retain the same meaning regardless of national frontiers and despite the passage of time. No matter which ideas or values one turns to – ideas such as freedom, individuality, community, justice and nationality, for example – profound disagreement exists about their meaning, significance and desirability. The unity lies, rather, in the existence of a common postwar agenda to which thinkers in the main western European states have been compelled to respond, regardless of whether they favoured or opposed the items comprising it. The agenda will be considered more fully in the first chapter, but it will be useful to sketch its general nature briefly at the outset.

What shaped the postwar agenda was the decision to consolidate the defeat of totalitarianism by a major reconstruction of democracy made by all western European states, with the exception, initially at least, of Spain and Portugal. In Britain, it is true, the survival of the prewar constitution made the task of reconstruction less radical than it was on the Continent, but even there the demands of socialists, amongst others, left no doubt about the need for extensive restructuring of the state.

Although the reconstruction project was pursued in very diverse ways in different states, none of those which adopted it could avoid confronting four core items on the agenda which it involved. The first concerned the need to ensure that the postwar democratic state was a limited one securely based on the rights of the individual, in order to prevent any recurrence of totalitarianism. The second item concerned the need to ensure that postwar democracies ended the interwar fear of class conflict by creating a stable mass base through the provision of welfare as well as individual freedom. The failure of prewar democracies in this respect had meant that they were unable to dispel the suspicion that they were primarily concerned to protect the interest of property owners. The danger, however, was that the massive growth of executive power created by the pursuit of welfare would undermine the victory over totalitarianism by subverting the system of checks and balances on which limited politics had previously depended.

The third item was the need to create a more plural form of democracy in response to demands for recognition by various groups, such as women, who rejected the existing forms of toleration as too restrictive and condescending. As decades passed, the challenge of pluralism was to become increasingly radical, partly due to the influence of multiculturalism, but also due to the postmodern affir-mation of the claims of practically every form of difference. The question of how this challenge is to be accommodated remains, as in the case of the other items on the agenda, a matter for deep disagreement.

The fourth item involved deciding to what extent postwar democ-racies would remain sovereign nation-states in a new world order in which Europe no longer held the dominant position. Initially, the survival of the nation-state was generally taken for granted. By the end of the twentieth century, however, widespread doubts had emerged about the adequacy of the nation-state as the basic unit of European political life. These were reflected in attempts to revise the classical concept of state sovereignty which the postwar European world had inherited from the age of Bodin and Hobbes in ways that would take account of new sub- and supra-national forms of citizenship which some regarded as prefiguring a vastly extended kind of civil society, but which others saw as more likely to bring the erosion of freedom and democracy by a centralized bureaucracy.

It may be urged that there are other important items which should be included on the postwar agenda. Concern for the environment, for example, might be suggested as a notable candidate. Although an early postwar commitment to action on that issue would no doubt have been desirable, until the advent of the European Union a decision about whether to respond to it remained optional in a way which it was not in the case of the four items mentioned above. This qualification applies, I think, to any other themes that may be put forward for inclusion.

What must now be emphasized is that the postwar reconstruction project was constantly threatened with both theoretical and practical incoherence since the items comprising it were by no means compatible with each other. The rights stressed by the ideal of the limited state, for example, might threaten social solidarity; welfare provision might in turn threaten the limited state by encouraging planning on a scale that threatened to create a leviathan state; and European integration might destroy the democratic experience of self-government associated with the sovereignty of the nation-state. The search for a viable accommodation between the conflicting ideals on the democratic agenda – a search which has of course assumed different forms in different national traditions – is a primary concern of the book.

It remains to indicate briefly not only why the particular states selected were chosen but also how the choice of individual thinkers to be considered was made.

Since the principal concern of this study is with the European project of reconstructing the limited state on a more democratic and socially just basis after 1945, a criterion for determining which countries to include is implicit in the enterprise itself. Specifically, the European world can be analyzed in terms of a spectrum, on the eastern part of which the ideal of limited politics is either unknown (as in Russia), or weak, as in eastern Europe at large. At the opposite end of the spectrum, Britain, Germany, France and Italy all have long-established intellectual traditions in which the ideal is explored, although their degree of practical success in implementing it has of course varied considerably. It is for this reason that attention has been focused on them. Spain and Portugal have been omitted because their escape from authoritarian rule was relatively belated.

Between the extremes of the spectrum lie a number of countries which have had a moderately strong ideal of limited government, even if the implementation of it has generally been weak. Amongst them, Poland, the former Czechoslovakia and Hungary are the most notable. In particular, during the decades before the collapse of the Soviet empire in 1989 an impressive critical literature on totalitarianism was produced by émigrés from Poland, Czechoslovakia and Hungary. A chapter has been included on this literature, as well as on the course of debate about democratic reconstruction since liberation.

The final chapter identifies the main changes that occurred in the democratic agenda towards the end of the twentieth century, when globalization and European integration had come to dominate it. At that point, the central question facing European political thinkers was whether it was possible to develop a concept of European political identity which could preserve the ideal of the limited state in supra-national form, on the one hand, while also accommodating Europe's extreme cultural diversity, on the other. Whether such an identity can also ensure the survival of the democratic project itself, at a time when European institutions are notable for their lack of democratic legitimation, remains to be considered.

Having chosen the states to be considered and identified the overall agenda confronting them, the selection of individual thinkers was made with the intention of presenting a comprehensive portrait of the wide variety of responses to that agenda in the different European states. No attempt, it should be stressed, has been made to do justice to every aspect of the thinkers considered, since the primary concern is with the implications of their work for the agenda. Inevitably, therefore, some thinkers will have received more attention than scholars with a different interest would have given them, some will have received less, and some whom others would have included will not have been considered at all.

To attempt an overview of intellectual responses to the postwar European democratic project in both its earlier postwar stages and its later supra-national one seemed worthwhile because most of the available literature on the period since 1945 is relatively narrow in scope, focusing either on specific thinkers, or on particular topics and countries. There thus appeared to be a case for trying to bring the wood more clearly into view. If the book helps to clarify the agenda which has shaped debate during the postwar era, as well as indicating the principal strengths and weaknesses of the main responses to the items on it by most of the leading thinkers in the countries included, it will have served its purpose.

1

The Postwar Agenda

The end of the twentieth century was marked by a general mood of liberal triumphalism. The collapse of the Soviet empire, it seemed, meant that democracy had finally overcome the last of the ideological rivals which had previously challenged its claim to political hegemony. A contemporary historian has rightly observed, however, that complacency on this account is extremely dangerous, ignoring as it does the ambiguity of the modern western European political tradition and the fragility of the democratic system of government. What is ignored, in particular, is the fact that although democracy appeared to triumph in 1918, it

> was virtually extinct twenty years on...By the 1930s the signs were that most Europeans no longer wished to fight for it; there were dynamic non-democratic alternatives to meet the challenges of modernity. Europe found other, authoritarian, forms of political order no more foreign to its traditions...[1]

Even in the British case, so the American ambassador wrote in *The Times* in 1940, democracy was effectively finished.[2] Two years later, E. H. Carr expressed an equally bleak view, dismissing British democracy on the ground that it had failed to respond to the wider 'revolution of social and political order' which had given birth to totalitarian regimes like the Nazi one.[3]

After its near eclipse on the eve of the Second World War, democracy was rediscovered in 1945, revitalized 'by the challenge of war against Hitler, [and] newly conscious of its social responsibilities'.[4]

1

Having rediscovered democracy, however, western Europe faced an agenda on which two challenging items – the need to place the limited state on a secure basis, as well as creating a welfare structure which would give it a popular one – had to be confronted immediately. Two more were less pressing but acquired increasing urgency during subsequent decades. One was the need to make the structure of the democratic state more pluralist, in response to growing demands from minorities for recognition. The other was the need to adjust initially to a world order no longer dominated by Europe, and eventually to a globalized, post-Cold War order in which the advance of European unification made the nature of European political identity an issue of central significance.

The Limited State and the Problem of Moral Foundations

The most fundamental intellectual problem for postwar European political thinkers committed to the liberal-democratic ideal was to provide it with moral foundations which would be impervious to any resurgent totalitarian challenge. Although they disagreed about the meaning of the ideal itself, which was interpreted in very different ways in different national political traditions, as well as within each of them, there was widespread agreement that the issue of foundations must focus on the concept of human rights.

Chapter 1 of the German Basic Law of 1949, for example, reflected this agreement, being devoted to Basic Rights. It began by proclaiming that: 'The dignity of man is inviolable. To respect and protect it is the duty of all state authority.' The second article added that: 'The German people therefore acknowledge inviolable and inalienable human rights as the basis of every community, of peace, and of justice in the world.' In similar vein, Article 2 of the 1948 Italian constitution announced that: 'The Republic recognizes and guarantees the inviolable rights of man.' The opening words of the preamble to the French constitution of 1946 stated that 'On the morrow of the victory of the free peoples over the regimes that attempted to enslave and degrade the human person', the French people 'proclaim once more that every human being, without distinction as to race, religion or creed, possesses inalienable and sacred rights. They solemnly reaffirm the rights and freedoms of man and of the citizen ordained by the Declaration of

Rights of 1789 and the fundamental principles recognized by the laws of the Republic.'

Unfortunately, these confident proclamations of supposedly obvious truths about inalienable human rights were at odds with several striking features of western European culture in the postwar era. One was a growing doubt about the ability of reason to provide absolute, universally valid foundations for moral and political values. In Britain, Isaiah Berlin was one of the leading thinkers who continued to resist relativist tendencies. 'What has emerged from the recent holocausts?', he asked rhetorically in 1959, replying that the answer is 'Something approaching a new recognition in the West that there are certain universal values which can be called constitutive of human beings as such.'[5] Against Berlin, however, were ranged members of the British analytical school, whose positivist sympathies led its members to treat all values as subjective. As Bertrand Russell, one of the school's leading representatives, remarked, 'Whatever can be known, can be known by science; but things which are legitimately matters of feeling lie outside its scope.'[6]

British scepticism was further reinforced by the later work of Wittgenstein, which restricted the practical function of political philosophy to clarifying concepts by removing various misunderstandings of them that might get in the way of intelligent deliberation. This view received classic formulation not long after the Second World War in T. D. Weldon's *The Vocabulary of Politics* (1953). 'When verbal confusions are tidied up,' Weldon wrote, 'most of the questions of traditional political philosophy are not unanswerable. All of them are confused formulations of purely empirical difficulties. This does not mean that these are themselves easy to deal with, but it does mean that writers on political institutions and statesmen, not philosophers, are the proper people to deal with them.'[7]

On the Continent, a very different style of philosophizing prevailed, often characterized as 'hermeneutic', in contrast to the British analytical tradition.[8] What marks hermeneutic philosophy is a rejection of natural science as the model of all true knowledge, as well as of the related assumption that the philosopher can be a detached spectator of life, like the scientist conducting experiments in his laboratory. The philosopher, on the hermeneutic view, is not only in some sense a participant in existence, but also inevitably possesses a particular perspective which makes a wholly impersonal concept of objectivity, of the kind commonly attributed to the natural sciences, completely unattainable. One of the most important consequences of this difference between the analytical and the Continental approach to philosophy is the emphasis on the 'historicity' of all philosophical thought which is often found in the Continental tradition: the philosopher, that is, is not a disembodied observer, occupying a timeless vantage point, but is always embedded in a specific historical context. Despite this divergence from the analytical school, for which historicity was generally an alien concept, Continental philosophers were impelled by it towards a rejection of universalist theories of morality which converged with that at which the analytical school had arrived by a different path.

There were, of course, important differences amongst Continental philosophers, but what matters at present is that, regardless of whether they shared the concern for historicity, they were often unable to avoid scepticism about the ability of philosophy to construct rational foundations for moral and political values. Writing of phenomenology, for example, Alfred Schütz declared in 1945 that its aim is only 'to observe and possibly to understand [the world]'.[9] From within the idealist tradition, which had close conceptual links with phenomenology and had once abounded with members only too anxious to give practical advice, Benedetto Croce also restricted the task of moral and political philosophy to explanation, insisting on the existence of a logical gap between theory and practice. Yet another form of scepticism found expression in existentialist philosophy, for which subjective, non-rational commitment was the only source of value. Later, postmodern thinkers completed the philosophical rejection of universal theories of value by dismissing them as dependent on untenable 'metanarratives' – ideological claims, that is, to absolute truth.

Why, one may ask, did scepticism make such progress in postwar European thought, in both the analytic and the Continental traditions of philosophy? Many explanations are possible, such as the decline of religion in twentieth-century western European life and the loss of confidence which followed the end of the Eurocentric era, but amongst the most suggestive is one put forward by the Spanish-American philosopher George Santayana, who prophesied long before the Second World War that relativism would be the inexorable fate of twentieth-century European thinkers. The main reason Santayana gave for this was the emergence in the European world of what he termed a general 'insecurity about first principles'.[10] In politics,

Santayana noted, this intellectual uncertainty was reflected above all in a new attitude towards the enemy. In previous ages, he observed, 'No one sought to understand his enemies, nor even to conciliate them, unless under compulsion or out of insidious policy.' Instead, 'he merely pelted them with blind refutations and clumsy blows. Everyone sincerely felt that right was entirely on his side, a proof that such intelligence as he had moved freely and exclusively within the lines of his faith.'[11] In the course of the twentieth century, however, a new atmosphere of acceptance and understanding of the enemy has developed in the Western world, mainly because the early pattern of moral absolutism has been replaced by universal sympathy or, to use Santayana's own term, by tenderness. This tenderness, Santayana emphasized, is not so much the outcome of moral conviction as of the fact that the twentieth century represents

> the *Wanderjahre* of faith; it looks smilingly at every new face, which might perhaps be that of a predestined friend; it chases after any engaging stranger; it even turns up again from time to time at home, full of a new tenderness for all it had abandoned there...[12]

Santayana's benign description of this situation owed much to the fact that he wrote it before the ideological conflicts of the interwar years. During the decades following his death in 1952, however, the sceptical spirit has been intensified by the growing tendency of many postwar political thinkers to attach intrinsic value to difference as such, with no concern for the universality to which European defenders of values have traditionally aspired. As Ernesto Laclau observed towards the end of the twentieth century,

> In a post Cold War world, ... we are witnessing a proliferation of particularistic identities, none of which tries to ground its legitimacy and its action in a mission predetermined by universal history – whether that be the mission of a universal class, or the notion of a privileged race, or an abstract principle. Quite the opposite. Any kind of universal grounding is contemplated with deep suspicion.[13]

Although this particularistic emphasis is in principle perfectly compatible with confident self-assertion, scepticism about reason's ability to ground morality has made it difficult to escape a sense of intellectual unease. This was evident during the 1980s, for example, when

Alasdair MacIntyre advanced the dramatic thesis that not only the European world but the Western world at large is one in which 'we have – very largely, if not entirely – lost our comprehension, both theoretical and practical, of morality'.[14] At the close of the century, it was again evident, for example, when Ralf Dahrendorf concluded *The Oxford History of the Twentieth Century* by lamenting that scepticism had paved the way for 'a wave of relativism' which is now 'sweeping the world, especially the old developed word. Anything goes . . . '.[15]

Scepticism and relativism, however, were not the only intellectual problems facing those who sought to provide the postwar democratic project with rational foundations. Another was the growing realization that, despite more than two thousand years of philosophy, the western European world still lacks an adequate language with which to describe what a human being – or, more precisely, a rational, self-conscious agent – is. This was the message eloquently spelt out, for example, by Ernst Cassirer in his *Essay on Man* just before the war ended. The reason for this ignorance, he maintained, is that without realizing it, we make the mistake of applying concepts which only apply to things external to ourselves: we mistakenly apply the language of objects, that is, to the sphere of subjects. It was for this reason that Cassirer attacked the modern European tendency to idealize natural science, as expressed in the characteristically modern disciplines of economics, sociology and psychology. All of them attempt to treat human existence as if it belongs to the same order of reality as material objects. We lack, in consequence, an autonomous language of agency, which is the main requirement for understanding moral and political existence. In its place we have only a reductionist language of drives, instincts and socially conditioned responses.

Finally, defenders of democracy who sought coherent foundations for the reconstruction project were confronted by an intellectual challenge which struck at the very heart of the model of liberal democracy favoured by the triumphant Allies. This was the contention that the concept of the individual presupposed by the democratic project was nothing more than an illusion. That disconcerting conclusion was arrived at from a variety of directions, one of which was the revisionist psychoanalytic theory developed by Jacques Lacan. The immediate target of Lacan's attack was the uncritical way in which he believed that Freud had adopted the modern concept of the individual. In reality, Lacan maintained, this rests entirely on an illusion which arises at some point during the first eighteen months of childhood, when the child sees his reflection in a mirror. The reflection presents to him a creature which looks unitary and self-contained. Having formed this impression of his identity, the child spends the rest of his life trying to implement it in practice, in the face of an experience of life which constantly reveals that the self is neither unitary nor self-contained. The concept of the individual self, then, is no more than an illusion derived from a deceptive reflection in a mirror.[16]

More influential on the Continent than Lacan's psychoanalytic critique of the concept of the individual, however, was the structuralist one, which drew on the linguist theory of Saussure in order to establish that individual existence has meaning only in the context of relationships which it presupposes, and outside which the individual can be conscious neither of himself nor others. As a commentator sympathetic to structuralist method put it, one result is 'the "decentring" of the individual subject, who is no longer to be regarded as the source or end of meaning'.[17] From a somewhat different standpoint, so-called communitarian theorists were also to reject the pre-social, pre-relational identity whose existence more extreme forms of individualist theory took for granted.[18] This multifaceted attack on the individual was completed by the postmodern 'deconstruction' of the subject, despite the fact that a leading postmodern thinker, Jacques Derrida, has dismissed the idea that deconstruction means the destruction of the subject as a caricature of his view. Unjustly, however, Derrida has often been taken to be pursuing a programme of wanton demolition.[19]

The outcome of relativism, of a defective language of agency, of structuralism and postmodern deconstruction, then, was that it was very hard to defend the universalist conception of human rights incorporated into postwar European constitutions. In practice, however, the memory of totalitarianism combined with the new threat from the USSR and growing postwar prosperity to ensure that theoretical problems did little to undermine the democratic reconstruction programme. A more pressing issue, indeed, was the need to give that programme mass appeal by underpinning it with a welfare programme.

The Welfare State and the Problem of Growing Executive Power

What was amply evident by 1945 was that a relevant postwar form of democracy could not be based on the prewar bourgeois model but must be committed to mass welfare provision, instead of merely protecting property rights. In Britain, the main political parties acknowledged this before the war ended by accepting the Beveridge Report. In France, the preamble to the 1946 constitution of the Third Republic declared that 'The Nation guarantees to all, and particularly to the child, the mother, and the aged worker, protection of health, material security, rest, and leisure.' In Germany, Article 20 of the Basic Law proclaimed that the Federal Republic 'is a democratic and social federal state'.

General acceptance of a welfare state commitment must not, however, obscure the fact that it was derived from very different political traditions, by no means all of which were liberal-democratic. This was ignored, for example, by T. H. Marshall, who mistakenly generalized from the British case when he argued that the postwar welfare commitment marked the advent of a new deeper kind of democratic citizenship which he described as 'social', by contrast with the earlier, more restricted civic and political kinds. In fact, the welfare commitment of Continental states was often neither new nor rooted in democratic experience. On the contrary, it derived from three sources which played no part in the British version. One was prewar authoritarian politics. In West Germany, for example, the welfare state could be traced back to Bismarck's 'state socialism' of the 1880s. The second was the interwar totalitarian state. In West Germany, once again, Nazi pronouncements of the early 1940s had included a commitment to comprehensive provision for old-age pensions, as well as to a massive postwar housing programme. In postwar Italy, likewise, the welfare system drew heavily on institutions created by Mussolini's regime. Having noted the continuity of some Continental versions of the welfare state with undemocratic prewar ones, however, it must be added that, after 1945, the welfare ideal was harnessed to the cause of implementing individual social rights, rather than to illiberal ends such as Nazi biological objectives or the fascist goal of merging the individual in the nation.

A third major source of Continental welfare theory was Christian social thought, which rested on ideals of solidarity and natural hierarchy hostile to liberal individualism and popular sovereignty alike. In the postwar decades, however, Christian Democratic doctrine compromised with both – often swayed less, it is true, by social idealism than by the pragmatic consideration that the existing social order might best be preserved by such an accommodation. In particular, the West German CDU came, under the influence of Ludwig Erhard, to accept his conviction that the free market is the only beneficial institution to create just and maximal distribution, even though this claim appeared to conflict with the ideal of 'organic' social unity. Despite the general acceptance of the market, however, the Christian Democratic ideal of social solidarity retained such widespread influence that the massive attack on the welfare state launched during the 1970s and 1980s by the 'Thatcherite' New Right in Britain never threatened to overthrow the dominant collectivist and consensualist orthodoxy to which it lent vital support on the Continent. One aspect of the New Right onslaught nevertheless properly focused attention on an issue which had been of concern to thoughtful critics as soon as the postwar welfare commitment had been made. This was the constitutional implications of the massive growth in state power brought about by centralized provision, rather than the economic ones. The danger, critics like F. A. Hayek argued, was of inadvertently creating a version of the totalitarian form of government against which the Allies had fought.

What accentuated the constitutional danger still further, as Geoffrey Barraclough commented two decades after the war, was the tendency of highly organized mass parties, combined with skilful use by governments of the mass media, to increase the centralization of power.[20] In order to prevent the collapse of postwar democracy into oligarchy, Barraclough observed, it was a matter of urgency to find new ways of re-establishing democratic accountability. Although neither he nor other defenders of constitutional democracy were able to propose any convincing solutions, an important check on plebiscitary democracy was eventually to emerge from a non-democratic direction he had not foreseen. This is the strong juridical emphasis of the European integration project, whose implications for democracy will be considered later.

Although postwar criticism of the welfare state was initially motivated by fear of growing executive power, subsequent experience created additional sources of anxiety. Amongst them was the fear that, instead of helping those in need to stand on their own feet, welfare measures merely created a culture of dependency; that demographic trends were creating an ageing population whose health and pension requirements the state could no longer afford; that increasing social fragmentation created a growing underclass likely to be a permanent burden on the state; that the high cost of new drugs and health technologies could not be supported by the state; and that declining European global economic competitiveness made the post-1945 welfare settlement even more unviable. By the end of the twentieth century these considerations, which will reappear in subsequent chapters, had combined to create a situation in which major revision of the welfare dimension of democracy was necessary. At present, however, it is necessary to complete this outline of the principal items on the postwar reconstruction agenda by turning to the third, which concerned the need to rethink the nature of citizenship in the light of increasing social diversity, especially of a multicultural kind.

From Social and Cultural Homogeneity to Radical Pluralism

Shortly after the war, a British Royal Commission on Population recommended that 'immigration on a large scale into a fully established society like ours could only be welcomed without reserve if the immigrants were of good human stock and were not prevented by their religion or race from inter-marrying with the local population and becoming merged with it'.[21] As this passage indicates, Mark Mazower remarks, racial sentiment remained widespread in the postwar European world. Indeed, it intensified, as the early postwar enthusiasm for immigration inspired by economic growth disappeared as the economic climate worsened from the late 1960s onwards. From 1968, Mazower notes, 'British citizenship was, for the first time, made dependent on having a British parent', departing in this respect from a largely civic conception to a more markedly ethnic one, while the 1971 Immigration Act 'contained provisions for "repatriation", although these were never publicized or promoted, to avoid jeopardizing "good race relations"'. [22] In France, further immigration was stopped in 1974, while in West Germany, the 1965 'Foreigners' Act' 'was an even more stringent measure than the National Socialist legislation it replaced: expulsion no longer depended on the behaviour of the individual worker but simply on the needs of the state'.[23] More generally, European states possessed 'no anti-discrimination machinery, and in most countries the state believed that encouraging migrants to return home was the best answer to racial tensions (as in Bonn's 1983 Act to Promote the Preparedness of Foreign Workers to Return)'.[24] If eastern Europe avoided the challenge faced by the western part, it was only because most ethnic minorities had been eliminated, first by Nazism and then by communism.

It was against this background that the evolution of multiracial societies 'became as great a challenge to postwar democracy in Europe as the struggle for gender equality'.[25] What made it difficult for western European states to meet this challenge, however, were two assumptions which had been fundamental to European moral and political thought since at least the Enlightenment.[26] One is that human nature is the same for all human beings, the result of which was a tendency to play down the significance of cultural diversity, making it especially difficult to develop conceptions of citizenship that come to terms with the large-scale post-1945 migrations. The difficulty of accommodating cultural diversity was increased by a second assumption shared by all twentieth-century ideologies. This is that a political order is only legitimate when it reflects the cultural identity of an homogeneous moral community. At the present day, nationalist ideology expresses the most influential version of the latter assumption.

The impact of the demand for a new pluralism was especially profound in Britain, where it contributed to the end of 'the top-down, centralised and unitary version [of national identity], with its old supporting props of Britishness: English myopia, obsession with sovereignty, and a general failure to understand its own nature'.[27] The optimistic view was that the end of the old Britain paved the way for a new one which will be 'loose and untidy, with power organised at different levels, a home to experiment and diversity'.[28] The more sceptical view, however, was that the new ideals of inclusion, experiment and dialogue were based on the sentiments of a small minority of the population and showed little regard for the darker side of the historical process by which unity had been created. As J. C. D. Clark remarked, national identity rested on a shared understanding of ancient growth which is 'not easily or quickly reformulated'.[29]

In Germany, the adjustment to a pluralist conception of democracy was impeded by a conception of citizenship based (after unification in 1871) on *jus sanguinis*, according to which only those of German blood were eligible to be citizens of Germany. This meant, for example, that although over a million immigrants from Eastern Europe and Russia who arrived between 1988 and 1991 were immediately granted full citizenship, the large number of Turkish residents actually born in German was virtually excluded. In France, a very different concept of citizenship has been inherited from the monarchy of the *ancient regime*, which based citizenship not on blood but on territorial jurisdiction (*ius solis*). Although this has meant that all those born on French soil can become citizens, regardless of their ethnic origin, French tolerance of cultural diversity has nevertheless been severely restricted in practice by the republican tradition, which assumes the cultural uniformity of 'the people', whose sovereignty was proclaimed in 1789.[30] Despite the *jus solis*, then, republican senti-ment has made it as difficult for many of the French to come to terms with multiculturalism as it has been for the Germans. This is the case in relation to their Islamic minority in particular.

The demand for recognition of cultural diversity, it must be added, is only one aspect of an increasingly insistent postwar demand for a radical pluralism affirming practically every form of diversity. This demand found its most extreme expression in postmodern political thought, in which the commitment to diversity and multiculturalism threatened to become a challenge to authority in every form. In the eyes of critics, radical pluralism was accordingly synonymous with social fragmentation, or even anarchy. In the eyes of its defenders, however, it was regarded as a triumphant breakthrough to a deeper, more positive form of freedom. Which view is correct is a question that is likely to continue to divide liberal and conservative thinkers just as much in the future as it has in recent decades. Whether multi-culturalist defenders of radical pluralism in particular have succeeded in proposing a viable way of combining unity and diversity will be considered in subsequent chapters. In the final chapter, as was indi-cated, the problem of accommodating cultural pluralism will be con-sidered in relation to the quest by the European Union for a new, supra-national concept of political identity.

The End of Eurocentric History and the Search for a European Political Identity

The fourth challenge facing the reconstruction project concerned the need of postwar European nation-states to come to terms with a 'post-European' era of world history. The interwar era, George Lichtheim observed, could still be called a European one, 'in the sense that the pre-eminence of Europe at the centre of global politics was not seriously in question'.[31] By 1950, however, 'European hegemony was gone, the former colonies were becoming independent, the Soviet Union had turned into a Eurasian giant, and China [had begun] to modernize in earnest under the aegis of Communism'.[32] The end of the Eurocentric era brought with it, in addition, the growing economic might of Japan. But what exactly was the nature of the new world order by which postwar European states found themselves confronted?

A decade before the war, Paul Valéry had already identified the most novel feature of the age as the advent of a new 'period of interrelation' which was replacing the former 'period of discovery'.[33] What marks the new period is the fact that 'The age of uncharted areas, of unoccupied territories, of places which nobody owns, and therefore the age of free expansion, is at an end ... *The age of a finite world is now beginning*.'[34] Is there anything more remarkable, Valéry asked rhetorically, than this 'linking together of all parts of the globe'? The inevitable result is that

> We must henceforth relate all political phenomena to this new universal condition, since they all represent a resistance or compliance to the effects of this final delimitation and increasingly close interdependence of human dealings. The habits, ambitions, and loyalties we have acquired in the course of our past history have not ceased to exist, but, moving imperceptibly into a society of very different structure, they are losing their meaning and becoming the source of fruitless endeavours and mistakes.[35]

The intensified pattern of international interrelationship which Valéry had remarked upon did not, however, completely clarify the precise nature of the postwar world order which confronted Europe. This was not only because he did not foresee the new era of space exploration which vastly extended the 'finite world' whose coming he forecast. It was also because he remained insensitive to the distinction between an 'international' and a 'world' economy drawn some two decades after the end of the Second World War by a thoughtful American author. An 'international' economy, Peter Drucker wrote in 1968, is one in which each country remains 'a separate unit with its own economic values and preferences, its own markets, and its own largely self-contained information'.[36] During the second half of the twentieth century, however, an 'international' economy has been transformed into a 'world' economy marked by the development of common appetites, common demands, and a large body of common information.[37] No doubt Drucker exaggerates the extent to which non-economic differences have disappeared, but his distinction between an international and a world economy draws attention to the fact that European states were increasingly faced, after 1945, not only by a change in the external order of power relationships. They were faced, in addition, by a breakdown of the boundary which once existed between cultures, in some degree at least, as well as that between internal and external economic considerations.

How were European states to respond to this new situation? There were three options. The first, most idealistic option was the dream of creating a world government which would prevent war from ever occurring again. In the light of the interwar experience of the League of Nations, however, this option was viewed with general scepticism. Even when Jacques Maritain, for example, tried to make his vision of world government more realistic by presenting it as the logical continuation of growing world economic interdependence, he remained an isolated figure.[38] Maritain referred those who might be doubtful about the merits of a world government to the *Preliminary Draft for a World Constitution* printed in 1948 by a committee set up at the University of Chicago. It did not occur to him that the world out- side the USA might find it hard to accept that nearly all the drafters were American, and that the world constitution they drafted had an uncanny tendency to mirror the American constitution. Although the creation of the United Nations in 1945 provided an echo of the dream of a world order, it was in practice rarely the centre of unreal- istic expectations of Maritain's kind.

The second option was to try to retain the nation-state as the most appropriate basis for European life and, beyond that, for any world order. As Alan Milward has argued, however, this option required a massive rescue operation in order to make good the almost complete collapse of the nation-state on the eve of the Second World War. 'Of the twenty six European nation-states in 1938', Milward observes,

> by the close of 1940 three had been annexed, ten occupied by hos- tile powers, one occupied against its wishes by friendly powers, and four partially occupied and divided by hostile powers. Two others had been reduced to a satellite status which would eventually result in their occupation. The only one which had extended its

power and triumphantly dominated the continent offered as little
hope to mankind as any political organization which had existed.[39]

In a controversial thesis, Milward has maintained that not only is the
rescue of the nation-state 'the most salient aspect of Europe's postwar history' but that European integration was merely an aspect of
that rescue process. If the surrender of national sovereignty which
the rescue has involved looks more like the death of the nation-state
than its rescue, Milward's reply is that that surrender is 'but a small
part of the postwar history of the nation-state'.[40] Although he fully
acknowledges that 'some national policies aiming at national reasser-
tion had to be internationalized in order to make them viable',[41] and
that 'national citizens have developed a strong secondary allegiance
during the Community's existence',[42] Milward nevertheless maintains that nationally based democracy continues to flourish as the
primary reality beneath the new dual system of allegiance that has
emerged.

Milward's account of the rescue of the nation-state has been
criticized on various counts,[43] of which the most telling is that his
'nationalistic' account of European integration only applies to its
early stages. By the 1980s, Robert Bideleux observes, 'the supra-
national dynamic of integration crossed a threshold which allowed it
to escape inter-governmental control and take on a life of its own'.[44]
From that time, the integration project could no longer plausibly be
regarded as an unqualified ally of democratic reconstruction within
a national framework. The fact that neither could it properly be
scapegoated as the enemy of the nation-state is a matter which will be
considered later: what is mainly relevant at present is that in the later
stages, European integration could no longer be presented as an
instrument of purely national purposes.

In between the two extremes of world government and rescuing
the nation-state lay a third option which was eventually to become
the one that would shape the European political word in the twenty-
first century. This was a programme of European integration which
recognized from the outset that the goal was a federal polity. In
retrospect, Europhiles have sometimes presented this option as the
logical continuation of a long process of growing national interdependence that extends back to the eighteenth century, or as an
enlightened attempt to prevent the resurgence of fascism by locating
the nation in a more comprehensive political unit. Critics, however,

have emphasized the complex strands of thought on which the integration project drew, stressing in particular its fascist roots.

According to one of the most impressive explorations of the darker side of the integration project, 'Nazis, Vichyites, Italian Fascists and others spent many of the war years – as they or their spiritual fathers had done in the 1930s – developing sophisticated programmes for European economic and political integration.'[45] To those who object that the fascist version of European integration was essentially based on national domination, John Laughland replies that the aim, on the contrary, was supra-national unity, although it is true that the principle of nationhood was not dismissed outright.[46] To those who object that it was based on coercion, he replies that the fascist view of European unity was conceived in essentially voluntary terms.[47] The fundamentally pacific character of the fascist project, indeed, was emphasized by both Hitler and Mussolini in a joint communiqué issued in August 1941. The Axis victory, they declared, would create a New European Order in which all the causes of war which had previously rent the European world would be removed.[48] Goebbels further clarified the nature of the new order when he indicated that German regionalism could provide the model for harmoniously integrating European states in a federal system which would not infringe their identity.[49] Göring, who had launched the Nazi project for European economic union in 1940, envisaged fixed exchange rates, the abolition of customs barriers and the protection of agriculture.[50]

The point of dwelling for a moment on the less attractive face of the European integration project, Laughland emphasises, is not to reach the absurd conclusion that contemporary pro-Europeanists are latter-day fascists in disguise. It is to emphasize, rather, that some of the strands of European thought on which the postwar integration project relied, originally at least, owed nothing to liberal or democratic values. Whether those values have subsequently found contemporary expression in a securely democratic conception of European political identity, or retain only an ambiguous position in the integration project, is a question which will be considered in the last chapter.

The Problem of Amnesia

It is now necessary to consider a phenomenon which has been held to doom both postwar democratic reconstruction and European integration to failure from the very outset, on the Continent at least. This is the collective moral and political amnesia cultivated by those who had colluded extensively with totalitarianism.[51] The reason it doomed the reconstruction project was that it prevented postwar states which were party to it from considering objectively the problems confronting them. Instead, they opted for myths of national innocence and passive victimhood which transferred sole responsibility for atrocities committed both during and after the war to the Germans. After the war in particular, Tony Judt has argued, this strategy enabled non-German nations in Continental Europe to pursue their own 'final solution' to the nationality problem by expelling their own German minorities with little resistance from the Allies.[52] The figures are worth recalling:

> As a result of the shifting of Poland's frontiers agreed on at Potsdam, the expulsion of the Volkesdeutsche from the Balkans, and the collective punishment visited on the Sudeten Germans, some 15 million Germans were expelled in the postwar years; 7 million from Silesia, Pomerania and East Prussia; 3 million from Czechoslovakia; nearly 2 million from Poland and the USSR; and a further 2.7 million from Yugoslavia, Rumania and Hungary.[53]

Although racially motivated purges were unacceptable when committed by the Nazis, they became acceptable, it might seem, when committed by postwar democracies.[54] The misgivings this might inspire about some aspects of postwar democracy in parts of Europe were one of the things conveniently veiled by amnesia.

To note the importance of amnesia as a somewhat rickety foundation stone of postwar democracy is not, however, to deny it a positive dimension. In Germany in particular, a rigorous postwar anti-fascist purge would not only have created a dangerously disaffected outsider group with a vested interest in subverting the new democratic order but would also have removed a large part of the administrative class, leaving only a relatively poorly educated body of personnel to staff public institutions. Amnesia was the only way of avoiding this. A similarly sympathetic view can be taken of the indulgent view of amnesia taken by de Gaulle in France and de Gasperi in Italy, both of whom regarded it as a patriotic duty to draw a veil over disquieting aspects of their national past. How well a European postwar democratic order erected on a foundation of amnesia could succeed in achieving stability and legitimacy, however, remained to be seen. To a sceptic like Judt, there is no doubt about the answer: the postwar ideal of European unity was from the beginning no more than a fragile piece of myth-making, relying as it did on a theory of European victimhood which minimized the extent of the postwar problems faced by defeated and occupied European states by attributing them entirely to German aggression in the first instance, and thereafter to Soviet aggression.[55]

   In the event, it was not until a relatively late stage in postwar history that European countries at last became willing to jettison the veil of amnesia and face up to their past.[56] Although significant steps in that direction were discernible in the mid-1960s, it was only in the 1990s that the heritage of Vichy began to be candidly faced in France, for example. In 1991, René Bousquet, the head of the Vichy regime's police, and an active participant in the expulsion of foreign Jews, was finally charged with 'crimes against humanity' (he was murdered in 1993, while awaiting trial). Bousquet had originally been tried for treason immediately after the war, but was convicted only of the lesser offence of 'national indignity' – a sentence which was then almost immediately commuted because of his help to the resistance movement.[57] In West Germany, as late as 1977 'Not a single West German obituary made mention...of the fact that Hans-Martin Schleyer, chairman of the (West) German Confederation of Employers and victim of a terrorist attack, had made his fortune as the Nazi commander of a slave-labour factory in the eastern territories.'[58]

   Amnesia, however, was not the only postwar intellectual obstacle to a clear-sighted approach to democratic reconstruction. A further one, especially marked in Germany, was a degree of cultural and political alienation which led to suspicion of democracy even amongst those opposed to totalitarianism. It was not the case that the defeat of Hitler led to an upsurge of democratic sentiment; there was, on the contrary, a widespread feeling that the Allied occupation (and especially the denazification programme) merely meant more of the same totalitarian diet – a feeling which naturally disappointed the United States in particular, since the American assumption had been that the Germans would enthusiastically embrace democracy.

   To amnesia and spiritual alienation must be added two further intellectual obstacles to a realistic assessment by its supporters of what democratic reconstruction involved. One, which relates more especially to France and Italy, consisted of a radical idealism which made it difficult for those who shared it to view the limits and possibilities of the democratic project with lucidity. In the case of the postwar French intellectual establishment, for example, radical idealism veered between a heroic cult of personal authenticity and a collectivist enthusiasm which could shade over into support for Stalinist modes of government. In Italy, for reasons which will become clear later, Stalinism did not have the same attraction, but collectivist sympathies nevertheless prevented a principled (as opposed to pragmatic) commitment to democracy.

The remaining obstacle to clarity about the requirement of reconstruction concerns Britain. In this case, it had nothing to do with amnesia, alienation or radical idealism: it took the form, rather, of a danger to which victors are always exposed – the danger, that is, of excessive complacency. The ways in which complacency displayed itself in postwar British political theory will be examined in the next chapter.

Conclusion

The agenda confronting European political thinkers from 1945 onwards, then, was dominated by the need to provide a coherent theory of human rights, to devise a welfare state which did not foster an over-mighty executive, to develop more pluralist concepts of citizenship, and to determine the extent to which the nation-state should continue to be the basis of European political life. Needless to say, political thinkers in each European country responded to this agenda in the context of their own specific cultures and political traditions, characterized by the pragmatism of the British, the republicanism and cultural confidence of the French, the division in Germany between defenders of ethnic nationalism and defenders of constitutional patriotism, and the fragility of national politics of any kind in Italy. In the case of the countries of east-central Europe, early hopes of democracy were shattered by the Soviet occupation, while liberation soon saw dreams of self-government rapidly replaced by a demand for membership of the European Union. Identification of a common agenda, however, provides an intellectual framework which transcends the differences in national traditions whilst also permitting the different individual responses of European intellectuals to the postwar democratic project to be examined in some detail.

2

British Political Thought since 1945: The Limitations of Pragmatism

Unlike Continental states, Britain faced the postwar world with an intact parliamentary constitution and none of the humiliation brought by defeat and occupation. Victory, however, brought with it the danger of complacency, from which the vanquished were automatically protected. This was expressed not only in an inability to accept that Britain's days as a great power were at an end, but also in a reinforced insularity and an excessive confidence in the merits of 'muddling through'.

From the standpoint of political thought, the most striking manifestation of British complacency was the postwar predominance of a linguistic and analytic approach to political theory which claimed to be essentially value-neutral and non-ideological. Rejecting the speculative style of Continental thought as prone to encourage a dangerous metaphysical worship of the state, British advocates of the analytic approach set severe bounds to the task of sensible intellectuals. Unlike that of the 'public' intellectuals of the Continent, this was not to expose exploitation and preach liberation but was merely to clarify the various ways in which different words can properly be used in ordinary language. Barely concealed beneath the surface of the British pretence of modesty and objectivity, however, lay a self-satisfied English form of nationalism which the émigré German political philosopher, Eric Voegelin, took delight in exposing in the political theorizing of J. D. Mabbott and T. D. Weldon in particular.

In *The State and the Citizen* (1948), Voegelin notes, Mabbott described his aim as 'to bring out the general principles of politics'. Voegelin caustically comments that one can hardly avoid envying the happy situation of a British political philosopher who immediately finds, as Mabbott does, that these general principles 'happen to be identical with those of his own civilization'.[1] He goes on to quote with amusement Mabbott's conclusion that, if other nations and civilizations should be debarred by circumstances from following these principles, 'I [Mabbot] cannot avoid the conclusion that, in the field of politics at least, they are condemned to lasting loss and sacrifice.'[2]

In T. D. Weldon's *The Vocabulary of Politics* (1946), Voegelin remarked, national complacency assumed an even more remarkable form. A fundamental feature of Weldon's work was the division of all political theories into organic and mechanical. Under the organic heading he lumped together a highly disparate collection of thinkers of whom he disapproved: these included not only Hitler and Mussolini, but Plato, Aristotle, and Catholic theologians. Under the mechanical heading he included an equally mixed batch of whom he approved. What united the latter was the influence of 'Christianity as developed since the Reformation, and especially in Puritan England during the seventeenth century'.[3] What this means, Voegelin remarked, is that everything ultimately 'boils down to the difference between Protestant England and the rest of mankind'.[4] In politics, only those blessed enough to stand in the English Protestant tradition, in short, are worthy of attention, since only the Protestant doctrine of conscience can protect the individual against claims by society to dictate what he ought to do.

If complacency was the first danger facing postwar Britain, a second was excessive faith in a long-established tradition of political pragmatism which sanctioned muddling through, at a time when deeper thought was required about how best to respond to the postwar situation. By the early 1950s, this faith had found expression in a 'middle way' consensus based on a combination of welfare and full employment policies. As subsequent decades were to reveal, the optimistic dream of a halfway house between capitalism and socialism which inspired the consensus proved to be a source not only of largely unforeseen social and economic problems but also of state planning on a scale that threatened to subvert the principle of constitutional balance which had shaped English politics since 1688. Unfortunately, however, the dominant analytic style of political theory discouraged serious intellectual scrutiny of the new consensus on the ground that it would be purely ideological. Any attempt to debate the ends of government, Anthony Quinton explained, would inevitably go beyond the analytic classification of key political terms and statements to which judicious postwar British political thinkers should confine themselves.[5] Curiously, Quinton identified the only contemporary piece of philosophical work to avoid being ideological as the 'substantial general survey of political theory from an analytic point of view' published by S. I. Benn and R. S. Peters in 1959, entitled *Social Principles and the Democratic State*. What is puzzling about Quinton's willingness to credit that work with being non-ideological is the fact that the whole purpose of the book was to defend a liberal-democratic commitment.

Although the analytic orthodoxy did not pass unchallenged, those who questioned it often did so from positions which were no less problematic. Ernest Gellner, for example, mounted a sustained attack from the standpoint of what he termed 'sociological realism', a position from which he announced that man's essence in the twentieth century is 'not that he is a rational, or a political, or a sinful, or a thinking animal, but that he is an industrial animal'.[6] Moving on from this dogmatic declaration, Gellner adopted a no less dogmatic conception of industrial functionalism, according to which what defines man is not his moral or intellectual or aesthetic attributes, but 'his capacity to contribute to, and to profit from, industrial society'.[7] Strangely, Gellner seemed not to notice that his functionalist standpoint made it impossible to criticize an industrializing totalitarian regime since, as he puts it, '[man's] essence resides in his capacity to contribute to, and to profit from, industrial society'. No less strange was Gellner's conviction that 'power rightly belongs to the possessors of the new [industrial] wisdom ... [that is, to] those who have acquired diplomas from the schools of the societies which are themselves already ... industrialized',[8] which ignored the possibility that an industrial elite might not automatically possess political wisdom. More generally, Gellner's sociological realism was notable for its complete indifference to such issues as the need to limit power by the rule of law and constitutional checks and balances.

What seemed at first sight to be a more profound critique of the stifling grip on political theory of the analytic tradition was advanced by John Plamenatz, whose starting-point was a rejection of Peter Laslett's famous announcement, in 1956, of the death of political philosophy at the hands of logical positivism.[9] What Laslett ignored, Plamenatz maintained, is society's need for *practical* philosophy

which, unlike the analytical approach, adopts a value commitment
that may be critical of established concepts and usages.[10] In order to
dent the analytic orthodoxy, however, Plamenatz had to show that
the practical philosophy he advocated was not just ideology. His
attempt to do so was unconvincing, however, since he characterized
practical philosophers as 'missionaries' whose business is 'to help
people commit themselves' – hardly a non-ideological business.
Although Plamenatz tried to veil the ideological dimension of his
thought by immediately adding that practical philosophies should
be 'realistic' as well as committed, his definition of realism was unsatisfactory: it consisted of 'tak[ing] account of the facts'.[11] Since 'the facts'
are a matter over which Marxists, fascists and liberals disagree, this
did not allay the suspicion that he had unwittingly surrendered to
ideology, albeit of a very conservative kind.

The British Left

It might be thought that the pragmatic mood which characterized
postwar British intellectual life would be challenged by those on the
Left. Unlike their Continental contemporaries, however, most leftwing
politicians and thinkers accepted the established constitutional order,
defended in 1951 by Harold Laski, for example, on the ground that
'the real alternative to the House of Commons is the concentration
camp'.[12] More generally, most differed entirely from Continental
socialists in preferring piecemeal change to revolutionary rhetoric.
Even John Strachey, who had been notable for his prewar revolutionary zeal, abandoned it in favour of a postwar commitment to
a (qualified) faith in the power of democratic politics to reshape
capitalism. If we have learnt anything in our epoch, Strachey wrote in
1956, 'it is that the means and methods profoundly condition the
goal. A socialism achieved by democratic means will inevitably be
a basically different thing from a socialism achieved by dictatorial
coercion.'[13] R. H. S. Crossman spoke for many Labour Party supporters
when he wrote that the 'true aim of the Labour Movement' had
never been 'the dramatic capture of power by the working class, but
the conversion of the nation to the socialist pattern of rights and
values...'.[14]

It was not only gradualism and consensualism which marked the
postwar Labour Party, however. Its greatest advantage was that,

from 1943 until the 1970s, it also occupied the moral high-ground it had acquired during the war as a result of the lukewarm reception given to the Beveridge Report by Conservative members of the coalition government on the ground that the devastated British economy could not support the full cost. Since it was Beveridge's enormously successful national promotion of his Report, more than anything else, which shaped the popular vision of the New Jerusalem that would follow the war, their misgivings led Conservatives to be completely discredited in the popular mind as reactionary defenders of the old prewar order of unemployment and poverty.[15] Against this background, Attlee's victory over Churchill in 1945 is easy to understand.

What is mainly relevant at present is that it was their privileged moral idealism, rather than a clearly thought out political position, upon which proponents of postwar social democracy mainly relied. In place of intellectual clarity, indeed, they fell back on a loosely linked body of assumptions uncritically taken over from three sources. One was Keynes' conviction that the state could regulate the economy in ways which ensured growth and full employment; the second was Beveridge's commitment to universal state provision of welfare and social security; the third was a Fabian tradition which held that only state action could place national above private interest. In combination, these sources were generally considered adequate to justify a highly centralized form of state collectivism whose potentially authoritarian character was rarely noticed by those committed to it.

Consider, for example, R. M. Titmuss, a leading socialist academic specializing in social policy research who has been criticized for anti-pluralist sentiments so intense that whenever he detected any signs of group autonomy, 'he saw it as being exercised against the public interest by powerful and secretive minorities'.[16] Or consider, from a somewhat different direction, T. H. Marshall, best known for extending citizenship to include 'social rights'. Marshall defended centralized action on the ground that the experience of universal state dependence made a major contribution to social unity. The fact that this was achieved in a way which echoed Kafka was irrelevant: 'All learn', Marshall wrote, 'what it means to have an insurance card that must be regularly stamped, or to collect children's allowances or pensions from the post office.'[17] The most extraordinary defence of centralized welfare provision, however, was provided by Barbara Wootton, who argued that 'showering benefits upon rich and poor alike' means that 'nobody need then know who is poor and who is not'.[18] Universal state handouts seemed, on this view, to be an almost magical way of creating the socialist society overnight.

Although the vision of these thinkers, as indeed of all those who supported the creation of the British welfare state, was inspired by noble sentiments, it was flawed from the outset by three features of the social democratic consensus which guaranteed that it would ultimately prove self-destructive. The first was the fact that British social democracy was mainly understood to be socialism 'from above'. No matter how good the intentions of those who implemented the ideal, it therefore did nothing to generate an active sense of involvement even amongst those who were its main beneficiaries. In the case of nationalization, for example, Raymond Williams argued that the situation of workers had actually been worsened by the tendency to reproduce 'sometimes with appalling accuracy, the human patterns, in management and working relationships, of industries based on quite different [i.e. capitalist] social principles'.[19]

The second self-destructive feature of the social democratic consensus was that it mistakenly assumed that high levels of economic production could be taken for granted. The major problems were assumed to relate only to distribution. This naïve optimism, which survived for several decades despite Britain's continuing economic decline, was particularly evident in Anthony Crosland's *The Future of Socialism* (1956). The possibility that collectivism might actually strangle the goose that laid the golden eggs was not seriously considered until the 1970s, when the relentless growth of the public sector finally became a source of concern even to Labour supporters. Closely related to this growth was the social democratic acceptance of high taxation, based on the optimistic hope that voters would think of themselves as receiving a 'social wage', rather than of having had their money taken from them by the state. Since few thought in those terms, the result was to intensify still further the alienation from socialism of the mass of the population already fostered by the top-down approach to welfare.

Finally, the social democratic consensus took for granted that, in principle at least, state planning could deal with any social problem. Although Crosland, amongst others, expressed unease about various aspects of central control, past planning failures did not dent his faith in state action. Any failure, he wrote, 'was essentially a *political* one, which reflects the difficulty of planning in a democratic society', and could be overcome by greater determination on the part of planners.[20] The logic of this claim was to 'de-democratize' social democracy by defining success in terms of steam-rolling opposition in a way usually associated with Stalinism.

There were, of course, thinkers on the Left who did not share the social democratic belief in the power of the state to create the New Jerusalem, but they had no viable alternative to offer. George Orwell, for example, veered between an early idealization of British working-class culture and a later more qualified view of what might be expected of those whom he referred to in *1984* (1949) as 'the proles' without being able to indicate how they might create a socialist society. Others demanded that the state should yield to the anti-centralist cause of workers' control, but had no remedy for the lack of mass enthusiasm their doctrine encountered.[21] The same indifference greeted the Marxist thinkers associated with the *New Left Review*.

The Marxists did, however, mount a theoretically impressive response to Crosland's claim that socialist radicalism had become irrelevant because postwar capitalism had already been socialized by two bloodless revolutions. One consisted of the separation of management from ownership which had replaced the nineteenth-century union of the two functions in the single person of the entrepreneur. Management, in brief, has passed into the hands of a new professional salaried class which has little interest in maximizing profitability, while ownership has passed to anonymous shareholders. The other bloodless revolution consisted of the new, active role of the postwar state in supervising the economy – a development which gave the lie, Crosland believed, to the Marxist belief in the primacy of the economic order.

In the eyes of Marxist thinkers, Crosland had been duped by what were in reality only superficial changes in the capitalist system. Beneath those changes, class domination and state oppression remained intact: capitalist exploitation, in short, had only changed its form. They acknowledged, however, that the state enjoyed a relative autonomy from the economic order mistakenly denied to it by classical Marxist theory, sympathizing in particular with the structuralist revisionism of thinkers like Nicos Poulantzas, who rightly maintained that the economic reductionism of classical Marxist theory made it impossible to understand the part played by the state in the genesis of twentieth-century totalitarianism, especially in its fascist form.[22] The problem, however, was that the revised Marxist doctrine failed to clarify the sense in which the state could be both relatively autonomous in relation to the economic order and yet ultimately determined by changes within that order. Although one leading British radical, E. P. Thompson, avoided this kind of theoretical difficulty by developing a purely indigenous form of revolutionary doctrine, based in particular on the socialism of William Morris, his efforts foundered on the reluctance of his fellow countrymen to respond to his appeal to 'build their own, organic community' and become 'societal' creatures, instead of 'acquisitive' ones.[23]

If these alternatives to postwar social democracy differed from it in crucial respects, they nevertheless shared with it a profound suspicion of the market which rendered socialist thought of every type unable to respond effectively to the New Right challenge of the 1970s. Only at the end of the following decade did David Miller produce the most philosophically impressive postwar restatement of social democracy, which endeavoured to strike a balance between the conflicting claims of personal freedom, the market, nationalism, community and distributive justice, all within a constitutional framework.[24] In order to construct a form of socialist identity capable of performing this ambitious task, however, Miller was compelled to stress the need for a 'transformative' politics which required two major changes in the British conceptions of democracy and industrial life. Politically, it was necessary to abandon the conception of democracy as merely a device for interest aggregation and adopt instead one based on a non-instrumental conception of citizenship as active participation in a public dialogue about policy. On the industrial front, it was necessary to move towards a cooperative system of production. Although Miller suggested that some existing trends already pointed in these directions, he acknowledged that his philosophical vision would not prove significant in practice unless a conscious decision was made to adopt the extensive transformation of prevailing values and perspectives required by his vision of social democracy.

In the event, there was no indication that any such decision was likely to be made. On the contrary, it was the highly untransformative politics of New Labour for which a large section of the electorate voted. Before considering that, however, it is necessary to examine several major critiques of the dominant social democratic orthodoxy which were mounted by a disparate group of liberal and conservative thinkers whose members included Karl Popper, Friedrich Hayek, Michael Oakeshott and Isaiah Berlin.

Liberal and Conservative Visions of the Free Society

The core of Popper's political vision is the concept of the 'open society' which he opposes to totalitarianism.[25] His defence of this concept is based on a 'fallibilist' theory of scientific method which eschews the search for absolute certainty and is instead content with the modest goal of falsifying hypotheses through a process of trial and error. The details of the fallibilist method are less relevant in the present context than the fact that Popper believes it to be applicable to both the natural and the social sciences. What characterizes the open society is the commitment to applying this method in every area of human experience, including the political. The whole of human existence is accordingly treated as an endless process of experimentation, in the course of which no aspect of life must remain uncriticized. Although this ideal links Popper to J. S. Mill there is a crucial difference, which is that Mill thinks of the process of experimentation as one in which citizens are ceaselessly pursuing truth, whereas Popper thinks of it instead as a process whose aim is the endless avoidance of error. It is from this standpoint that Popper interprets the totalitarian experience: totalitarians are defined as those who have attempted to apply non-fallibilist philosophies to politics.

Unfortunately, this definition of totalitarians is so broad that it applies to most leading political thinkers from Plato onwards. It is therefore not surprising to find that Popper's analysis of the origins of totalitarianism in *The Open Society and Its Enemies* (1962) amounted to little more than demonizing an arbitrary selection of very different thinkers drawn from the past two thousand years. With no sense of historical anachronism, Plato, Hegel and Marx in particular were labelled as the totalitarian forebears of Hitler and Stalin. Not long after the publication of Popper's book, G. R. Mure wrote that although many good men would sympathize with his liberal sentiments,

> nobody who has seriously studied the works of [his] alleged enemies [of the open society] could think Dr. Popper a reliable historian of philosophy. One would say, indeed, that he had flung scholarship to the winds in the pursuit of his thesis, could one be sure that he had any to fling; but his accounts of Aristotelian and Hegelian doctrine could only be defended from the charge of deliberate caricature on the plea that they are founded on an almost complete ignorance of the originals.[26]

Although Popper's account of the intellectual origins of totalitarianism is vulnerable to strictures of this kind, it remains possible that his account of the open society itself has a case to be made for it. Here, however, a great weakness soon becomes apparent, which is that his vision of the open society rested on an uncritical faith in the benefits to be derived from applying scientific method to politics by means of rational planning or what he termed 'social engineering'. Although Popper assumes that there is all the difference in the world between totalitarian planning and social engineering, his ground for making this assumption is not clear: he simply takes it for granted that planners in a liberal society can be trusted in a way that those in a totalitarian one cannot.

The source of Popper's otherwise inexplicable optimism in this respect is his belief that power is not a problem in the open society, since it is in effect a kind of seminar in which we encounter only contending arguments and ideas, rather than conflicting interests. It is therefore unnecessary to provide institutional safeguards such as the rule of law for the protection of liberty. The future of liberty is thus left at the mercy of the social engineers. What made the dependence of the open society on their wisdom and integrity even more disturbing was Popper's refusal to set limits to the range and scope of experimental political projects, provided that governments carry them out on a piecemeal basis.[27]

In the event, Popper's admirers believed that his faith in social engineering was vindicated by the apparent success of the social democratic ideal of the middle way. To the more critical eyes of Isaiah Berlin, however, Popper was guilty of naïve optimism, in so far as the open society took for granted the possibility of creating a largely conflict-free social order.

Whereas Popper had grounded liberalism in faith in scientific method, Berlin's originality lies in his attempt to ground it instead in a modified version of the tragic vision, according to which unavoidable conflict between values is an inescapable feature of the human condition. From this vantage point Berlin sought to develop a pluralist vision of the social order in opposition to the monistic one which he regards as 'the central current of western thought' at large, and the source of totalitarianism in particular.[28] The essence of monism is the belief that all human values can be harmonized within a single ideal of individual and social perfection. To it Berlin opposes the main contention of value pluralism, which is that values are multiple, incommensurable, and in potential conflict.

Although Berlin defends this doctrine with great subtlety, his attitude towards the moral relativism to which value pluralism seems to point is inconsistent. On the one hand, he embraced relativism when he emphasized, in a way reminiscent of existentialist contemporaries on the Continent, that arbitrary choice is the only means of coming to terms with the fact that 'ends equally ultimate, equally sacred, may contradict each other, that entire systems of value may come into collision without possibility of rational arbitration'.[29] On the other hand, Berlin insists at other times on 'the moral validity – irrespective of the laws – of some absolute barriers to the imposition of one man's will on another'.[30] As might be expected, the concept of 'absolute barriers' attracts him when he is, for example, discussing fascism.[31] Within the framework of his thought, however, no philosophical justification for the moral absolutism which this position involves is provided.

Closely related to the incoherence of Berlin's philosophy of value is the problematic nature of his distinction between negative and positive liberty. Negative liberty is freedom from interference by others in whatever one wants to do. This liberty is regarded by Berlin as the foundation of human dignity, although he emphasises that it is only one of a range of competing values between which a choice must be made. Positive liberty, by contrast, means the power to live in accordance with one's higher self and is compatible in principle with the imposition, either by persuasion or coercion, of some purpose or ideal regarded as good because it facilitates the realization of that self. In Berlin's eyes, this latter kind of liberty therefore constitutes a door through which despotism may enter into the heart of modern liberal democracy. Nevertheless, he does not maintain that positive liberty is invariably unacceptable, but only that it inevitably entails the sacrifice of negative liberty, with a consequent diminution of human dignity.

One of the most powerful criticisms of Berlin's distinction between negative and positive liberty is that his schema ignores a third concept of liberty which is potentially in conflict with the liberal-democratic institutions he set out to defend. This third concept, whose nature has been explored by Philip Pettit and Quentin Skinner, is what Skinner terms 'neo-Roman' freedom, which is freedom from dependence on others. The relevant point is that there can be freedom from *interference* by others – that is, Berlin's negative freedom – without freedom from *dependence* on them. At the extreme, for example, a subject might spend his whole life under a despot who never interfered with his liberty, yet his dependence on the will of the despot would prevent his condition from being described as free. This third, neo-Roman concept of freedom, Skinner argues, is of more than purely academic interest since it implies in practice the need for a republican constitution whose nature remains unexplored in Berlin's work.[32]

Sceptics have argued that this third concept of freedom is very difficult to distinguish from 'the old liberal ideal of equal freedom under the law'.[33] Even if the challenge to Berlin from neo-Roman theorists is disregarded, however, a further incoherence in his distinction between two kinds of liberty concerns his use of the term 'negative'. As Maurice Cranston rightly observes, 'the expression "negative liberty" does not serve well to designate the concept of liberty put forward by those philosophers Berlin is most eager to defend: Locke, Constant and Mill, who had each of them a distinctively positive concept of freedom, whether in terms of rights, autonomy or self-realization. Negative language may well be used in liberal "definitions" of freedom, but that does not make liberal freedom negative.'[34]

Why, one may ask, did Berlin insist on regarding liberal freedom as negative? The answer, in part at least, is the questionable picture of the relation between the self and the world which he takes for granted. More precisely, Berlin assumes, as Bhikhu Parekh comments, 'that men derive liberty from nature, not from society'.[35] The trouble with this view is that the whole of the social and the political order, which is of 'artificial' origin, automatically appears to be an intrinsic threat to the exercise of the 'natural' free will which negative liberty is intended to protect. There is, that is, an anarchic assumption at the heart of Berlin's social vision. This is the source, in particular, of his inability to theorize adequately the rule of law – the most vital of all the institutions necessary to implement the liberal pluralist position he himself upholds. As Berlin puts it, every law 'seems to me to curtail *some* liberty, although it may be a means to increasing another'.[36]

The unsatisfactory nature of Berlin's assumption that law necessarily curtails liberty was well brought out by H. L. A. Hart, for whom constitutional law does not curtail activity but merely defines a status, viz. that of citizenship.[37] Likewise, much contractual law does not curtail the activity to which it relates, but simply makes that activity possible. Marriage, for example, would be impossible without the body of law which defines what constitutes a binding contract.

It is not only the nature of law which Berlin misinterprets, however. His fundamentally asocial concept of the individual also creates a more general confusion about sovereignty and civil association particularly evident in his comments on Hobbes, the most important early modern theorist of those concepts. Hobbes, Berlin writes, is to be praised for his candid admission that sovereignty enslaves: 'he [Hobbes] justifies this slavery, but at least did not have the effrontery to call it freedom'.[38] Hobbes, however, could not possibly make the admission with which Berlin credits him, because he does not consider that sovereignty enslaves. Far from destroying freedom, Hobbes regards sovereignty as creating civil society, and in that way protecting the very pluralism to which Berlin himself is committed. Sovereignty in civil association does this, for Hobbes, because it creates *civil* freedom, not Berlin's negative freedom. More precisely, civil society is the friend of civil freedom because it does not consist, *pace* Berlin, of orders and commands promulgated by power, but of authoritative rules which do not impose substantive restraints upon the aims and purposes of subjects.

Despite Berlin's limitations, two achievements may be credited to him. One is that, unlike many contemporaries, he recognized that the defeat of fascism did not herald the end of ethnic nationalism. If Berlin is open to qualified criticism in this respect, it is on the ground that he tended to believe that nationalism of the ethnic kind was more likely to be important outside the Western world than within it.[39] The other achievement was to challenge, through value pluralism, the assumption of social homogeneity taken for granted by the early postwar ideal of consensus. It is in this respect above all that his vision transcends its original Cold War context, despite his failure to clarify the concepts and institutions necessary to implement value pluralism.

For Hayek, the critiques of totalitarianism mounted by Popper and Berlin share a common flaw, which is the failure to appreciate fully that a free society must inevitably be a capitalist one.[40] In his eyes, neither thinker is sufficiently aware of the folly of social democratic belief in the possibility of a middle way between collectivism and capitalism – a belief involves a constant leftward shift, as more and more planning is resorted to in a desperate attempt to make good the failure to which it is doomed. Social democratic aspirations thus threaten to subvert the Allied victory over totalitarianism by creating what Hayek terms 'the road to serfdom', the ultimate origin of which is the mistaken assumption that because society is *made* by man, it can be *designed* by him.[41] To this belief Hayek opposed his vision of the

Great Society, in which social integration is largely spontaneous and unplanned.

How convincing, one must ask, is Hayek's attack on planning, which many regard as a valuable tool for securing welfare, social justice and economic growth? His claim that history reveals an iron link between planning and totalitarianism ignores the fact that it was quasi-religious ideological visions, not economic planning, which inspired both the Nazi and communist regimes.[42] He also ignores the fact that liberal-democratic welfare planning does not typically take the form of orders and commands but of progressive taxation, which is quite compatible with the rule of law. The main problem, however, is Hayek's claim that only spontaneous, unplanned social integration is truly rational. This applies in particular to the market, which is not just a crude, badly organized means of exchange but is, on the contrary, a highly sophisticated information system that synthesizes a vast body of knowledge dispersed amongst a mass of separate individuals. What advocates of planning fail to grasp is that this dispersed knowledge can never be gathered into a body of explicit propositions and placed at the disposal of a central authority: the knowledge on which social integration depends is of an essentially practical kind that always remains embedded in pre-conceptual forms of social existence.

Unfortunately, Hayek's defence of spontaneous social integration seemed to conflict with disturbing historical facts. The record of Weimar Germany, for example, indicated that the maintenance of liberal political institutions could not be achieved merely by leaving the spontaneous order to go its way. Hayek himself, indeed, implicitly acknowledged that the spontaneous order was by no means fully self-adjusting when he demanded extensive financial and constitutional reform in contemporary Britain, in order to protect the free market against democratic governments which constantly undermine it by pursuing inflationary financial policies. Ironically, Hayek's advocacy of such reform has exposed him to the charge of doing little more than replace one kind of planning by another.[43]

If Hayek's attack on planning paradoxically turns out to involve quite a lot of it, his distinction between the state and the spontaneous order is also difficult to make. His attempt to sustain the distinction parallels, in an equally paradoxical way, the classical Marxist distinction between the material base of the social order and the ideological superstructure. In both cases, the political order is dismissed as possessing only a secondary or derivative reality. In Marx's case, this is because it is simply a mask for bourgeois power; in Hayek's, it is because it is assigned only a functional value, based on its contribution to the evolution of the spontaneous order. Both Hayek and Marx veer in consequence towards an anarchist position, in which no ethical justification of the state's coercive dimension is possible. For Marx, who wishes to get rid of the state, this is not a problem, whereas for Hayek, who does not wish to abolish it, inability to distinguish the state from a merely coercive organization is a major source of incoherence in his thought.

The structural similarity between Hayek's thought and Marxism extends still further. Just as Marxism dismisses nationalism as a form of false consciousness, so Hayek dismisses it as merely an atavistic echo of an earlier, tribal stage of social development.[44] Unfortunately, nationalism has refused to perform the vanishing act Hayek hoped for. More plausibly, it might seem, Hayek assumed that a vanishing act was also due to be performed by socialism, which he regarded as another atavistic survival from the tribal era. Although history might seem to have been on his side in this case, it is not at all clear that the disappearance of socialism means the death of the collectivist mentality which inspired the statist mentality Hayek feared: this has deep roots in the modern democratic tradition.

Perhaps the two greatest weaknesses in Hayek's political thought concern the concept of freedom at the centre of his vision of the Great Society. One arises from his recognition that freedom 'never worked without deeply ingrained moral beliefs'.[45] The problem, however, is that the market may erode the moral beliefs on which its own existence depends by sanctioning purely egoistical and acquisitive attitudes.[46] To this Hayek gives no answer. The other problem – the biggest of all – is the *ambiguous* nature of the freedom Hayek wants to defend. He describes this as freedom from coercion, but uses the term 'coercion' in two very different senses. One is a narrow sense, in which coercion refers to government orders and plans incompatible with the rule of law. In this sense, the freedom Hayek defends is perfectly compatible with capitalism. The other sense of coercion, however, is much broader: it consists in 'such control of the environment or circumstances of a person by another that, in order to avoid greater evil, he is forced to act not according to a coherent plan of his own but to serve the end of another'.[47] Now this, it can be argued, is exactly the kind of freedom which led Marx to demand the abolition of capitalism on the ground that the employment relation makes it impossible for the majority to enjoy it.[48] Ironically, then, it is not at all clear what Hayek's 'Great Society' is actually about. Nor is it at all clear why the majority, whom Hayek accepts are unable to lead their own lives, should commit themselves to it.

The main postwar means for ensuring that the majority do commit themselves, instead of feeling alienated, has taken the form of theories of social justice. Hayek, however, dismisses these as mere rhetoric on the ground that they involve the impossible task (impossible, that is, for everyone except God) of deciding who deserves what. The result is that he completely fails to provide any social 'glue' – the need for which was acknowledged by Plato, for example, in the form of what he termed a noble lie, and by Aristotle, in the form of what he described as a 'watery friendship' amongst the members of the body politic.

Although Hayek fails to develop a coherent vision of the Great Society, his scepticism about the benefits of planning has now become widespread. Even though enthusiasm for the free market alternative he advocated has been restricted mainly to New Right intellectuals, some compromise with it is generally regarded as necessary. Of the last of the four thinkers to be considered, Michael Oakeshott may be seen as offering a more coherent theory of liberal democracy by developing an ideal of civil association released from the dependence on capitalism and, more generally, on the problematic concept of the spontaneous order in which Hayek had entangled it.

As in Hayek's case, the target of Oakeshott's attack was the postwar British collectivist mentality which had embraced central planning and threatened in the process to destroy 'the diffusion of power inherent in the rule of law' by 'a lavish use of discretionary authority'.[49] Like Hayek, he believed that the collectivist faith in planning reflected a pervasive rationalist mentality the result of which, he wrote of British political life shortly after the war, was that

> We have the spectacle of a set of sanctimonious, rationalist politicians, preaching an ideology of unselfishness and social service in which they and their predecessors have done their best to destroy the only living root [viz. tradition] of moral behaviour; and opposed by another set of politicians dabbling with the project of converting us from Rationalism under the inspiration of a fresh rationalization of our political tradition.[50]

Unlike Hayek, what Oakeshott opposes to rationalism is not a concept of the spontaneous order grounded in a naturalistic philosophy but a concept of civil association underpinned by an ethical commitment to freedom, in the form of a self-chosen life. This, at least, is the position developed in Oakeshott's mature writings. In his earlier work, which was more polemical and less philosophically precise, what he opposed to rationalism was a concept of tradition, rather than the model of civil association he developed later. The defence of tradition which was the theme of *Rationalism in Politics* (1962) did not, however, prove very successful, for a number of reasons.

One was that Oakeshott tended to give the impression that the true understanding of tradition was only possible for 'an aristocracy who, ignorant of ideals, had acquired a habit of behaviour in relation to one another and had handed it on in a true moral education'.[51] In the postwar world of predominantly middle-class politics, this could only mean a retreat into reactionary nostalgia. A second reason was that Oakeshott wrote as if an existing national consensus about the established order was being disrupted by a few rationalist politicians who foolishly believed that what he termed 'abridgements' of British political practice could be used as recipes for political action. In reality, there were deep national divisions about the nature and purpose of the state which could not be satisfactorily dealt with in this dismissive way.

In addition, Oakeshott seemed to be judging postwar British politics from the standpoint of a more neutral ideal of government than could ever exist. Ideally, he wrote, government stands above party, treats politics as a 'conversation', and acts mainly as a 'referee', imposing generally accepted rules and refusing to take sides.[52] The fact that Oakeshott knew very well that British reality fell short of this ideal does not remove the difficulty in principle of ever applying it to a world in which power, party and conflict have an unavoidable place. Finally, the most theoretically ambitious part of Oakeshott's political essays, which consisted of clarifying the concept of tradition, involved defining tradition so broadly that rationalists turned out to be unwitting traditionalists.

The subsequent publication of Oakeshott's *magnum opus*, *On Human Conduct* (1975), however, made clear that his main project was not so much to castigate rationalism as to move to a deeper level at which a crucial tension could be exposed between two different models of politics which have dominated modern European thought. One

is the formal or procedural ideal of civil association, the other is
what he termed 'managerial' politics. Managerial politics, of which
the totalitarian regimes are the most striking embodiment, is incompatible with freedom because it imposes an overall purpose on the
whole of society.

The basis of Oakeshott's concept of civil association is not an abstract
theory of human rights, or a substantive vision of the political good,
or an appeal to the tradition of a particular society. It is, rather, an
ethical problem he believes is central to modern western political life.
Briefly put, this is the need to explain how membership of the state,
which is a non-voluntary association, can be the source of obligation
amongst citizens who possess what he considers to be the three defining
characteristics of modern western men. These are that they do not
agree on fundamental values; that they hold a radical concept of
natural equality which precludes any privileged claim to authority;
and that they wish to remain free, in the sense of living self-chosen
lives. It was these characteristics which Oakeshott believed Hobbes
had clearly identified in his portrait of the state of nature. Taken
together, they give rise to the problem of political obligation, in the
sense in which classical political thinkers from Hobbes to Kant
formulated it. This problem also stands at the centre of Oakeshott's
own thought, although he was dissatisfied with the answers the earlier
thinkers had given.

The answer Oakeshott himself proposed was that citizens can only
be obligated to the state in so far as it is a civil association governed by
formal, non-instrumental rules they acknowledge to be authoritative.
These rules do not infringe individual freedom because they only
specify general conditions to be observed, not purposes or ideals to
be put into practice. The rules must be non-instrumental, in the
sense that they do not serve an extraneous purpose, interest or ideology,
because they would otherwise restrict freedom. As it is, they simply
define the obligations of citizenship. In so far as the rules of civil association may be said to 'do' anything, it is to constitute, and thereafter
maintain, the civic identity itself.

In this respect, Oakeshott broke with a long line of political thinkers, from Plato onwards, who have made state authority dependent
on the nature of the laws it makes. For Oakeshott, however,
acknowledgement of the authority of the rules of civil association
does not require that they should be rational (as Plato required), or
that citizens should approve of them (as modern consensual theory

has frequently held). Nor does he require that citizens should approve of the outcome of the laws, or believe in the intelligence and integrity of those who make them. This concept of authority is perhaps the hardest aspect of Oakeshott's model of civil association to accept. Sympathy for his position may increase, however, when it is noticed that it is only because approval is not required for civil authority that the civil model can accommodate the extreme diversity of interests and values that characterizes modern societies. The only forms of diversity it excludes are those which are incompatible with acknowledgement of the rules of civil association, whatever they may be. Relationships are not excluded, that is, simply because they are indifferent to the civil bond, or even because they challenge it, provided that the challenge respects the civil framework within which it is made.

A no less striking feature of Oakeshott's version of the civil model is the way he treats one of the most controversial issues in the liberal tradition, which concerns the distinction between 'public' and 'private' life. He rejects as untenable, for example, John Stuart Mill's claim that private and public acts are in some way intrinsically different from each other. He also rejects Hannah Arendt's claim that there are intrinsically different spheres or realms in which private and public acts occur. For Oakeshott, the distinction rests on the fact that every act necessarily has two dimensions, viz. a public dimension, in so far as every act can be seen from the standpoint of its compliance or non-compliance with the rules of civil association, and a private dimension, in so far as every act is the successful or unsuccessful pursuit of some substantive purpose on the part of a particular agent. For Oakeshott, then, the liberal distinction between private and public acts is not an optional or contingent one but is, on the contrary, a necessary feature of civil association.

Finally, Oakeshott is perfectly clear that it is impossible to equate civil society with the state. It is impossible, because the state cannot be reduced to making and implementing the system of formal rules that constitutes civil association. There will inevitably be situations, such as war, in which any state acquires a purposive or 'managerial' character. Oakeshott does not wish to deny this, but only to insist that 'For rulers to become managers even of an undertaking such as this, and for subjects to become partners or role-performers in a compulsory enterprise association such as this, is itself a suspension of the civil condition.'[53]

These then are characteristics of civil association which Oakeshott believes a democracy must preserve in so far as it wishes to remain a limited state. There are, however, several major difficulties presented by his version of the civil model, of which the first is that it is a purely moral relationship which leaves the distinctive feature of the state, viz. coercive power, unexplained. A second is that the model tends to narrow politics down to debate about considerations relating to constitutionality, thereby eliminating the 'stuff' of modern political disputes, which consists in conflicts that extend far beyond the constitutional sphere. A third difficulty is that although Oakeshott fully recognizes the ambiguity of the modern European tradition, he systematically privileges one side of it – the civil side – without establishing why this is intrinsically superior to the 'managerial' side for any but the relatively small number of citizens who place the desire for a self-chosen life above all other concerns.

It will be useful to restate the last problem from a slightly different perspective, which is in terms of how well the civil model corresponds to the postwar concerns of contemporary European democracies. The answer is that, in at least two crucial respects, it does not fit them well at all. One is that civil association requires a very special kind of citizen – a citizen characterized, above all, by the ability and inclination to think of his political identity not in terms of benefits or interests or even rights, but in terms of a non-instrumental commitment to preserving the formal conditions which make freedom possible. This way of thinking, however, is a minority one in modern mass democracies. The second is that civil association as Oakeshott understands it takes for granted the moral authority of what he terms a 'prevailing educated moral sensibility' as the final point of reference in debate about the nature of justice. Oakeshott describes the nature and function of what is in effect a moral elite in his portrayal of what is required in order to make the rule of law just:

> the *ius* [justice] of *lex* [law] cannot be identified with its faithfulness to the formal character of law. To deliberate the *ius* of *lex* is to invoke a particular kind of moral consideration: neither an absurd belief in moral absolutes ... which should be recognized in law, nor the distinction between the rightness and wrongness of actions in terms of the motives in which they are performed, but the negative and limited consideration that the prescriptions of the law should not conflict with a prevailing educated moral sensibility capable of

distinguishing between the conditions of 'virtue', the conditions of moral association ('good conduct'), and those which are of such a kind that they should be imposed ('justice').[54]

In this passage an echo may be discerned of Coleridge's call, a century and a half earlier, for a 'clerisy' whose moral authority would underpin social unity amid the increasing diversity of the modern state. By the 1960s, however, the last vestiges of moral consensus and social hierarchy which this mode of thinking took for granted were beginning to disappear. Unsurprisingly, therefore, Oakeshott experienced the growing despair about the fate of civil association evident, in particular, in his late essay 'The Tower of Babel' (1983). There, he seemed to turn his back on modern European democracies as wholly given over to a consumer mentality and completely devoid of any commitment to civil association.[55] The tentative conclusion must be that his despair was perhaps self-induced by the excessive purity of his version of that ideal.

What emerges from this review of four of the most impressive postwar attempts to clarify the nature of the limited state? In the case of Popper, the answer has to be not much. In the case of Berlin, Hayek and Oakeshott, however, misgivings about postwar social democracy led them to rediscover, by different paths, the continuing relevance of a central theme of such earlier thinkers as de Tocqueville, John Stuart Mill and Dostoevsky. This was the tension between democracy, on the one hand, and the conditions for individual freedom, on the other. What Berlin, Hayek and Oakeshott failed to do, however, was to indicate a viable basis for a postwar consensus which could accommodate not only freedom but other values as well. Berlin largely ignores the problem; Hayek is too optimistic about the possibility of securing widespread commitment to a free market society; and Oakeshott is unable to indicate the source of motivation which will lead the bulk of the population to commit themselves to the rules of civil association. Not surprisingly, therefore, a younger generation of thinkers began, during the 1970s, to search for an ideal of consensus which could include social justice as well as freedom. Other thinkers insisted, in addition, that the postwar generation had failed to appreciate fully the increasingly pluralist character of British society, despite the sensitivity Berlin had shown in that respect. It is these objections which must now be considered.

The Quest for a Rational Consensus

At the beginning of the 1960s Bernard Crick commented on the spread of a new, more idealistic mood in Britain. Far from rejoicing about this, however, he expressed deep misgivings about its likely political implications. Despite its morally admirable aspirations, Crick wrote, the new idealism might in practice only serve to undermine the liberal aspects of the existing political order by bringing politics itself into disrepute, on the ground that it involved compromise and might, more generally, be viewed as creating unnecessary obstacles to the realization of the good society. This danger could only be avoided, Crick maintained, by recalling that politics itself is 'a great and civilizing activity', with 'a life and character of its own'.[56]

A few years after Crick wrote, R. D. Laing, one of the most colourful representatives of the British New Left that emerged during the 1960s,[57] bore out his fears by dismissing politics in any form as nothing more than a source of alienation. This was scarcely surprising, in view of the fact that the only kind of relationship Laing valued was so direct and pure that it would be impossible even in heaven. Describing this relationship, Laing claimed that we are both separated and joined

> by our different perspectives, educations, backgrounds, organizations, group-loyalties, affiliations, ideologies, socio-economic class interests, temperaments. These social 'things' that unite us are by the same token so many *things*, so many social figments that come between us. But if we could strip away all the exigencies and contingencies, and reveal to each other our naked presence? If you take away everything, all the clothes, the disguises, the crutches, the grease paint, also the common projects, the games that provide the pretexts for the occasions that masquerade as meetings – if we could meet, if there were such a happening, a happy coincidence of human beings, what would now separate us?[58]

Although idealism of Laing's extreme sort serves to illustrate the changed mood of the 1960s, it was in a far more muted and intellectually subtle form that the new mood eventually began to penetrate the mainstream of British political theory. In its most influential form, it assumed the guise of a call by Brian Barry for a new 'politics of principle' that would subject all basic social institutions to the requirements of social justice.[59] Sweeping traditional political philosophy to one side as a useless 'rolling [of] the classics round [the] tongue like old brandy',[60] Barry set out to show that analytic philosophy was not eternally condemned to the practically inconsequential study of concepts but could be combined with rational choice theory in a way that would permit it to yield normative conclusions.[61]

Despite Barry's iconoclastic tone, the task he initially assigned to the new politics of principle was a relatively modest one, restricted to 'rather refined distributive questions'.[62] During the next two decades, however, Barry's modest early view was replaced by a far more ambitious one, according to which the proper task of political philosophy is the construction of 'a universally valid case in favour of liberal egalitarian principles'.[63] Barry qualifies his position, it must be added, in an important respect: he insists that the conception of justice as impartiality 'has no pretensions to being a complete political ethic, let alone a complete personal ethic'.[64]

Barry's addition of a normative dimension to the analytic tradition found support in the even more influential work of John Rawls in the USA. To the many sympathizers with the justificatory or 'foundationalist' project which they jointly pursued, it seemed that the 1970s had witnessed an almost miraculous rebirth of political philosophy, following upon years of decline. Objections, however, were not far to seek. At the most fundamental level, critics have questioned the concept of rationality upon which Barry relies to underpin the ideal of justice as impartiality. The problem, David Miller remarks, is that 'what people can reasonably accept seems to depend very largely on their prior sense of justice, so as a way of deriving principles of justice this approach is open to the charge of circularity'.[65] No less seriously, Barry's concept of rationality has been criticized for relying upon an unattainable ideal of moral and political neutrality. The trouble, Glen Newey observes, is that 'it is far from clear why [the rejection of neutrality] by those who favour a non-neutralist political good is *necessarily* unreasonable, or in other words why neutrality is a political [ideal] which nobody can reasonably reject'.[66] Others have noted (as Newey does) that Barry's neutralist ideal amounts in reality to a flight from politics into morality,[67] or else into an equally non-political process of judicial review,[68] leaving Barry wholly unable to come to terms with the central political phenomenon of power. Power, within the framework of justice theory, figures only as an incidental feature of politics which serves to obstruct or facilitate the quest for justice; the fact that it is an inescapable feature of the human condition is not considered. The most radical critiques of Barry's work, however, reject the entire rationalist framework within which his project is conceived. Since those who have developed these critiques have done so as part of a broader quest for a non-rationalist consensus, it will be best to consider them separately.

The Quest for a Non-Rationalist Consensus

Amongst the full-scale assaults launched on rationalist thinking, those of Roger Scruton and John Gray are of particular interest. For Scruton, the principal error of the new rationalist orthodoxy is its inability to recognize the central place of nationalism in the constitution of political identity. The blindness of progressive thought in this respect, he maintains, may be traced back to a disastrous confusion which has bedevilled liberalism from the outset. This consists of a failure to distinguish the conditions for political legitimacy from the conditions for political unity. More precisely, liberalism correctly sees the state as the source of legitimacy, but incorrectly concludes that it is *also* the source of unity. In fact, the source of unity '[is] in the normal instance social rather than political, and ought also to be national'.[69] This is an important insight, but what is problematic is Scruton's attempt to explain the precise sense in which unity is social and national rather than political by invoking a concept of pre-political 'membership'. This concept, which is the lynch-pin of his political thought, comes, above all, from a sense of common destiny and common culture that can properly be described in racial terms, although race in this sense is a wholly historical and cultural phenomenon, not a biological one.[70]

The difficulty is to know how pre-political membership of the nation is related to membership of the state – a question complicated by the fact that the modern nation was itself created by the policies of early modern states. The problem is that Scruton appears to regard the state as a secondary and parasitic creation, dependent upon the 'underlying social unity' of the nation, hidden beneath 'the opinionated crust which smothers it'.[71] Elsewhere, he is careful to insist that pre-political membership of the nation is not based on racial but on cultural and historical unity. This, however, leaves the problem of the relationship between nation and state unresolved. The source of

Scruton's apparent uncertainty about this issue seems to be his reluctance to accept that the civil bond, which is law, is by its very nature an impersonal bond, and therefore cannot satisfy his desire for the deeper and more personal one provided by the nation. Unlike civil identity, he believes, national identity is capable of providing 'roots' that can protect individuals from feelings of spiritual alienation by giving meaning to their existence.[72] The danger created by giving priority to the quest for roots, however, is that it risks the potential reduction of politics to neo-tribalism by destroying the autonomy of civil identity.

The conclusion must be, then, that Scruton does not succeed in making his fundamental concept of pre-political membership intelligible. Despite this, his emphasis on the importance of nationalism has rightly provoked belated attempts to incorporate it into both liberal and socialist theory, after several decades in which its existence was largely ignored. David Miller, for example, has made a sustained effort to integrate more moderate forms of nationalism into socialist thought by exploring the relationship between welfare politics and a shared sense of national identity.[73] More generally, Margaret Canovan has documented the failure of postwar liberal theorists at large to recognize that their ideals were parasitic upon the existence of nation-states which were created, and could only have been created, by forms of power they could not countenance. 'Hobbesian truths about the need for a stable body politic', as she put it, have been ignored.[74]

Unlike Scruton, John Gray does not challenge the primacy of civil association in contemporary western politics. On the contrary, the only kind of political unity relevant to Western societies today, Gray maintains, is one that combines 'the Oakeshottean account of civil association' with 'Berlinian liberalism...founded on radical pluralism'.[75] This combination leads Gray to reject universalistic liberalism in favour of an agonistic version 'in which not [rational principles] but radical choice among incommensurables is central, and in which the particularistic character of human identity and reasoning is fundamental'.[76] The difficulty, however, is that the more recent development of Gray's thought has created two sources of tension with his commitment to civil association. The first is his growing belief that the deepest need of human beings is not for liberty but for 'a home, a network of common practices and inherited traditions, that confers on them the blessing of a settled identity'.[77]

Any attempt to promote the 'organic' kind of society Gray desires, however, either involves piecemeal measures that change little or confers powers upon government which endanger the civil order to which he is committed.

The second source of tension with Gray's civil commitment is his belief that the entire world is now permeated by a nihilistic will to power, in the form of global capitalism, which is in danger of completely destroying civilization.[78] Since the only solution to this malaise is a spiritual revolution, Gray is confronted by a difficult choice. On the one hand, he can opt for a revolt against modernity, of the kind pioneered by Heidegger, whom Gray has written sympathetically about in this connection. On the other, he can pursue the suggestive reformulation of liberalism sketched out in *Two Faces of Liberalism* (2000), in which his aim was the relatively modest one of defending a *modus vivendi* politics that seeks only 'to reconcile individuals and ways of life honouring conflicting values to a life in common'.[79] Even if he adopts the latter strategy, however, it is difficult to reconcile his concern for civil association with his quest for community and for a less spiritually and environmentally destructive mode of life.

The value pluralism which Gray shares with Berlin has been challenged during the last two decades of the twentieth century by demands for a still more radical pluralism, more sensitive to cultural diversity, to group rights, to the claims of ethnic minorities, and to claims based on sex and gender. Whether British political institutions, even in an extensively modified form, can accommodate identity politics of this kind without being destroyed in the process is the question that must now be considered.

Identity Politics: The Search for a Radical Pluralist Consensus

Although many thinkers have argued for a more radical pluralist consensus in recent decades, attention will be restricted to four who have presented the principal versions of it in particularly persuasive form. The first is Anne Phillips, whose concern is to reformulate liberal-democratic theory on the basis of a 'politics of presence' more sympathetic to feminist issues in particular. The second is Chantal Mouffe, whose aim is to provide an even more ambitious restatement of liberal-democratic theory on the basis of a radical democratic programme. The third is Joseph Raz, who has extensively revised the established liberal tradition to accommodate multiculturalism. The fourth is Bhikhu Parekh, who has incorporated an even more radical multicultural philosophy into it.

For Phillips, the only legitimate form of consensus is one sensitive to what she terms the 'politics of difference', which is the only kind of politics that can provide a satisfactory solution to feminist concerns in particular.[80] Unlike earlier feminists, she does not believe in a single, unchanging female essence; does not demonize men; does not indulge female feelings of victimhood by invoking the concept of patriarchy; and does not reject liberal-democratic institutions out of hand. Her concern, rather, is to create a new *modus vivendi* politics based on a 'politics of presence'. Until now, Phillips observes, what has existed is an excessively abstract 'politics of ideas', in which difference has been confined to differences in opinion and belief, with the result that an unrealistic degree of social homogeneity has been ascribed to the social order. In particular, differences such as those of race, religion and sexuality have been ignored.[81]

The remedy for this major defect in the established political tradition, Phillips maintains, is to inject into it a 'politics of presence' that will represent the concrete multiplicity of identities, instead of sacrificing them to an abstract 'politics of ideas'. In this modified system of representation, 'ideas will no longer be separated from presence',[82] and one person will therefore no longer be able to represent others as completely as the classical liberal 'politics of ideas' permits.

How successful is Phillips' attempt to portray a political system more genuinely representative of difference by a compromise between the old politics of ideas and the new politics of presence? The main problem is her requirement that representatives should 'mirror' more accurately the characteristics of the person or persons they represent.[83] If this idea is taken literally, the danger is that *all* representation is in principle open to rejection – a conclusion reached long ago by Rousseau – on the ground that one person can *never* represent the concrete will of another. Although Phillips herself wishes to avoid that conclusion, she fails to show how the logic of her argument can resist it. As a result, the terms upon which a feminist commitment to liberal democracy can be made remain unclear.

There are, however, further difficulties. One relates to Phillip's insistence that active participation in politics is vital for female liberation, a claim which appears to rest on precisely the kind of essentialism she rejects. Another concerns her belief in group rights, despite the danger of locking individuals into group identities, as well as of creating an incentive for them to invent fictitious group identities if that attracts state benefits.

Phillips' 'politics of presence', then, does not offer a coherent alternative to the existing representative system. For a more consistent, albeit no less problematic position, one must turn to Chantal Mouffe's programme of radical democratic reform. Like Phillips, Mouffe rejects any attempt to reduce the identity of either individuals or groups to a single core or essence, whether in the form of class, race or gender.[84] For this reason she also rejects the term feminism itself, on the ground that 'There are...by necessity, many feminisms, and attempts to find the "true" form of feminist politics should be abandoned.' What then is to be the basis of the democratic pluralist social order Mouffe seeks? Like Phillips, she refuses to reject the liberal tradition in its entirety, although she shares Phillips' scepticism about forms of liberalism based on universal principles of rationality or ideals of impartiality. Unlike Phillips, however, what she wishes to conserve is not certain aspects of a 'politics of ideas' but is, rather, the classical model of civil association as reformulated by Oakeshott – provided, Mouffe insists, that Oakeshott's model is first modified in one vital respect. Specifically, it must first be fully democratized, by being recast in terms of her own 'project of radical and plural democracy'.[85]

The difficulty is to know why the various contending groups 'struggling for an extension and radicalization of democracy' in Mouffe's project should commit themselves to the ideal of civil association.[86] In response, Mouffe maintains that the only possible source of integration is the transformative impact of actual participation in the democratic process.[87] Participation, however, is likely to convert only a few to democratic activism of the kind Mouffe desires: for most citizens, their private identity is likely to remain their most important one. Even when attention is restricted to converts to her programme of radical democracy, moreover, it is not clear why they should favour the Oakeshottean ideal of civil association, rather than a form of democracy based on what Oakeshott terms enterprise association.

An even more radical vision of pluralism, however, has challenged the British quest for a consensual basis for the political order. This has been developed by advocates of multiculturalism, a form of political theory which has polarized political thinkers more than any other, being dismissed by one, for example, as merely 'an exercise in political correctness by a *bien pensant* elite'.[88] At least two British presentations of the multicultural position demands consideration, however. One is that of Joseph Raz, who has made a notable attempt to restate liberalism in a way more sympathetic to multiculturalism. The other is that of Bhikhu Parekh, whose more radical version of multiculturalism is the most ambitious philosophical formulation of it.

Multicultural Political Theory

The great defect of the established European liberal tradition, according to Raz, is that it remains rooted in an impersonal 'culture of urban anonymity' which is no longer appropriate to an age challenged by the emergence of 'subcultures of anomie, alienation from society and its institutions, and the emergence of a growing underclass'.[89] Liberalism's deficiency in this respect is evident above all, he maintains, in its failure to respond adequately to the phenomenon central to the emergent multiculturalism of recent decades, which is the group identity other cultures commonly take for granted: this is unintelligible to a political tradition which is about the emancipation of the individual from all traditional ties.[90]

In order to enable liberalism to cope with increasing cultural diversity, Raz seeks to reformulate it by incorporating two evaluative judgments. One is 'the belief that individual freedom and prosperity depend on full and unimpeded membership in a respected and flourishing cultural group'. The other is 'a belief in value pluralism and in particular in the validity of the diverse values embodied in the practices of different societies'.[91] A liberalism based on these two beliefs, Raz claims, will ensure no one will talk any longer of 'a minority problem or of a majority tolerating the minorities' but will instead think of the state as consisting of diverse communities, of which none can claim the state as its own.[92]

The main problem presented by Raz's multicultural revision of liberalism is to know how any kind of unity will be created amongst the diverse cultures it sanctions. The answer, he suggests, lies in the creation of a common culture.[93] The trouble, however, is that Raz fails to give a very coherent account of how this culture is to be constructed, largely due to his paradoxical belief that it must be firmly based on several peculiarly western foundations. Foremost amongst these foundations is a 'perfectionist' moral ideal which attaches ultimate value to individual autonomy. A second is value pluralism which, once again, is peculiar to the modern western tradition. A third is the western European liberal ideal of toleration and non-discrimination in the public realm.

The principal theoretical problem presented by Raz's vision of a common culture based on specifically western values lies in his explicit universalization of the latter, which he identifies as 'true values'.[94] Why, one must ask, does he feel justified in elevating western values to this absolute status? Unfortunately his answer, which is that they are grounded in 'right reason', appears merely to be a reaffirmation of his belief in their absolute character, rather than a defence of that belief. Even if the philosophical difficulties presented by the concept 'right reason' are ignored, however, Raz's multicultural liberalism presents a further problem. This is his highly problematic assumption that the culturally diverse members of a multicultural society who have agreed on the need for an authority that succeeds 'in getting people to conform to right reason'[95] would be able to agree on the kind of institutions that could convert their agreement into concrete policy proposals. When Plato was faced by the need to make rule by right reason acceptable, it will be recalled, he had to introduce the idea of a myth of the golden, silver and bronze natures. In the absence of the kind of emotional underpinning such a myth provides, Raz's belief that diverse cultural groups can be harmonized by a universally binding concept of rationality appears somewhat optimistic.

What impels Raz to adopt this implausible position? The answer ultimately seems to be traceable to his fear that multiculturalist liberalism may end in cultural relativism. Fear of relativism is evident, above all, in his claim that only what he terms a 'non-relativized' concept of authority can be truly legitimate.[96] The problem with a 'non-relativized' concept of authority, however, is that it obligates its subjects *quite independently of whether they themselves regard it as authoritative*. Raz consequently saves himself from relativism only by adopting a potentially authoritarian position which appears incompatible with his liberalism. More generally, as has been noted, he relies upon a concept of rationality which ameliorates the problem of multicultural diversity by assuming that conflicts can be resolved by resorting to an extra-political 'view from nowhere' which appears to be unattainable. It is his endeavour to overcome problems of this kind that lends particular interest to Bhikhu Parekh's *Rethinking Multiculturalism* (2000), one of the most ambitious postwar works of political theory.

Liberal efforts to deal with multicultural diversity, Parekh maintains, involve unacceptably restricting multiculturalism to valuing cultural minorities. A truly multiculturalist perspective, by contrast, must create a standpoint from which the very concept of a majority/ minority division is eliminated. Progress in this respect, Parekh believes, has been impeded not only by the fact that liberalism can never provide an impartial framework for conceptualising other cultures, but also by its inability to appreciate the positive value of interaction between them. He emphasizes, however, that multiculturalist concern with cultural diversity should not be mistaken for a concern 'about difference and identity *per se*'; its concern is rather with 'differences that are embedded in and sustained by culture'.[97] The first major challenge confronting Parekh, accordingly, is to provide a definition of culture.

A culture, he writes, is 'a body of beliefs and practices in terms of which a group of people understand themselves and the world and organize their individual and collective lives'.[98] This definition is so broad, however, that it fails to provide multiculturalist theory with the distinctive concern Parekh claims for it since the gays, feminists and vocationally distinct groups (such as fishermen and miners) whose 'cultures' he wishes to differentiate from multiculturalist concern are all 'embedded in and sustained by culture' as he defines it. In order to characterize the distinctive nature of multiculturalist theory more precisely, Parekh therefore adds that the groups with which it is specifically concerned not only possess their own culture but also live in separate communities. The trouble, however, is that religious groups such as monks and vocational groups like bear trainers in India meet that condition. This does not mean, of course, that such minorities are not worth protecting; what it means is that the distinctive nature of the multiculturalist theoretical position is not made clear, since the concept of culture invoked is so comprehensive that there appear to be few kinds of minority that do not come under it. It is difficult, in consequence, to avoid the suspicion that multiculturalism is merely another term for an extensive pluralist commitment, rather than the distinctive philosophical position Parekh takes it to be.

The more theoretically ambitious dimension of Parekh's thought only emerges, however, when the difficulties presented by his broad definition of culture are disregarded and attention is focused on the ethical theory with which he underpins multiculturalism. The core of this theory is his claim that cultural diversity is an intrinsically valuable part of the human good because every culture realizes only a limited range of human capacities and values, with the result that different cultures 'correct and complement each other, expand each other's horizon of thought and alert each other to new forms of human fulfilment'.[99] The difficulty with this claim is that it equates *cultural particularity* with *intrinsic imperfection*. Since many would object to this identification, the second great challenge confronting Parekh is to defend it.

In order to do so, Parekh adopts the Enlightenment belief in a universally valid ideal of progress and commends, in particular, latter-day Enlightenment enthusiasts like John Stuart Mill on the ground that they 'have always held, and rightly, that diversity is the precondition of progress and choice, and that truth can only emerge from a peaceful competition between different ways of life'.[100] The problem with this position is that the Enlightenment ideals of progress, choice and truth on which it rests, along with belief in the merits of peaceful competition, are all rooted in a secularized Judaeo-Christian tradition which not all cultures share: they are all, in fact, ideals that are deeply contestable. Adopting them, moreover, implies a simple division of history into societies that make a positive contribution to progress and truth, on the one hand, and those that do not, on the other. Such a division ignores the complexity of the political world, in which the reality of power creates considerations with which only practical wisdom, rather than truth, can deal. Finally, it is difficult for those unconvinced by Parekh's equation of cultural particularity with imperfection to sympathize with his claim that the promotion of particular cultures is a duty for governments and individuals alike. There may of course be prudential reasons why particular cultural minorities should sometimes receive special political treatment, but the case for such treatment is more easily made out in terms of the pragmatic concessions necessary for political integration than in terms of the duty, wherever possible, to foster cultural perfection upon which Parekh's ethical doctrine depends.

It is indeed in the course of Parekh's conversion of his ethical doctrine into a political one that he encounters his third and greatest philosophical challenge. Applied to the political order, he maintains, multiculturalist ethical doctrine means that 'The state should obviously treat all its communities equally', although 'that need not involve identical treatment'.[101] Equality of treatment, however, is downgraded to an ideal which may be overridden when Parekh remarks that 'In a multicultural society one might sometimes need to go further and grant not only different but also additional rights to some groups or individuals' in order 'to achieve such worthwhile collective goals as political integration, social harmony and encouragement of cultural diversity'.[102] What is mainly relevant at present, however, is Parekh's recognition that a major obstacle to the multiculturalist political programme is created by 'ineliminable inequalities' which arise from the fact that every society has an

> historically inherited cultural structure which informs its conduct of public life. While it has a duty to modify it to accommodate the legitimate demands of its minorities, it cannot do so beyond a certain point without losing its coherence and causing widespread disorientation, anxiety and even resistance. This is likely to lead to unequal treatment of its cultural minorities in certain areas, about which in spite of all its good intentions it might be able to do little.[103]

Since the 'certain point' to which Parekh refers might be reached very quickly, the risk seems to be that multiculturalist political theory might rapidly be condemned to impotent 'good intentions'. Parekh manages to avoid this conclusion by the optimistic claim that the difficulties encountered are best dealt with 'by discussion, negotiation and compromise'.[104] This admirable commitment to peaceful political methods can only be presented as defensible in the face of intractable inequalities, however, by retreating into an effectively 'depoliticized' vision of a multicultural society in which the sources of social conflict are assumed to be ultimately non-antagonistic.

Parekh's retreat from politics is especially pronounced in his attempt to avoid relativism by subjecting governments to universal moral truths which set limits to cultural diversity. 'It is of course true', he writes, 'that some traditional societies have grossly outrageous practices and customs which obviously need to be changed...'[105] But to whom exactly is this 'of course true'? In order to make clear that it is not merely to confident western liberal theorists like John Rawls, Parekh claims to base his own universalism on what he terms 'a freely negotiated and constantly evolving consensus on universally valid principles of good government' which can call on support from a large range of different cultures.[106] This cannot, however, conceal the remarkable convergence between Parekh's vision of a rational international consensus on the conditions of good government and Enlightenment faith in the ability of reason to construct a global order based on human rights – a convergence which is especially striking when he praises references in the 1948 United Nations Declaration of Human Rights to 'respect for human rights and dignity, equality before the law, equal protection of the law, fair trial and the protection of minorities' as exemplifying his ethical ideal.[107]

Does this impressive statement of multiculturalism constitute, as Parekh claims, a coherent distinctive philosophy with a more genuinely inclusive and affirmative attitude towards cultural diversity than anything the established liberal-democratic tradition can hope to provide? From a philosophical standpoint, perhaps the main criticism is that Parekh fails, as was noticed above, to acknowledge the extent to which his position is shaped at nearly every point by Enlightenment assumptions which he rejects in their more specifically liberal guise; and that his multiculturalism shares, in particular, the central characteristic of the Enlightenment, which is the vision of an ideal society (Parekh is fully aware that there may in practice be insuperable obstacles to it) in which conflict and power have been subjected to control by reason, in this case in the form of cross-cultural dialogue. Ironically, as Slavoj Žižek remarks, the result of this Enlightenment inheritance is that the 'multiculturalist celebration of lifestyles' tends merely to reproduce, in a modified form, the very sameness which it sets out to reject. In order to diminish the significance of radical difference, that is, it postulates an underlying social uniformity, in the guise of 'a non-antagonistic Society [that] is the global "container" in which there is enough room for all the multitude of cultural communities, lifestyles, religions, sexual orientations...'.[108] This does not mean, it should be emphasized, that the multiculturalist political theory is an error; it means, more precisely, that it is inspired by a faith, rather than derived from the coherent philosophical position its defenders claim. Nor does it mean that Parekh fails to qualify his Enlightenment idealism by significant concessions to the established social order. When he does so, however, his views are so eminently cautious and prudent that there appears to be little difficulty, given sufficient goodwill, in accommodating them (in Britain at least) within the established framework of government, without the need for the radical revision of contemporary political categories for which his philosophical position calls.

Beyond Identity Politics: Republican Theory

Although Phillips, Mouffe, Raz and Parekh are committed to radical pluralist positions, they do not offer convincing solutions to the problem of social integration this creates. What must now be considered is the response to this problem by contemporary British defenders of republicanism, a political theory which has enjoyed a revival during the last decade of the twentieth century. Like the thinkers just considered, republican theorists maintain that only some form of political participation can prevent the fragmentation of the social order. Unlike those thinkers, however, republican ones do not tie the case for participation to the advocacy of a particular form of identity politics. Their starting point is, rather, the conviction that a sense of identification with political institutions can only be created through participation in the political process itself.

David Miller, for example, emphasizes that a public practice of impartiality can only be generated by participation in political discourse. Precisely because the participation is public, those involved cannot appeal to purely personal interests but are compelled to argue their case by giving public reasons – they are compelled by the political process itself, that is, to become impartial.[109] In similar vein, Richard Bellamy has stressed that only the experience of political participation can overcome the traditional liberal tendency to regard constitutions as little more than mechanisms for securing individual interests and rights. Republican theory, by contrast, regards constitutions as the non-instrumental framework for a dialogue in which fellow citizens constantly define and redefine the nature and implications of their mutual identity as fellow citizens.[110] Participation alone, Bellamy maintains, can create the sense of intrinsic value this perspective confers upon constitutionalism.

Amongst the most persuasive defenders of republicanism are members of the 'neo-Roman' school, according to whom it is only when the ancient Greek model of direct democracy, with its history of internal conflict, is copied that doubts arise about the integrating capacity of participation.[111] The neo-Roman concept of participation, by contrast, is firmly committed not only to the rule of law but to the division of powers and institutions of responsible government, and therefore escapes the difficulties confronted by republicans who put their faith in the ancient Greek experience. Even the neo-Roman school, however, cannot escape the problem, identified long ago by Constant, created by the political apathy of modern western man, whose interests are predominantly social and private. A particular merit of Quentin Skinner's thought is the directness with which he confronts this. Machiavelli, he maintains, was right to insist that civic virtue can only be ensured if the law is used 'to force us out of our habitual patterns of self-interested behaviour, to force us into discharging the full range of our civic duties, and thereby to ensure that the free state on which our own liberty depends is itself maintained free of servitude'.[112]

Unfortunately, the historical evidence indicates that even when interest in political participation is awakened, it is only in the face of a threat to national survival, and is therefore essentially temporary. Even if that view is too pessimistic, the use of legal compulsion to counter political apathy envisaged by Skinner is likely to produce only outward conformity, without the inner enthusiasm and intelligent commitment at which republicanism aims. Even if this misgiving proves to be misplaced, however, two other major problems are presented by republican theory.

One is that the continued existence of the private realm in a republican society would be in constant danger, since there would be a tendency to regard it as merely a sphere for personal self-indulgence, to which only those without a sense of social and political responsibility withdraw. Although republican theorists may regard this misgiving as ill-founded, the institutions upon which they rely are likely to be staffed by civic enthusiasts, and therefore provide little reassurance. The other problem is that, as de Tocqueville eloquently maintained, a desire to participate arises only when doing so confers significant power. This would require a degree of decentralization which conflicts so greatly with long-established patterns of government that it is unlikely to happen, no matter how desirable it may seem.

Despite the problems just indicated, what is salutary is the republican reminder that concepts of consensus based solely on rights, interests, abstract rationality or *modus vivendi* are unlikely to provide adequate protection for the institutions of a free society. What is needed, in one form or another, is widespread civic sentiment. Perhaps

the greatest merit of the third way ideal of the New Labour government is its recognition of this fact – at the ideological level, at least.
How seriously the ideology is to be taken in practice remains to be
considered.

The Politics of the Third Way

To its defenders, the third way programme represents a visionary
modernization project aimed at redefining the postwar British ideal
of social democracy in ways that empower citizens and renew their
civic sense of duty, whilst also alerting them to the new realities of
a globalized world. To its critics, it is merely an empty body of rhetoric
masking an enormous growth of the regulative state and the destruction of parliamentary government by a demagogic presidential style
of rule based on media manipulation. In order to decide which view
is correct, it is necessary to look more closely at the view of defenders
of the third way, as well as what critics say its implementation has
thus far involved.

From within the ranks of New Labour politicians themselves, the
clearest account of the third way has been offered by Gordon Brown,
the Chancellor of the Exchequer. The aim, Brown has explained, is
to go beyond both social democratic reliance on central state provision
of welfare and the neo-liberal faith in unregulated markets by nur-
turing 'a new civic patriotism', expressed in the form of 'a renewal of
civic society, where rights and responsibilities go together'.[113] The
third way envisages, that is, 'A new era – an age of active citizenship
and an enabling State'. More precisely, reliance will mainly be on
'community-based services where the accent is on the one-to-one
approach and the greater flexibility to innovate in which voluntary
organisations often excel – whether it is in coaching teenagers,
motivating former truants, or mentoring new business'.[114] By 2005,
Brown has enthusiastically declared, two-thirds of adults may be
expected to do at least two hours' voluntary activity a week.[115] In
England too a million flowers may yet bloom.

There is, however, a fundamental aspect of third way theorizing
that Brown did not touch on. This is the essentially global perspective
emphasized by Anthony Giddens when he observed that 'The [new]
welfare society...is not just the nation, but stretches above and
below it. Control of environmental pollution, for example, can never

be a matter for national government alone, but it is certainly directly relevant to welfare.' In a similar vein, David Held has insisted that any theory of legitimate power must now inevitably be 'the theory of the democratic state within the global order and the theory of the impact of the global order on the democratic state'.[116]

Such, in outline, is the framework of the ambitious new consensus sought by theorists of the third way. In practice, however, attempts to implement it have not produced Gordon Brown's ideal of civic patriotism but have instead vastly extended state regulation through the setting of targets throughout the public sector, with related monitoring requirements, and an extensive programme of redistribution, with elaborate paperwork on eligibility conditions. After Gordon Brown's 2002 budget, for example, it was calculated that his additions to the already complex system of tax credits would mean that before long about thirteen million adults – the majority of parents, pensioners and the disabled, amounting to nearly one-third of the total adult population – would receive state benefits of some kind.[117] Whether this constitutes empowerment or dependency is no doubt arguable, but what is less contestable is the lament of the commentator who remarked that what the third way meant in practice is that 'We are being made into a nation on means-tested benefits.'[118]

Is the quest for a third way consensus to be dismissed, then, as mere rhetoric? So far as globalization is concerned, critics have maintained that, far from third way aspirations heralding the emergence of a supra-national civil society, they mark the stark division of the world into the haves and have nots.[119] So far as domestic politics are concerned, Mr Blair himself has expressed disappointment with progress to date. Confronted early in his second term with the charge that the New Labour ideal had not taken root in Britain, his response was to blame the recalcitrant natives: 'People', he said, 'have not tried to understand it here.' More appreciative electorates, he added, could be found 'in parts of South America for example, [where] it is still seen as a ground-breaking moment for the centre-left'.[120] For those stuck in the UK there was perhaps some consolation in recognizing, as a thoughtful commentator remarked, that despite the failure of third way policies, third way thinking was nevertheless correct to emphasize the need for 'a new relationship between the individual and the state, moral choices that cannot be fudged and a wholesale decentralisation of health, education and social services with a new role for voluntarism and mutual aid free of government control'.[121] How to put this programme into action remained, needless to say, unclear.

The Constitutional Issue, the Problem of British Identity and the European Union

At the end of the twentieth century, a major British work on political theory concluded with the encouraging thought that our present situation reveals 'a state form reconciled to human limitations ... but still aimed at mitigating the vulnerability of its subjects and serving their more commonplace and insistent practical concerns'.[122] So far as Britain itself is concerned, the questionable aspect of John Dunn's relatively optimistic position was its failure to take account of what is perhaps the greatest change in British political thought since the war, which is the decline of the constitutional concern taken for granted by almost all thinkers in 1945. In the absence of that concern, 'a state form reconciled to human limitations' might prove to be one with little regard for freedom.

The decline of constitutional concern was the result of various features of postwar British political life, amongst which the most important intellectual ones were the initial dominance of conceptual analysis, for which such issues were not an appropriate subject of attention, and the subsequent concern of normative theory with social justice and rights. In so far as constitutionalism continued to attract attention, it did so only to the extent that it seemed to be connected to those issues. This is evident, for example, in Richard Dworkin's definition of constitutionalism as nothing more than 'a system that establishes legal rights that the dominant legislature does not have the power to override or compromise'.[123] The result, as Richard Bellamy has remarked, was that concern for the political mechanisms associated with the British ideal of a mixed or balanced constitution was quietly abandoned, and that postwar Britain gradually moved in consequence towards a situation in which effective political checks on the potentially despotic doctrine of absolute parliamentary sovereignty inherited from Dicey were no longer of central concern.[124] This, then, was how it came about that a constitutional revolution described early in the new millennium by the Downing Professor of the Laws of England at Cambridge University as 'more serious than anything experienced since the 17th century' proceeded with little attention or opposition.[125]

The origins of this situation were not, of course, of postwar making: they lay rather in the centuries-old failure of British political thought to comprehend the state as an impersonal public structure that transcends those who staff its offices. The state, as one commentator observed, has been 'personalized' (or 'privatized'),[126] with the result that government officials claim the rights of private citizens but fail to recognize clearly the public responsibilities which attach to the state offices they hold. The root of the problem, in a word, was the British lack of a systematic body of public law. Due to this, Prosser notes, 'we have a "stateless" society' in which attention has been primarily concerned with 'the exercise of power in particular instances', rather than with the responsibilities and limits of public power as such.[127]

It was hardly surprising, in this situation, that a land which prided itself on its tradition of individual freedom should discover, towards the end of the twentieth century, that the European conception of public law might offer better protection for the citizen than the British doctrine of parliamentary sovereignty.[128] What undermined British self-confidence still further, however, was a deepening sense of crisis about the very nature of British national identity which emerged during the final decade of the century.

The nature of this crisis was aptly summarized in the editorial introduction to a special edition of the *Political Quarterly* on 'Being British' published in 2000. 'The twentieth century ends, and the twenty-first begins', it read, 'with the idea of Britain in deep trouble... Muddling through no longer seems adequate or even available.'[129] The problem, more precisely, is that 'The traditional support systems of Britishness have all weakened. The collective endeavour and sacrifice of total war is a fast-fading memory. The lived experience of empire is even further distant. Polls show that most people do not think the monarchy will still exist in fifty years' time.' In addition, there is the solvent impact of postwar immigration, globalising trends and supra-national European institutions.

What was to be done about the British identity crisis? The response of the editors was to propose a new form of British nationalism, based on 'a new politics of identity, culture and territory'. In this new British identity, the old 'top-down, centralised and unitary version, with its old supporting props of Britishness' would be replaced by a multinational kingdom which 'will be loose and untidy, with power organised at different levels, a home to experiment and diversity. It will be a union state, but not a unitary state. A part will no longer confuse itself with the whole. Its inhabitants will be easy with the idea of overlapping identities and multiple loyalties.'

So far as concrete ways of constructing this new, more pluralistic sense of national identity are concerned, one of the most suggestive emphasized the need for a more 'dialogic' kind of politics, inspired by a republican commitment to forging a political identity in and through the political process itself.[130] Critics, however, were not slow to point out that optimism about such a radical reconstruction of British identity assumed a degree of plasticity in political affairs for which history gave little support. The existing identity, they noted, had not only been long in the making but had also involved violence, so there was no reason to assume that a new one could easily be forged.

Confronted in particular by devolution, as Scotland acquired its own parliament and Wales a national assembly, some thinkers and publicists were tempted to stake their hopes on the English identity. Krishan Kumar, for example, contrasted its 'civic' character with the primarily cultural and ethnic ones of Wales, Scotland and Northern Ireland, and noted England's consequent ability to absorb 'a wide variety of peoples – Celts and Jews, Irish and Poles, Asians and Africans'. If England now 'at last needs to see itself as a nation among other nations', he concluded, 'it can by example still show the world that nationalism need not mean only narrowness and intolerance. English nationalism, that enigmatic and elusive thing, so long conspicuous by its absence, might newborn show what a truly civic nationalism can look like.'[131] For more sceptical admirers of England, however, it was too late in the day to dream of an English civic revival of this kind.

For David Marquand, for example, 'British civil society, which was once one of the strongest in the world in the nineteenth century, is now one of the weakest in the democratic west.'[132] Marquand's pessimism was not an isolated affair. For Kenneth Minogue, the pursuit of social justice and (more recently) the affirmation of diversity have ended by creating a society weighed down by political correctness and regulation.[133] For Roger Scruton, things appeared to be worse even than they were in T. S. Eliot's wasteland, since England is 'becoming a no-man's-land . . . managed by executives who visit the outposts only fleetingly, staying in multinational hotels on the edges of the floodlit wastelands'. All the old loyalties (notably, the religious one) on which English civic patriotism was built have disintegrated, he maintained, have been replaced by the most corrosive of human emotions – a universal sense of resentment.[134]

Faced by such dismal sentiments, those bent upon finding a ray of hope for the future of the United Kingdom might turn in desperation to the broader identity offered by European integration. For Europhiles, not the least attraction this offered was that the new British pluralism appeared to be an important step towards implementing the 'Europe of rights' to which Britain had signed up when it incorporated the European Convention on Human Rights into British law in 2000. More generally, Europhile historians like Norman Davies and Linda Colley argued that the sense of British specialness which continued to be an obstacle to embracing European integration was based on outmoded and ill-founded forms of nationalistic sentiment that failed to grasp the extent to which British history has been interwoven with that of the Continent. In particular, Colley maintained, what has united Britain since the eighteenth century is a combination of factors no longer relevant to British political life: hostility to France, Protestantism, war and imperial expansion. The disappearance of these factors means that that there is now a greater prospect of the public realizing that membership of the European Union merely formalized existing historical realities, rather than destroying a non-existent tradition of insular national autonomy.

For Eurosceptics, by contrast, the prospect of signing the draft European constitution meant the end of a distinct English political identity of any kind, since the UK would dissolve into independent regions. Challenged to hold a referendum because of this, the British government argued that there was no need, since the draft constitution was merely (in the words of Peter Hain, the chief British representative at the drafting convention) a 'tidying up' operation. In reality, Noel Malcolm replied, the European constitution 'is the greatest alteration in the rights and powers of government in this country since 1688', since 'the powers of the European Union, which were previously based on treaties, will now be based on a constitution. With this change,... something that could not legally be considered as a state ... most definitely can [be]'.[135] The British Government, Malcolm notes, is proud of the fact that it has inserted an amendment stating that the powers of the EU were 'conferred' on it by the member states, which therefore retain their national sovereignty. Malcolm rightly responds, however, that this claim 'conflicts with basic constitutional theory', according to which any amendment of the EU constitution is authoritative 'only because of the intrinsic authority of that constitution itself'. Despite the approaching moment of truth, Malcolm notes, 'in the hearts of the British people, the new European Constitution has hardly made any impression at all; it is viewed with either vague apprehension or almost complete indifference'.

Conclusion

When these conflicting views of Britain's future are weighed in the balance, what do they suggest about the likely course of British politics? Two things at least seem abundantly clear. One is that, regardless of whether the future lies with a new pluralist Britain or a revitalized England, the old constitutional system of checks and balances which postwar Britain inherited from centuries past will no longer remain central to its political tradition. In other words, the commitment to the limited state which was for several centuries the distinctive feature of British political life is likely only to survive as, at best, a somewhat marginal and unprincipled one. The second concerns the implications of signing the draft European constitution. In that event, the crucial issue is whether the supra-national state thereby created (assuming the validity of Malcolm's compelling analysis) retains some continuity with the British past by virtue of embodying the ideal of civil association which formerly played a central part in British political theory and practice. Whether it is plausible to interpret the EU in terms of a supra-national form of civil society, however, is a question which will be taken up in the final chapter.

3

From Revolutionary Idealism to Political Moderation: The French Search for an Accommodation with Liberal Democracy since 1945

By the time of the Liberation in 1944, French domestic politics had descended into a condition of virtual civil war between collaborators with the Vichy regime and members of the Resistance movement. At the very centre of postwar French political life, in consequence, was an acute problem of national identity. Although this problem was hardly new, rooted as it was in the original profound division of modern France caused by the Revolution in 1789, one aspect of the postwar political situation was nevertheless novel. This was the fact that the only viable answer to the problem of reconstruction seemed to be the revolutionary one offered by the radical Left. How did this extraordinary situation come about?

The answer is not far to seek: three alternative conceptions of national unity that had previously been available were for the time being no longer significant options. The republican one, which consisted of expressing the national will through a popular assembly, had been discredited by the weaknesses of the prewar Third Republic, which had finally come to an ignominious end in 1940 when most of the deputies and senators had voted for the abolition of the republic and transferred absolute power to Marshal Pétain. The socialist one did not succeed in winning the working class away from its prewar support for Communism, as well as suffering from the fact that the Socialist Party had not developed a particularly impressive record of participation in the Resistance. The Right, finally, was tainted by association with the Vichy regime. De Gaulle alone was able, because of his resistance record, to offer a credible alternative to the domination of debate by the Left. It was against this background that the revolutionary Left was able to step into the political vacuum and rapidly establish its sway over political discourse.

This situation was to last for nearly three decades, after which the disintegration of Left domination permitted a search for a non-revolutionary framework for national political debate. Whether this search has resulted in the replacement of revolutionary idealism by a coherent commitment to political moderation, however, is a question about which opinion varies. In particular, the question of whether an acceptable alternative to the revolutionary vision of political integration can ever be provided by the kind of liberal compromise with democracy found in the Anglo-Saxon world remains a matter on which French thinkers have not been able to agree. In order to understand the complex issues involved, it is necessary to begin by considering the nature of the radical sentiments against which the quest for a non-revolutionary politics had to be defined.

Radical Political Thought

Although the thinkers associated with the radical Left did not constitute a homogeneous group, their thought displays a common structure which will be useful to consider before examining the strands within the radical fold. This structure is marked, firstly, by opposition to constitutional democracy. As Sunil Khilnani has remarked, although constitutional values had all been affirmed in France as early as 1789, the Revolution, and in particular the Left it created,

> proved to be the best enemy of these values... To the intellectual Left, constitutional representative democracy, 'bourgeois' or 'formal' democracy, was a contemptible and mystifying illusion; only... in the late 1970s did it gradually come to be accepted as a political form in its own right.[1]

In fact, there is an element of exaggeration in Khilnani's portrait of the fate of consitutionalism: it has found important French representatives, such as Constant and de Tocqueville, throughout French history, although it is true that they have very much been a minority.

The belated revival of constitutionalism in the postwar era, following the decline of revolutionary enthusiasm amongst the French intelligentsia, will be considered later in this chapter.

The second characteristic was a nationalist zeal no less strong on the Communist Left than on the Right. Since orthodox Communist doctrine had always rejected nationalism as a bourgeois phenomenon, this might seem puzzling. The integration of nationalism into the revolutionary Left's orthodoxy was facilitated, however, by two considerations. One was the belief, expressed for example by Merleau-Ponty, that to be a Marxist is 'not to renounce all differences, to give up one's identity as a Frenchman, a native of Tours or Paris, or to forego individuality in order to blend into the world proletariat. It is indeed to become part of the universal, but without ceasing to be what we are.'[2] The other, even more telling consideration, was the belief that the Russian Revolution of 1917 was merely a further step along the revolutionary path originally charted by the French themselves in 1793. The torch of freedom previously carried by the French Jacobins, in other words, had for the time being passed into Soviet hands. Understandably, the French Left's enthusiasm for Russia was enhanced still more by Soviet opposition to Nazism during the Vichy era.

The third structural characteristic of postwar radical discourse was a tendency on the part of radical intellectuals to treat political conflict as a struggle between the forces of darkness and light, represented by the bourgeoisie and the proletarian masses, respectively. In this respect, the Left was adopting a mode of thought which could once again be traced back to 1793. Specifically, it originated with the proclamation of the doctrine of popular sovereignty, according to which all legitimate power derives from the people. The difficulty from that point onwards has been that reactionaries, liberals, socialists and communists naturally define the 'people' to suit their own ideological purposes. In each case, the outcome was a simple reduction of politics to a struggle between insiders and outsiders. After 1945, this dualism was given a particularly vicious character by continuing hostilities between collaborators and members of the Resistance. More generally, a postwar politics structured around the division between insiders and outsiders offered no prospect of ever ending the division of the French nation inherited from the Revolution of 1789.

The final structural characteristic of radical thought, which was not peculiar to the radical tradition but received special emphasis in it, consisted of conferring almost canonical status on the political pronouncements of favoured intellectuals. This did little to encourage a spirit of political compromise, encouraging instead arrogant claims to moral purity in a corrupt social world. After 1945, this arrogance was intensified by the conviction that being engagé was the only sure sign of philosophical integrity. The intellectual, Sartre indicated, is not a detached spectator, as the French Cartesian tradition held, but a concrete historical creature who cannot turn his back on politics. In times like the present, he 'is necessarily involved in the march of history. His task [is that] of presentation, of criticism, of setting ideologies face to face with freedom'.[3] This view was supported by, amongst others, Merleau-Ponty, who declared that the chief lesson to be learned from the Occupation and the Resistance was that men are not abstract consciousnesses 'naked before the world' but historical beings with specific cultures and territories which they must fight to defend.[4]

Such, then, was the structure of the radical orthodoxy which characterized French political debate during the first three postwar decades. Within it, however, were three conflicting visions of the human condition, represented by existentialism, personalism and Marxism. Of the three modes of radical thought, existentialism appealed in particular to members of the Resistance and those, more generally, who subsequently experienced postwar social and political dislocation. Its attraction was that it made freedom an inner achievement, independent of adverse social circumstances. To those who recognized that national reconstruction involved more than personal salvation, however, it offered little inspiration. The limitations of Sartre's philosophy in this respect had indeed been identified at an early stage by the Italian thinker, Norberto Bobbio, when he distinguished between the revolutionary and the rebel. The revolutionary, he remarked, 'fights one form of society in order to create a better', whereas the rebel 'fights every possible form of society', with the result that 'If he exerts any influence on the world, it is due not to his activity in itself, but to his example.'[5] As Bobbio noted, Sartre was a rebel rather than a revolutionary. As such, he shed little light on how a reconstruction programme with national appeal might be created.

The key to Sartre's rebel posture is the theory of consciousness developed in *Being and Nothingness*, in which he effectively stood the traditional western view of freedom on its head. According to the traditional view, freedom is an essentially positive human characteristic.

For Sartre, by contrast, freedom is merely a lack, or void, or 'hole of being at the heart of Being'[6] which dooms man to a life of futile endeavour since the hole can never be filled. Sartre made this futility explicit towards the end of *Being and Nothingness* in the brief remark that 'Man is a useless passion'.[7]

One of Sartre's most acute French critics, Gabriel Marcel, had little difficulty in identifying the principal flaw in his negative concept of freedom. This is, that it is not arrived at by a comprehensive study of human nature but by improperly generalizing from the highly restricted experience of a relatively small group of unfortunate people. This is evident, for example, when Sartre concludes in *Huis Clos* that 'Hell is other people' on the basis of a selection of the human race confined to three untypical human beings, viz. Garcin, a deserter; Ines, a lesbian who is guilty of the death of her friend's husband; and Estelle, who has infanticide on her conscience.[8]

Even more harshly, but with acute insight, Marcel maintains that Sartre's vision of life is restricted to 'the world as seen from the terrace of a café'.[9] By this he means that Sartre is unable to attach value to such ordinary features of social existence as being a father, which many non-café dwellers value. Worse still, he continues, the father of a family must always appear to Sartre 'as someone who is ... playing a part', simply because Sartre has insufficient human sympathy to find it natural that anyone should actually want to be a father and embrace the burdens it involves.

Sartre's vision, in short, is impoverished by his lack of sympathy for anything but an extreme and very limited range of human experience. This is especially evident, as Marcel notes, in 'his inability to grasp the genuine reality of what is meant by *we* ...'.[10] This, indeed, is the main feature of Sartre's political thought: the complete absence, that is, of any concession to human sociality. In *Being and Nothingness* in particular, all human relations are presented in sado-masochistic terms. Even something as innocuous as a gift, for example, is described by Sartre as always and inevitably 'a primitive form of destruction ... To give is to enslave'.[11]

Although Sartre's later work, in which he struggled to combine existentialism with Marxism, reveals a more benign view of human nature, it remained unclear how his individualism could be reconciled with Marxist historicism. He must, he wrote, 'dissolve myself practically in the process of human development' by somehow seeing his own life 'as the Whole and the Part, as the bond between the Parts and the Whole, and as the relation between the Parts, in the dialectical movement of Unification'.[12] This was the language of mysticism rather than of political theory: addressed to God, such thoughts would be admirable, but 'dissolving' oneself in history, where power is a reality, is a different matter.

Sartre's extreme individualism meant, in particular, that he always identified the state with violence, which is the only way of combining individuals in a group identity. The sovereign, he wrote in *The Critique of Dialectical Reason*, is merely 'the pure unity of integrating violence', used by a dominant group to secure obedience from the passive social order below.[13] If the political order rests only on violence, however, it is difficult to avoid sanctioning violence against it by individuals or groups who pose as liberators. At the extreme, this meant that Sartre's rebel posture was in constant danger of degenerating into a defence of terrorism. The development of his political thought is instructive in this respect. Not long after publishing *Critique of Dialectical Reason*, he committed himself in his preface to Fanon's *Wretched of the Earth* to defending the legitimacy of violence as a weapon in the Third World struggle for liberation. Thereafter, Sartre was unable to resist legitimizing the use of revolutionary violence in France itself following the events of May 1968. It is true that his attitude towards it was often disapproving, as in the case of the Baader-Meinhof terrorist group, against whose treatment by the German authorities he commendably protested. In the end, however, his political thought oscillated between expressions of his personal view of when violence was acceptable, on the one hand, and acceptance of what the veiled violence of the state dictated, on the other. As Bobbio noted, the 'rebel' posture did not permit the development of a concept of citizenship capable of integrating France in a non-coercive way.

Emmanuel Mounier's personalist philosophy, in contrast, seemed to offer the possibility of a more balanced combination of individualism with socialist solidarity. Although social democracy in the British form, as Pierre Rosanvallon has remarked, was generally rejected by the postwar French Leftist intelligentsia as too bourgeois and revisionist to represent a genuine political option, the relatively moderate character of Mounier's personalism made it perhaps the nearest that France got to the British and German social democratic compromise in the years immediately following the war.[14] In addition, personalist sympathy for religion appealed to Christians.

For Mounier, the greatest need of the present age is for a spiritual and social revolution of a far deeper kind than existentialism had envisaged. 'Personalism' is the term he gives to this revolution, which is necessitated by the collapse of 'the two great religions of modern man, Christianity and rationalism'.[15] In order to respond positively to the consequent danger of nihilism, it is necessary to understand the profound change in man's self-understanding that has occurred in the modern period. What has happened, to be precise, is that modern European man has left behind the closed and finite view of the universe which characterized the pre-modern era and stepped into an open, infinite universe.[16] From this universe he can no longer seek refuge in what used to be thought of as the objective order of nature because the only world he can now know is one of which he is the maker. Modern man, that is, is essentially 'the *artifex*, that is to say, the creator of forms, the maker of artifices'.[17] Paul Valéry was therefore correct, Mounier remarks, to observe that modern Europeans 'have flung themselves into a terrific adventure that consists in modifying the initial, natural conditions of life . . . to create an utterly artificial form of existence . . . '.[18]

Western modernity, then, is in the midst of a revolutionary transition from the pre-modern world of fixed destinies to a world of radical freedom. Yet none of the dominant ideologies of the present age, Mounier maintains, has responded adequately to this novel situation. Existentialism retreats into a wholly negative conception of human freedom, liberalism reduces life to egotistical self-indulgence and Communism stifles human creativity by subordinating it to the Party. In order to construct a viable response, Mounier drew on three sources, viz. Christianity, the socialism of Péguy, and the thought of Pascal, Kierkegaard and Nietzsche. Reflection on these sources revealed, he maintained, that the origin of nihilistic despair is individualism, which conceives of man as a solitary creature living in a self-created world of values, in relationships of inescapable hostility to others.[19] To individualism Mounier opposes a concrete concept of the self, in which values do not originate in momentary acts of will treated in isolation but surge up out of the whole character. This personalist self, moreover, does not regard institutions negatively, as merely a source of Sartrian *mauvaise foi*, but as a positive setting for the full development of personality. The task which still remains, however, is to create an organic society in which the creative, integral personality can flourish.

For this, Mounier turned to the ideal of a 'third way' between individualism and collectivism which relied on a combination of syndicalism and enlightened government. Syndicalism, however, presupposed the existence of a degree of industrial harmony which did not exist in postwar France, while enlightened government meant entrusting government to a politically unaccountable bureaucracy. The main thing that condemned personalism to political marginality, however, was Mounier's elitism. Although he claimed that personalism is a philosophy of spiritual ordinariness completely opposed to the heroic sympathies of Kierkegaard and Nietzsche, his conception of what spiritual ordinariness involves is so demanding that the personalist ideal can never have a mass appeal. In politics, indeed, Mounier insisted that what personalism meant was a sustained attempt to transform the populace from egotistical into communal beings. The potentially totalitarian nature of this project was evident in his qualified sympathy for fascism (in so far as he saw in it an ideal of spiritual regeneration) and Soviet Communism (in so far as it offered an ideal of social solidarity). How to enjoy the positive aspects of totalitarianism whilst avoiding the negative ones was a problem Mounier never solved.

Ironically, Mounier's enduring impact was through the politics of two Catholic admirers, Jacques Delors and Robert Schuman, who, far from being radicals, were bureaucrats mainly concerned to implement the European integration project.[20] This was far removed from Mounier's desire for a revolutionary spiritual awakening that would break completely not only with bureaucracy but with elitism of every sort.

The most intellectually influential version of revolutionary thought in postwar France was Marxism. In the decades after the Second World War, however, a deepening crisis confronted those who turned in this direction. Ever since 1917, French Marxists had embraced Soviet Communism as a legitimate continuation of the revolutionary tradition they themselves had begun with the French Revolution. By the 1950s, however, reports of deportations and concentration camps could no longer be dismissed as a capitalist travesty of Soviet reality. French radicals who nevertheless remained determined to cling to their revolutionary commitment were compelled to resort to desperate intellectual stratagies unrivalled by the legendary ostrich: that creature merely buried its head. The thought of Louis Althusser is perhaps the most striking example of outdoing the ostrich in this respect.

According to Althusser, Stalinism was the product of an unscientific understanding of history which had failed, in particular, to take account of a new theory of knowledge developed by Marx. According to this, knowledge is not the result of an empirical encounter between a passive subject and object but is the product of a variety of intellectual practices, all of which are used to interpret theoretical raw materials presented in the course of historical experience. Since knowledge assumes different forms in different areas of social experience, it is absurd to try to explain history in terms of a single set of causes, such as economic ones, since history – Althusser maintained – can have no 'causes' in the conventional sense. Putting the same thing slightly differently, the only intelligible historical concept of 'cause' is the overall system of knowledge practices that constitutes history.

As a philosophical contribution to the nature of historical inquiry, Althusser's theory might be welcomed. As an explanation of Stalinism, however, it seemed naïve, since it implied that the Soviet dictatorship was the product of an intellectual mistake that other revolutionaries could avoid simply by a better understanding of Marxist texts.[21] The appearance of naïvety increased when Althusser wrote an introduction to the first volume of Marx's *Capital* in which he sternly instructed future readers exactly how they must approach the text in order to avoid erroneous interpretations of the Stalinist kind.[22] Perhaps the most extraordinary feature of Althusser's position, however, is that he found the secret of avoiding despotism in the philosophy of Lenin. If one asks why Althusser saw nothing humorous about this, the answer is that what mattered to him was not liberty but objectivity, which he believed Lenin possessed in the highest degree. Lenin alone, he wrote, was sufficiently free from petit bourgeois instincts to enable him to draw a genuinely philosophical dividing line between true and false ideas, as well as an objective political one 'between the people (the proletariat and its allies) and the people's enemies'.[23] Althusser completely failed to see that the supposedly scientific philosophical and political dividing lines he claimed to be drawing, with Lenin's guidance, were a formula for creating despotism, rather than ending it.

Althusser's grandiose claim to have put postwar French radicalism on a truly scientific basis marked the zenith of postwar French radicalism. What must now be considered are the reasons for its decline and the quest for a moderate alternative.

Towards a Non-Revolutionary Political Discourse

There were several reasons for the weakening of the stranglehold of the Left on French political discourse during the late 1960s and early 1970s. One was growing disillusion with both the Soviet and Chinese forms of communism. In the Soviet case, this was due in particular to the widely read French translation of Solzhenitsyn's *Gulag Archipelago* published in 1975. In the Chinese case, Pasqualini[24] revealed in the same year the existence of camps there, while in the following year Philippe Sollers, a leading member of the *Tel Quel* circle, not only rejected Maoism but did the unthinkable: he made his first visit to that sink of cultural mediocrity, the USA. A second reason was disappointment with the French working class, which had failed in the aftermath of May 1968 to display any of the revolutionary tendencies previously ascribed to it. A third was generational change and growing prosperity, which appeared by the late 1960s to be creating a new 'identity politics' that Marxist theory could not accommodate. It was this last development in particular that led Gilles Lipovetsky to break the radical mould by proclaiming that in 1968 French democracy had entered a new era, marked by what he intriguely termed the 'empire of fashion'.[25]

The real significance of the events of 1968, Lipovetsky argued, has nothing to do with class conflict: they were not in any sense a last flicker of proletarian yearnings for solidarity. What actually happened was that the dominant principle of modern western life, which is individualism, was rediscovered. As Louis Dumont and Marcel Gauchet have also pointed out, Lipovetsky notes, individualism is not a bourgeois perversion of modern western life, as Marxism holds, but is on the contrary its very foundation. It follows, Lipovetsky maintains, that 'The effort to conceptualize the individual – and to give conceptual legitimacy and sociopolitical efficacy to the principle of autonomy that is coextensive with the individual – constitutes one of the most innovative and promising trends to appear on the French intellectual scene ...'[26] In the new phase of French democracy marked by the rediscovery of individualism, what emerges is a wholly new kind of social relationship characterized by 'the empire of fashion'.[27] Tradition, in other words, is replaced by the rule of ephemera, a cult of the new and the influence of seduction, in the form of the desire to attract.

Looking back on 1968 two decades later, Lipovetsky saw the intervening years as a period of progress towards democratic maturity. In the France of May 1968, he wrote, individualist passions were celebrated on city walls...Individualism sought to change the world, to change life. Today, it has settled down and become "responsible"...It has gotten rid of the utopian matrix and it rejects all political perspectives, all party affiliations, all overarching worldviews...In fact, the student movements of the 1980s brought no evidence of a struggle against competitive individualist society and its flagrant inequalities; quite to the contrary, it brought evidence of the individualist desire to be integrated into society as it is, with its hierarchies and its injustices...[28]

The problem at the heart of Lipovetsky's thought was that he did not view the new empire of fashion as merely the final triumph of mass mediocrity, as de Tocqueville had done, but embraced it sympathetically. Why he regarded it so positively remains unexplained. As his thought indicates, however, the events of 1968 marked the advent of a new, post-revolutionary mood in French intellectual life. One of the most notable indications of this change was the emergence of a group of renegade revolutionaries who rapidly became known as the 'new philosophers', amongst whom the best known was the former Maoist, Bernard-Henri Lévy. In *Les Aventures de la Liberté*, Lévy attributed the uncritical faith of French intellectuals in revolution during previous decades to a kind of political blindness motivated, in particular, by a quasi-religious yearning for an impossible ideal of moral purity supremely illustrated by Althusser, whose disciple he had once been. The result of the final extinction of the revolutionary star, Lévy concluded, was that 'French intellectuals [have] suddenly rediscovered ideas which, until recently, had appeared outdated and absurd.' These ideas were hardly novel, including as they did morality, the Rights of Man, 'and even the old idea of democracy'.[29]

The danger with the anti-revolutionary fervour which inspired the new philosophers was that it threatened to give fanaticism a new lease of life, rather than pointing to a more moderate alternative. Signs of fanaticism were evident, for example, in the use made by them of the concept of totalitarianism, which had for long been a staple topic of British and American political theory but had previously been largely excluded from French intellectual life by widespread sympathy for the Soviet regime. For Jean-François Revel, for example, the struggle between democracy and totalitarianism was elevated into the key to contemporary world history, even though more critical theorists like J. L. Talmon had shown that democracy itself might easily become totalitarian.[30] As Revel's *The Totalitarian Temptation* made clear, an important attraction of the totalitarian concept was that it provided an easy way of distracting attention from the continuing deep divisions in French political life: simply situating France in the democratic camp, it was assumed, automatically freed it from all the nasty authoritarian elements found in the opposing Communist camp.

A second, more intellectually ambitious critique of postwar radical fervour was provided by postmodern political theory, in so far as it sought to rehabilitate power as a central concern of postwar French political thought. The revolutionary rhetoric of the early postwar decades had marginalized power by treating it as an essentially transient feature of the social order which would disappear as soon as reactionary elements were removed from it. The merit of Foucault in particular was to introduce a note of realism which viewed power as both ubiquitous and inescapable. From the postmodern standpoint, therefore, to aim at the wholesale abolition of power is futile. Foucault's theory of power suffered, however, from a grave defect, which was a systematic failure to distinguish power from authority.

Foucault's inability to differentiate between these two concepts meant, in particular, that his treatment of the state was open to the charge of travesty. The primary error of political theory to date, he maintained, has been that it has placed excessive emphasis on a narrowly juridical theory of sovereignty that is wholly unable to take account of the complex forms of social power which structure modern individual identity. Historically, Foucault writes, 'the process by which the bourgeoisie became . . . the politically dominant class was masked by the establishment of an explicit, coded and formally egalitarian juridical framework, made possible by the organisation of a parliamentary, representative regime . . . [But] the real, corporal disciplines constituted the foundation of the formal, juridical liberties.'[31] In place of the narrow juridical approach traditionally adopted by political theorists, Foucault put a much richer historical one that focused attention upon the growth of such integrating institutions as the hospital, the asylum and the prison, which he termed the 'disciplines'.

Whilst Foucault's expansion of the historical study of forms of power is suggestive, his presentation of the classical view of the state as narrowly juridical misrepresents classical political theory in a vital respect: whereas Foucault's concern is with the empirical study of power structures, the primary concern of classical theory was with the ethical problem of legitimacy, which could only be dealt with through the rule of law. Since Foucault's own conception of the nature and scope of political theory ignores this problem altogether, the discourse of power he provides cannot, in the end, define power itself satisfactorily since it is unable, as was remarked, to distinguish power from authority. For Foucault, that is, there is in principle no way of distinguishing between being arrested by a policeman and being mugged by a thief, since in both cases the situation is defined principally in terms of power.

Other postmodern thinkers, like Gilles Deleuze and Jean Baudrillard, have pursued the analysis of power in ways that make the revolutionary project seem, if anything, even more futile than Foucault does. Deleuze argues, in particular, that Foucault's analysis of power fails to go far enough because he continues to rely on the traditional assumption that power is basically external to us, or in some way transcends us. In reality, Deleuze maintains, we are now in the throes of a new 'machinic enslavement', the essence of which is that the machine is no longer external to the self but has become an integral component of human identity.[32] The trouble with Deleuze's analysis of the new machinic form of power, however, is that, like Foucault, he ignores the dimension of legitimacy. The result is the same willingness Foucault displays to dismiss juridical forms as nothing more than oppressive techniques of integration; the possibility that they might instead be regarded as positive procedures for securing freedom by checking arbitrary power is never entertained.

The postmodern analysis of power, then, suffers from conceptual crudeness. This assumes its most extreme form in the thought of Baudrillard, who completely inverts the classical Marxist emphasis on economic determinism by stressing instead the all-pervasive influence on postmodern man of non-referential signs. To be precise, the postmodern world is like a bubble in which we are now

all bubble children, like the boy who ... lived in his [NASA bubble] protected from all infection by the artificially immunized space; his mother caressed him through the glass with rubber gloves, as he laughed and grew up in his extraterrestrial atmosphere under the observation of science ... This bubble-child is the prefiguration of the future ... He is the symbol of existence in a vacuum, until now exclusive to bacteria and particles in laboratories, but which will increasingly become ours ... We will be thinking and reflecting in a vacuum, as illustrated everywhere by artificial intelligence.[33]

The postmodern analysis of power ends, then, by replacing the revolutionary dream of the *liberation* of man with a vision of the *end* of man, who now lies buried beneath a network of information and communication systems. The fact that power in its contemporary form may take the gentle form of 'seduction', as it does for Baudrillard, rather than overtly coercive forms, only enhances its ability to crush radical sentiment of any kind.[34]

Before proceeding further, it is necessary to consider one of the most influential aspects of the fascination with power produced by disillusion with revolutionary thought, which is postmodern feminist theory. Although this only provides a further illustration of the inability of postmodern theory to offer a coherent alternative to the exploitation it claims to expose, it is instructive in one respect. Specifically, the form of feminism developed by postmodern sympathizers like Julia Kristeva, Hélène Cixous and Luce Irigaray has involved such an elaborate and all-pervasive extension of the concept of power that it proves to be counterproductive, in so far as it risks portraying women as invariably victims of patriarchal civilization who are wholly incapable of leading independent lives. Luce Irigaray, in particular, is open to this charge.

The central aim of Irigaray's work is to refine the concept of patriarchal power by combining Lacanian psychoanalysis, Saussurian linguistics and Heideggerian philosophy in a way that permits her to expand it into every nook and cranny of western history. It follows that a woman does not have a distinct identity of her own but merely mirrors the male one, in terms of which she defines herself.[35] As just noted, this form of feminist theory tends to convert women into passive, childlike creatures incapable of independent initiative. If other postmodern feminists, like Kristeva, nevertheless manage to avoid this undignified outcome, it is only by a pragmatic accommodation to the existing social order that can easily be presented as selling out to the bourgeoisie. A good example is provided by Kristeva's discovery of the unheroic, unliberated delights of bourgeois ordinariness. As Kristeva informed her interviewer in a media session:

> People say: 'There was this group of people who were so intellectual, who were there in' 68, and where are they now? At home having children! *Quel malheur*! What conformism!' But I say that this is not to be less, it is to be more.... I'm getting to know the banality in myself.[36]

Kristeva, the interviewer noted, 'finds [banality] a pleasing discovery'. In this respect, the postmodern analysis of power, it might seem, has led at least some French intellectuals to a belated rediscovery of the wisdom of Montaigne. The finest lives, Montaigne concluded in his essay 'On Experience', 'are, in my opinion, those which conform to the common and human model in an orderly way, with no marvels and no extravagances'.

From the broader standpoint of postwar French political theory as a whole, the importance of postmodern theory lies not so much in the vague concept of power it has deployed as in the need to which it has pointed for a more pluralistic model of democracy. It is from this point of view, for example, that sympathetic interpreters of Derrida have argued that his political writings provide a suggestive exploration of an 'agonal' model of democracy, in which conflict is embraced, rather than suppressed in the interest of an oppressive consensus.[37] Although his admirers have tended to exaggerate the progress Derrida has made in clarifying the kind of pluralist democracy he believes France should be seeking to construct, their positive assessment of his work is better founded than the negative one of critics who have dismissed it as merely 'the ultimate post-structuralist fantasy'.[38]

If postmodern theorizing has helped to point French political thought towards an accommodation with pluralism, it has nevertheless failed to provoke sympathy for constitutionalism as a way of implementing it. The tendency, inherited from the revolutionary decades, to view constitutional forms as mere obstacles to liberty and community remains deeply rooted. It is evident, for example, in Foucault's insistence that the ideal society demands 'the radical elimination of the judicial apparatus, and anything which could reintroduce its ideology and enable this ideology surreptitiously to creep back into popular practices...'.[39] In part at least, it was this hostility to constitutional forms which permitted Foucault to dream of a new, non-juridical form of 'proletarian' justice, of the kind he naïvely assumed Ayatollah Khomeini would create in Iran following the revolution of 1979.[40] More generally, inability to recognize that civil and juridical forms are a way of checking the abuse of power and not merely a means of facilitating oppression has meant, as two thoughtful French critics remarked, that Foucault seemed to have criticized the 'disciplines' of modern Western society only to end as an apologist for 'a spirituality which punishes and disciplines'.[41]

The disintegration of the postwar radical intellectual hegemony marked by the new philosophers and postmodernism was completed by a third dramatic development. This is the dethroning of *les intellos*, as the media now refer to public intellectuals, by sceptical attacks on their claim to absolute knowledge. Ironically, those who have contributed most to this have not always abandoned their own claim to canonical status. Their reluctance to do so is particularly evident in the work of Jean-François Lyotard. In a volume with the graphic title *Tombeau de l'intellectuel et autres papiers* (1984),[42] Lyotard explained that the intellectuals whose tombs he was preparing had mistakenly believed in the possibility of 'metanarratives', of which the religious metanarrative of Christianity, the rationalist metanarrative of the Enlightenment and the historical metanarrative of Marxism have been the most influential forms. In opposition to the oppressive politics associated with metanarratives, Lyotard defends the 'politics of the *différend*', in which diversity is affirmed instead of suppressed by a forcibly imposed consensus.

Lyotard's politics of diversity, it might be thought, would surely point towards a democratic pluralism sympathetic to all repressed minorities. This, however, is not the conclusion Lyotard himself draws. A democratic system, he observes, provides no guarantee that minorities are able to represent their own position adequately. He therefore wants, not a democratic politics, but a 'politics of justice', which involves listening carefully to the silent sections of society repressed by the established order. Unfortunately, a 'listening' politics permits intellectuals and governments to project whatever views they wish onto the mute citizens whose interests they claim to articulate. Lyotard has accordingly been accused of doing little more than replace the oppressive metanarratives of the past with a new, no less potentially oppressive metanarrative of the '*différend*'. Nevertheless, he may be said to have 'relativized' the classical concept of the intellectual in a way which reduces him to the status of an ordinary citizen by depriving him of the authority conferred by the old metanarratives to dismiss bourgeois society as merely a system of exploitation and alienation.

What must now be considered is whether alternative, more moderate models of political integration are availabe to fill the void left by the disintegration of radical thought. Before considering more recent models, however, it will be useful to explore the efforts to indicate what they involve made by some notable thinkers in the years immediately after the Second World War.

Voices of Political Moderation

Amongst the most impressive early postwar assaults on radical ortho-doxy were the five very different theories of political moderation advanced by Claude Lefort, Albert Camus, Bertrand de Jouvenel, Jacques Maritain and Raymond Aron. Of these thinkers, the first two – Camus and Lefort – were renegades from the revolutionary camp, while the third, de Jouvenel, was a renegade from the fascist camp with which he had flirted during the 1930s.

In 1943 Claude Lefort, then still a student, joined the French Trotskyist Party (PCI). Five years later he broke with it and established (with Cornelius Castoriadis) a new, independent group which was to issue, from 1949 until 1965, the journal *Socialisme ou Barbarie*. Although Lefort retained radical sympathies, his reason for abandoning Trot-skyism was expressed in one of the most profound critiques of radical thought to emerge in postwar France. The immediate source of that critique was Lefort's dissatisfaction with the acquiescent attitude towards the Soviet regime of the French Left. What the Left failed to appreciate, Lefort maintained, was that the Soviet bureaucracy was not a removable piece of flotsam perversely inflicted on Soviet society by malign individuals like Stalin; it was, on the contrary, the tip of a structure of domination deeply rooted in the whole enterprise of the Bolshevik party, and was an inescapable aspect of a totalitarian project that found its complete expression in one party rule.[43] But exactly why was Stalinist oppression inescapable?

Lefort's answer was the most suggestive part of his political thought: it consisted, he said, in 'the repression of the question of the political' by French intellectuals.[44] It consists, more precisely, in the inability of socialism to comprehend the irreducible reality of power and conflict. Lefort explained how socialists repress 'the question of the political' in the following way:

> As soon as [socialists] saw private property abolished, as soon as class antagonism could no longer be deciphered in the known context of capitalism, their thinking was disarmed. They were quite capable of concluding that the Soviet state was loaded with vices; but they could identify nothing more than vices, whose origins were imputed to accidents of history. The Left lacked a theory of the State, or more profoundly still, a conception of political society... Because they had circumscribed the sphere of reality within the

limits of the economy, they were blind to the structure of a system of production which was explicitly embedded in the political system.[45]

The Left's repression of the political, Lefort adds, is not unique to socialism: on the contrary, much liberal theory displays the same defect, in so far as it tends to see the political order as a purely instrumental device for securing person and property. But what precisely is meant, it must be asked, by 'the political' in this connection? Lefort's reply is that the Left repressed the political in the sense that 'it misunderstood the symbolic nature of power in democratic society and the symbolic nature of the modern state'.[46] By introducing the concept of 'the symbolic', Lefort means to stress that the political can only be understood in terms of the subjective language of self-interpretation used by modern democratic citizens to describe their institutions, values and purposes. Instead of attending to that language, the Left claims to possess an objective standpoint which permits it to dismiss the actual view of citizens as false consciousness. Once the symbolic language of self-interpretation is ignored in this way, however, it is impossible to make the distinction between naked power and justifiable forms of authority upon which the Left itself relies. What happens, in a word, is that a necessarily authoritarian and coercive standpoint replaces a political one. This, then, is the explanation for Stalinism: it follows inevitably from the repression of the political.

Lefort's rehabilitation of the symbolic language of ordinary political life led him, in turn, to sympathize with the concept of rights in terms of which the political realm is structured in modern liberal democracies – a language, that is, which Marxism had dismissed as a form of bourgeois alienation.[47] What limited his quest for moderation, however, was the fact that he could not ultimately accommodate his thought to the existing social order. The explanation for this was simple: despite his break with Trotskyism, Lefort always retained the radical dream of a world free from domination. For that reason, the restraint his thought exerted on revolutionary zeal ended in political paralysis, rather than in a viable conception of citizenship. A somewhat similar paralysis was to be the fate of Albert Camus.

Whereas Lefort's background was in the Marxist strand of revolutionary theorizing, Camus' lay in the existentialist one. The novelty of his political philosophy lies in his attempt to derive a theoretical ground for moderation from what might seem to be the most improbable source of all – namely, the experience of nihilism from which existentialism derives much of its inspiration.[48] His aim, putting the same thing slightly differently, was to extract a theory of limits from a world of absolutes in which limits appear to have no place. Camus had originally explored the world of moral absolutes in *Caligula*, the initial version of which he had completed shortly before the war. One of the most dramatic moments in the play is the opening scene in which Caligula, who has been mysteriously absent from his court for several days, returns in a dishevelled condition. A diffident courtier finally musters sufficient courage to ask where Caligula has been. Caligula replies that he had been trying to possess the moon. The courtier respectfully asks whether he succeeded. Caligula impatiently replies that of course he didn't, because it would be impossible. In that case, the courtier asks, why did he try at all? Caligula replies that his reason consisted precisely in the unattainability of his desire. The theme of the play, in a word, is the search for absolutes, taken to the extreme in Caligula's nympholepsy.[49]

Camus' most ambitious theoretical work, *The Rebel*, which appeared well over a decade later (in 1951), is mainly notable for his rejection of his early sympathy for Caligula's quest for absolutes. In it, however, he embarks on a quest for moderation which ultimately leaves his understanding of the meaning of moderation questionable, to say the least. Crucial to this quest is a distinction between two completely different responses to the experience of absurdity. One is rebellion, which is creative, spontaneous and essentially *limited in its objectives*. Above all, rebellion does not seek to conceal the absurdity of human existence by trying to create a world of absolute justice. Rebellion is therefore a positive response to man's social condition. The alternative response is revolution, which is always destructive because it clings to the ideal of absolute justice, refusing to compromise with other ideals and acknowledge the proper limits of moral and political idealism. Because it refuses to do this, it inevitably ends in dictatorship.

Camus' main political message, then, is that Europe must replace revolutionary ideologies by the spirit of rebellion. The problem, however, is that it is by no means easy to distinguish rebellion, which Camus equates with moderation, from revolution. Strangely, Camus identifies Kaliayev, a fanatical member of a young Russian terrorist group who murdered the Grand Duke Sergei at the beginning of the twentieth century, as the model rebel, and hence the key to what moderation implies. Kaliayev and the other members of this terrorist group, Camus maintains, were exemplars of moderation because they were 'fastidious assassins' – murderers, that is, who 'were always prey to doubts'.[50] One may even speculate, he remarks, that 'while recognizing the inevitability of violence, [they] nevertheless admitted to themselves that it is unjustifiable. Necessary and inexcusable – that is how murder appeared to them!'[51] The main reason why Camus credits the fastidious assassins with moderation, however, is that they always matched a murder with a suicide. In that way, Camus writes, Kaliayev and his fellow terrorists asserted the equal value of all human lives, even as they murdered.[52] What is problematic is Camus' assumption that two negatives somehow make a positive – that by committing suicide whenever they murder, in other words, the fastidious assassins create a positive value.[53] Even if the value they create is positive, what matters at present is that the idea of a suicide in exchange for a murder can hardly be described as a formula for moderation.

So far as Camus' broader vision of politics is concerned, he was vague, merely espousing a rather nebulous concept of solidarity. The problem, more precisely, was that he had no way of explaining how solidarity could be reconciled with his central, highly individualistic concern with authentic personal morality. It was the search for authentic morality which dominated, for example, the characters of Meursault in *The Outsider* and of Dr Rieu, in *The Plague*. In both cases, however, the experience of solidarity only arose when confronted by the prospect of death, or an event threatening it. Whereas Sartre had turned to state power to generate solidarity, Camus, as Tony Judt remarks, was always 'peculiarly uncomfortable' with 'the very idea of power'.[54] In order to overcome this discomfort he turned away from politics – the world of power – and fell back on an ideal of solidarity produced by wholly unpolitical means. By doing so he inevitably exposed himself to the charge of political illiteracy.

It is necessary, then, to look elsewhere for a viable French philosophy of moderation. One of the most promising postwar sources is the thought of Bertrand de Jouvenel. Whereas Camus found the key to polit-ical moderation in a philosophical concept of limits, Jouvenel turned instead to an ideal of constitutional balance between liberty and authority. What threatens this ideal, he believed, is the democratic tendency to equate authority with *authoritarianism*, and to identify it in consequence as the enemy of liberty and liberalism. In fact, authority would only be 'authoritarianism' if it involved power. Properly understood, however, authority is not power; what it refers to is the ability of one man to have his proposals willingly accepted by others in the context of an impersonal framework of constitutional rules. Understood in this way, authority is a condition for the enjoyment of freedom, not the enemy of it.

For Jouvenel, then, democracy only represented a viable postwar option if it was balanced by constitutionalism. What Jouvenel neglected, however, is a problem which Jacques Maritain placed at the centre of his Thomist version of constitutionalism. This is that a constitutional balance might only be possible in a democracy in which civic virtue has a religious underpinning. That, indeed, was Maritain's thesis: civic virtue requires Christian virtue. What was problematic about his position, however, was his conviction that civic and Christain virtue can only be united by 'small dynamic groups ... which would not be concerned with electoral success but with devoting themselves entirely to a great social and political idea'.[55] From the ranks of these potentially fanatical groups would come 'prophets', whom Maritain believes will guide the people into the paths of virtue.[56] Strangely, Maritain appeared to have learned little from Weimar Germany, which posed the crucial question of how the people are to distinguish good prophets from bad ones, as well as call the good ones to account. These were problems to which he offered no convincing answer.

For Raymond Aron, balance was also the key to moderation. In his view, however, the character of the balance required is far more complicated than either Jouvenel or Maritain appreciated. 'The Western societies of our time', Aron wrote, 'have a threefold ideal: *bourgeois citizenship*, *technological efficiency*, and *the right of the individual to choose the path of his salvation*. Of these three ideals not one must be sacrificed.' We must not, Aron added, 'be so naïve as to believe that it is easy to achieve them all'.[57] The main obstacle to achieving a balance between these potentially conflicting ideals, he believed, is not so much a lack of civic virtue as an intensely moralistic and ideological outlook to which the decline of religion has made contemporary European politics especially prone. Aron's aim, in his own words, was to 'renounce the abstractions of moralism and ideology and look instead for the true content of possible choices, limited as they are by reality itself'.[58] In this respect, Tony Judt has astutely remarked, Aron, unlike other French intellectuals, 'took utterly seriously the original meaning of engagement'.[59]

Aron described his own concept of engagement as a search for realism, modelled in particular on the ethic of responsibility developed by Max Weber as the point of connection between thought and action. Weber, he wrote, grasped the true nature of political philosophy, which can be 'nothing but a more profound understanding of temporal action, a reflection upon the conditions within which our desires are expressed and an analysis of political choices in their relation both to reality and to our ideal'. Above all, what Aron admired about Weber's standpoint was the fact that he was prepared at any moment to answer the question, 'What would you do if you were a Cabinet minister?'[60]

To dismiss Aron's realism as mere pragmatism would be unjust: at the heart of his thought is a deep ethical commitment to the value of personal and political liberty, and his realism always aims to clarify the social and political conditions for its preservation. It is focused, in particular, on the concept of 'industrial society', which Aron believed is now confronted by only two possibilities: one is constitutional democracy, in which a viable balance is struck between liberty, economic growth and political authority; the other is totalitarian democracy, in which balance is destroyed by the subordination of all modern concerns to rule by a single party. The truly prophetic element in Aron's thought, however, was his fear that the future of industrial democracies might consist in enjoying prosperity and high levels of social benefits, on the one hand, while showing little concern for the forms and procedures on which freedom depends, on the other. For this danger, he saw no remedy.

Aron's defence of political moderation owed much to the constitutionalism of classical French liberal thought, especially that of de Tocqueville. A younger thinker, François Furet, was later to be led in the same direction by his conviction that French radicals (to whose ranks he had once belonged) had completely failed to appreciate the main problem which the heritage of the French Revolution had created for French politics. What the Revolution had done, he maintained, was expose deep divisions on fundamental values which can never be eliminated, as radicals assume, but only accommodated within a system of constitutional democracy that actually protects them by institutional safeguards for individual rights.

The connection between Furet's historical work and his commitment to constitutional democracy is evident in *Penser la Révolution Française*,[61] the aim of which was to expose the grossly simplistic assumptions of Marxist historiography. The principal defect of this historiography is its obsession with the idea that the French Revolution was a crucial transition of some kind – from a feudal to a capitalist society, for example. The real problem created by the revolution, however, has nothing to do with such issues: what it gave rise to, Furet maintained, is a ceaseless dispute *about the nature of legitimacy*. This dispute, which lies at the heart of every revolution, is one which every revolutionary group seeks to solve by despotic control of the entire social order. The only alternative to despotism, as Constant and de Tocqueville realized long ago, is a constitutional democracy, since that alone can respond in a non-coercive way to the problem of legitimacy. The main task facing contemporary French thinkers and politicians, in consequence, is to rediscover the French classical liberal heritage and use it to place the Fifth Republic on a constitutional foundation acceptable to the whole of the French nation.

The achievement of Aron and Furet, then, was not only to demolish the irresponsible moralism and historiography upon which the post-war revolutionary consensus had relied, but also to provide the basis for an alternative concept of French political identity inspired by the classical French tradition of constitutional democracy.[62] What remains to be considered is how the political thinkers who currently dominate French debate have responded to this challenge. Before turning to that question, however, it is necessary to consider the challenge to the whole ideal of political moderation posed from the 1970s by the so-called Nouvelle Droite, represented in particular by Alain de Benoist.

Alain de Benoist and the Nouvelle Droite

By means of various books and three journals he edits, viz. *Eléments*, *Nouvelle Ecole* and *Krisis*, de Benoist has broken with the traditional French Right in three crucial respects. He has attempted, firstly, to provide a new, 'pagan' basis for conservative thought in place of the old Christian one generally adopted in the past. This new basis is reflected in particular in a Nietzschean cult of the heroic, which is opposed to the decadent materialism and mediocrity now said to dominate the Western world. Secondly, de Benoist abandoned the traditional nationalism of the Right in favour of a European cultural and political identity deemed to be better able to respond effectively to the political threat posed by both the USA and (until recently) the USSR, and to the continuing cultural threat posed to Europe by the influence of American mass taste. Finally, he has renounced violence, rejecting in that respect the discredited politics of the Action Française. This does not mean, however, that he has committed the movement to political moderation: on the contrary, he is deeply committed to a revolutionary strategy taken over from the leftwing publicist Antonio Gramsci, the aim of which is to prepare the way for political revolution by an extended process of cultural indoctrination.

In the event, the intellectual challenge of the Nouvelle Droite has not proved very significant, partly because the Nietzschean heroic cult has little appeal in peacetime social life, and partly because Nouvelle Droite theory does little more than perpetuate in conservative dress the discarded dream of salvation through political action usually associated with the Left. There is, it is true, another challenge from the Right, which is the one presented by the National Front. This exploits, in particular, widespread hostility to immigrants, ethnic minorities, rising unemployment, and the (partially related) 'law and order' issue posed by disaffected urban youth. There is, however, nothing of intellectual interest in National Front theorizing to detain one. What is of more significance is the contemporary French struggle to come to terms with liberalism, and it is this theme, accordingly, which will now be taken up again.

Towards a New French Liberalism?

In the autumn of 1989 three Muslim girls contravened French educational laws by veiling their heads while at school. This incident immediately provoked a national debate about the nature of French political identity. The essential issue was summarized by Régis Debray, who declared that France was confronted by a choice between the alien Anglo-American liberal-democratic model and the native French republican ideal. For those who favoured the Anglo-American model, Debray explained, the incident presented no problem: they predict-ably respond to the veil incident by praising human rights, toleration and multiculturalism.[63] Defenders of the French republican ideal, however, cannot move so easily in the liberal direction since, for them, the issue is not just about rights, toleration and diversity but is, rather, about an ideal of citizenship that involves emphasizing a common culture, solidarity and duties. Perhaps the best way of describing the difference between the republican and the liberal-democratic ideals, Débray remarked, is by characterizing republicanism as the full form of democracy, since it not only takes into account 'the first need of man, which is the cultural order', but also pursues social justice and solidarity. The Anglo-American democratic ideal, conversely, can be characterized as what is left when everything that the republican one seeks to realize is stripped away.[64]

The debate between republicans and liberal democrats has continued ever since, but without yielding a coherent response to the multicultural diversity that now marks French society. In this debate, liberalism in anything like the Anglo-American form remains the object of widespread suspicion. The source of this suspicion is the republican emphasis, powerfully defended by Débray, on the need to achieve a perfect identity between the citizen and the community, especially through assimilation by education. It is concern over republican pressure for cultural uniformity which led Joël Roman, for example, to observe in the journal *Esprit* that: 'What threatens [French society] is its refusal to accord a place to its differences, its forced homogenization.'[65]

During the 1980s and 1990s, widespread misgivings about the ability of established forms of republicanism to respond adequately to the increasing diversity of French society led to various revisionist strategies, of which three in particular merit close attention. The first, and most radical, consists of abandoning the French republican tradition altogether, in order to pave the way for an *etat de droit* on the Anglo-Saxon model. This strategy is illustrated by the review *Esprit*, which has displayed considerable interest in the work of leading American and Canadian liberals such as Michael Walzer, Charles Taylor and Michael Sandel. To a lesser extent, it is also illustrated by belated interest in the work of the American philosopher, John Rawls, on the nature of justice.[66] The attempt to secure a hearing for Rawls, it may be noted, has provoked particularly savage criticism. Pierre Manent, for example, observed in 1988 that 'Two evils have arrived from America: Eurodisney and *A Theory of Justice*'.[67] The hostility is easily explained: either Rawls is regarded as too individualistic for his thought to be relevant in the French context, or (as Bernard Manin has maintained)[68] as too insensitive to the fundamental role of discussion in the political process. Republican sympathizers must be ignored for the moment, however, in order to focus on the work of Marcel Gauchet, who is the most impressive defender of the radical strategy.

For Gauchet, whose Anglophile sympathies are indicated by the scholarly edition of Benjamin Constant's political writings he published in 1980 (Constant himself being a notable Anglophile),[69] the main problem of contemporary French democracy arises from an inability to accept that the era of social consensus has now been replaced by ineradicable conflict. As Gauchet puts it, the political paradox of our age is that 'Democratic society is formed out of deep conflict, yet is populated by people who conceive of it solely in terms of social unity.'[70] Gauchet's response to this situation is a reformulation of liberalism notable mainly for the sweeping historical vision he uses in order to present western modernity as inevitably doomed to ceaseless moral conflict. In a way reminiscent of Hegel, he interprets history as the story of a demonic struggle to end man's original spiritual 'dispossession' in the earlier, religious stage of western experience.[71] Man's victory over religion, however, does not bring enlightenment and peace, as earlier thinkers had hoped. On the contrary, it merely renders conflict ineradicable by abolishing any external point of reference (God) by reference to which it can be settled.

In a sobering conclusion, Gauchet maintains that the kind of political order appropriate to modern conflictual democracy may well be authoritarian or totalitarian, rather than liberal. This is because the end of religion does not bring the end of the 'externality' characteristic of the religious era but creates a constant temptation for the state to transfer it from God to itself – with potentially disastrous implications for personal liberty.[72] So far as prospects for the future are concerned, much depends on whether western man can bring himself to 'renounce the dream of his own divinity', instead of clinging to the idea that the death of God entitles man to take his place.[73]

Gauchet's attempt to construct a radically pluralist model of democracy creates two main problems. One is his view of religion, which Charles Taylor has maintained he misunderstands.[74] The other is his neo-Hegelian view of history, which Pierre Manent, for example, has maintained misrepresents the history of the modern state.[75] Perhaps the most telling criticism, however, is that, so far as political analysis is concerned, Gauchet attempts far more than his purpose requires. It is, indeed, precisely her greater intellectual

modesty that lends interest to the alternative revisionist strategy of
Blandine Kriegel, who mounts an equally devastating attack on
the French republican tradition but without creating the problems
about religion, the meaning of history and the nature of the modern
state to which Gauchet's critique gives rise. For Kriegel, the illiberal
aspects of the French republican tradition do not derive from the
nature of history at large but are rooted in a specific aspect of
the French state tradition, which is its failure to incorporate the
rule of law. To be more precise, the French state tradition *has*
incorporated the rule of law, but the law in question is *Roman* law,
which has always had a despotic core and has led, in practice, to an
absolutist concept of sovereignty in marked contrast to the English
one that issued from common law and has always been limited by
individual rights. Against this historical background, Kriegel characterizes the principal feature of the contemporary French state as
its 'hybrid' character, by which she means that constitutionalism
remains stifled by a concept of sovereignty that continues to sanction arbitrary administrative power. This is revealed, for example,
in the 'republican presidential' nature of the Fifth Republic. The
appropriate response, Kriegel maintains, is an extensive restructuring
of the French body politic, with a view to establishing a more truly
democratic concept of citizenship firmly based on the rule of law
and recognition of individual rights. Only in this way is it possible
to give the present French constitution a genuinely universal appeal.
It was with this programme in mind that Kriegel responded to
Mitterrand's invitation to submit a report on appropriate constitutional reforms.[76]

Despite the cogency of her analysis of the weaknesses of the French
state tradition, the reforms Kriegel has suggested are by no means
theoretically coherent. Two in particular are especially problematic.
One is her demand for a new institution to protect individual rights
against the indivisible power which the established doctrine of sovereignty takes for granted.[77] This institution she calls the *Haute Autorité
de protection des libertés publiques*. The difficulty is to understand how
the new institution would operate, since she wishes it neither to be
fully independent of the legislature nor completely under its control.
The formula she uses to describe its position amounts, indeed,
almost to a contradiction in terms: the *Haute Autorité* would, she writes,
be 'independent, but controlled, in line with the requirements of
a democratic society'.[78]

No less problematic is Kriegel's desire to create a more democratic, genuinely inclusive political order by re-establishing citizenship on a universally valid doctrine of the rights of man.[79] The difficulty, more precisely, is that Kriegel seems to take it for granted that all the problems associated with deciding what the rights of man are can be resolved by creating the kind of ideal harmony between individual and communal interests whose very possibility she herself contests when the republican concept of popular sovereignty invokes it. Nevertheless, Kriegel has been rightly praised for attempting to construct 'a new...conception of republican democracy, freed of Jacobin and imperial impedimenta'.[80]

The third revisionist strategy for liberalizing the republican tradition consists of Dominique Schnapper's exploration of the conditions for maintaining what she terms 'the community of citizens'.[81] Schnapper's starting-point is the contention that it is 'in the framework of the nation that the legitimacy and practices of democracy were built'.[82] This includes, it need hardly be said, French republicanism. Above all, Schnapper holds, it was national sentiment which created the civic pride that enabled individuals to rise above their particular interests and create a public realm concerned with the common good, as the republican tradition in particular reveals.

Nationalism could provide this civic motivation, Schnapper maintains, only because it was fundamentally a *political* or civic ideal and not, as is now widely assumed, a purely ethnic one. By characterizing the nation in political terms as a 'community of citizens', Schnapper is able to argue that the national ideal is not synonymous with pressure for cultural homogeneity but is in principle perfectly compatible with multicultural diversity.[83] Schnapper immediately seeks to limit this concession, however, by adding, that cultural particularity must not form the basis of a *political* identity, since that would 'dissolve national identity in the interest of particular communitarian belongings'.[84] Concern about the possibility of dissolution has led Schnapper, along with other French commentators, to regard the American model of multiculturalism with particular misgivings, on the ground that it accepts too uncritically the 'given' or 'natural' identity of groups. How far compromise with multiculturalism can go without creating political fragmentation remains, of course, a matter for argument, but Schnapper's fear that 'We are witnessing today a weakening of public spirit and political bonds',[85] partly because of globalization and partly because of the permeation of domestic politics by the acquisitive spirit, suggests that she might well feel that the limits of compromise could be reached quite rapidly.

Kriegel's qualified embrace of liberalism is shared, albeit for different reasons, by Pierre Manent who, like Kriegel and Schnapper, refuses to invoke a sweeping historical overview of Gauchet's kind. Manent's reason for this refusal is that, like Furet, he regards the problem of political legitimacy as the central issue faced by modern democracy.[86] Once this problem is fully appreciated, he maintains, the only appropriate response is the modern liberal ideal of the neutral state. What liberalism cannot avoid confronting, however, is a fundamental cleavage in the life of the modern individual between two different faces he presents to the world, viz. a natural or social one and a civil or artificial one. The greatest challenge confronting the western liberal tradition, accordingly, is to keep these faces distinct whilst simultaneously acknowledging their intimate connection. Liberalism must wrestle, that is, with a tension between the natural order of society and the artificial order of the state that it must never seek to overcome.

Here, then, is yet another suggestive programme for a qualified liberalization of French republicanism. Its execution, however, is extremely problematic, requiring as it does a balance between the republican concern with solidarity, on the one hand, and the liberal concern with individual rights and freedom, on the other. How this synthesis might be achieved is not made clear by Manent.

What remains to be added is that French concessions to the liberal-democratic ideal are made more easily when it is presented as an entirely home-grown one. Gallic insularity is evident, for example, in the insistence by Alain Madelin, a leading politician and economic liberal, that the British and American liberal traditions are merely developments of what were originally French ideas. The originator of British liberal economic theory, for example, turns out to have been Turgot rather than Adam Smith, since Smith (Madelin maintains) borrowed extensively from the French thinker.[87] In like vein, Madelin argues that the American tradition of political economy established by Jefferson was basically French, having been heavily influenced by the work of Destutt de Tracy. The most philosophically ambitious example of this Gallic pride is

provided, however, by Luc Ferry and Alain Renaut.[88] Their aim is
to make liberalism acceptable to the French by restating it in terms
of a revised, yet distinctively French, form of humanism which
rejects the Cartesian 'philosophy of the subject'. The need for this
revision, they maintain, has been created by the powerful critique
of classical Cartesian humanism mounted by such postwar thinkers
as Foucault, Lacan and Derrida, all of whom were right, Ferry and
Renaut admit, to reject it as ahistorical and asocial, just as they were
right to reject theories of liberal democracy which relied on the
Cartesian identification of the individual with the abstract subject.
Nevertheless, they maintain, the ideal of liberal democracy, once freed
from dependence on the concept of the subject and reformulated
on the basis of a new French humanism, remains perfectly viable.
Their aim, accordingly, is to construct a coherent, distinctively French
form of moderate humanism with which to underpin a specifically
French version of liberal-democratic theory.

The question, needless to say, is whether Ferry and Renaut manage
to carry out this enterprise. What is strange, as Alexander Nehamas
remarks, is that, after rejecting the concept of the subject, Ferry and
Renaut turn for inspiration to Sartre, who is firmly within the Cartesian tradition they reject.[89] What is equally strange is that their revised
humanism, far from having the distinctively French character they
claim, also owes much to the German philosophical tradition whose
postwar influence over thinkers like Derrida appalls them. Specifically,
they share with German philosophy at least some of Heidegger's
critique of modernity, sympathizing in particular with his contempt
for technology and mass society.

In short, it is difficult to conclude that Ferry and Renaut have
succeeded in constructing the wholly indigenous French version of
moderate humanism with which they set out to integrate the regard
for individual rights characteristic of Anglo-American liberal constitutionalism into the French republican ideal. It follows that any
French accommodation with liberal democracy is likely to continue
to incur deep republican hostility, on the ground that it involves
adopting alien Anglo-American institutions which destroy solidarity
and show no regard for the needs of cultural assimilation. Sadly, Luc
Ferry's career as Minister of Education, made possible by Chirac's
sympathy for his revisionist enterprise, did not look promising after
his latest book, *For Those Who Love Schools*, was burnt in public by striking teachers in 2003.

Conclusion

How successful has the French search for an alternative to radical idealism been? Although the most viable of the possibilities explored has been liberal constitutionalism, facilitated by the 'juridification' of French politics under the leadership of the Constitutional Council,[90] this still tends to be viewed as 'an alien import, accepted with a reluctant resignation rather than enthusiasm, damned by its "Anglo-Saxon" connotations and feared as a threat to French exceptionalism'.[91] Even the most impressive attempts to construct a native concept of liberal democracy by reviving neglected nineteenth-century French liberal thinkers have failed to overcome, Mark Lilla remarks, the 'air of strangeness, or exteriority, accompanying French analyses of liberal society, as if they were *in* liberalism but not yet *of* it'.[92]

Above all, the suspicion remains that the French republican tradition retains sufficient strength to make any stable compromise with individualism, pluralism or constitutionalism unlikely, with the result that no coherent formula exists for stabilizing the swings from Left to Right that have characterized the French search for a political identity since 1789. In practice, progress is likely to depend heavily on the fate of the deeply held belief in French exceptionalism. On the bicentennary of the French Revolution, Furet and others proclaimed with pleasure that belief in exceptionalism was at an end, thus permitting France to make a constitutional commitment previously precluded by a mistaken pride in the revolutionary heritage.[93] The final decade of the twentieth century, however, saw this embrace of the end of exceptionalism rapidly replaced by fear that crucial aspects of French identity – most notably, republican citizenship and the commitment to *dirigiste* capitalism with a strong welfare orientation – were being threatened by Europeanization and globalization. Nevertheless, the temptation to fall back into insular nationalism was offset by a tendency, eloquently formulated by Elie Cohen in particular, to accept that France was simply *different*, rather than exceptional, and that this difference might flourish, rather than disappear, in the broader context with which French politics now has to come to terms.[94] A thoughtful commentator concluded, however, that 'the embeddedness of the idea of French exceptionalism in ... her modern history surely means that the language of French exceptionalism will retain its resonance and mobilising capacity within the realm of French politics'.[95]

So far as accommodation with the European Union is concerned, the pervasive influence of the French administrative tradition on the entire project meant that this might prove less demanding than it was for other states, such as Britain, which did not share the centralizing Roman law tradition so ably explored by Blandine Kriegel.

4

Nationalism, Democracy and Unification in Postwar German Political Thought

Even before the German surrender in 1945, the Allies had committed themselves to creating a new, democratic Germany which would never again be able to initiate war. The story of German political thought since 1945 is the story of the German response to this project, and in particular of debate amongst Germans themselves about whether they should adopt the project in a form acceptable to them, or dismiss it as alien to German tradition. More recently, the story is of a continuing debate within Germany about whether reunification in 1990 marked a further advance towards a democratic and peace loving Germany, firmly integrated in the European Union, or an opportunity to return (in part at least) to the nationalistic ethos that characterized German history until 1945. Before considering the response of German thinkers to the Allied democratization project, however, it is necessary to consider more closely how the Allies themselves conceived that project since it was they, initially at least, who determined the framework for political reconstruction.

The Allied Plans for a New German Identity

The three years before the Russian occupation of East Berlin in 1948 were marked by an Allied consensus on one fundamental issue, which was that the political reconstruction of Germany was meaningless unless it was accompanied by spiritual reconstruction. As Montgomery put it, creating a new Germany meant creating new

Germans by completely changing 'the hearts, and the way of life, of the German people'.[1] Russia naturally disagreed with the western Allies about what the new Germans should look like, but what is mainly relevant at present is that the problem for the western Allies was to find a way of carrying out spiritual reconstruction without inflicting a new kind of totalitarian rule. This was the task to which the Allies sought a solution at the Potsdam conference in 1945.

The solution adopted involved, amongst other strategies, a denazification programme and educational measures intended to get all adult Germans to acknowledge their collective guilt for Nazism.[2] In the event, however, the project of spiritually transforming the Germans was quickly abandoned: General Lucius Clay, commander of US occupying forces, ordered in August 1947 that it was to end by 31 March 1948.[3] This was partly because the Allies, under pressure from younger German intellectuals in particular, had come to recognize the counterproductive nature of the denazification process. It was due above all, however, to the Russian occupation of East Berlin. Abandoning their desire to transform Germany spiritually, the western Allies sought instead to transform it into an ally against the new enemy. In order to do so, they began to consider seriously the Germans' own views of what their new identity should be, instead of simply imposing one on them.[4]

There was, however, a major obstacle to further progress, which was that most Germans disliked democracy, especially in its American and British forms. The American model was considered inseparable from a ruthless type of capitalism which many believed had been one of the most disastrous features of the Weimar Republic. The British model was associated with another disastrous feature of the Weimar Republic, which was the doctrine of popular sovereignty. Thoughtful German critics believed this had opened the door to Hitler's plebiscitary dictatorship.

Despite their lack of enthusiasm for democracy, however, the Soviet occupation of East Berlin in 1948 led Germans to a compromise with it, in the form of the Federal Republic created in the following year. On the one hand, the Federal Republic made major concessions to the Allied demand for a form of democracy which was wholly uncontaminated by nationalist sentiment, which protected individual rights, and which accepted, to some extent at least, a free market commitment. On the other, the Allies sought to win the support of moderate Germans by sanctioning the incorporation into the constitution of three indigenous German political ideals which had not been contaminated by Nazism. The first was the ideal of the *Rechsstaat* – a state, that is, ruled by legal procedures. The second was the ideal of a highly decentralized federal system of government which, by conferring many important powers on the *Länder*, would make its abuse more difficult. The third was a Christian tradition which accommodated socialist and other reservations about capitalism, partially at least, by subordinating individualism and unchecked competition to the requirements of an organic social order.

In 1949, then, Germany – or rather, the western half of it, since it was partitioned in that year – acquired a democratic constitution, described however as the 'Basic Law' due to fear that the word 'constitution' might appear to acknowledge the division of Germany as permanent. Having swallowed the bitter pill, unexpectedly rapid economic recovery soon lent the democratic system a certain sweetness.

The great question, however, was whether, in spite of Allied concessions, the Germans would continue to regard democracy as an alien imposition, as they had done after the First World War, or would gradually make a moral commitment to it. Even if the passage of time permitted liberal democracy to put down new roots, would it nevertheless remain a fragile graft onto a political tradition which remained fundamentally authoritarian and nationalist? In order to answer these questions, attention will be concentrated on thinkers in the Federal Republic. The justification for passing over those in Eastern Germany in this cavalier way is twofold. In the first place, although the eastern reconstruction project initially took the form of a quest for a genuinely independent and distinctive form of socialism, more humane than the Soviet one, the DDR's Russian masters were not prepared to tolerate any serious challenge to the Moscow party. Secondly, when reunification finally came in 1990, it was the constitution of the Federal Republic which became the foundation of the newly unified nation.

Turning to German intellectuals in the Federal Republic, then, it is necessary to begin by considering the hostility to democracy expressed by leading members of an older generation of conservative thinkers who continued to be influential in the immediate postwar period.

Conservative Critics of the Federal Republic: Cultural Alienation and Political Impotence

What linked conservative thinkers was a 'spiritual' interpretation of German identity which was difficult to reconcile with liberal democracy. Although this sometimes led to outright rejection of democracy, as in Heidegger's case, more moderate conservatives sometimes made a serious attempt at coming to terms with it. At the heart of their thought, however, was the belief that a tension exists between the ideals of self-government and good government which should be resolved in favour of the latter, with the result that their position remained tinged by authoritarianism. This was true, for example, of Karl Jaspers and Eric Voegelin, both of whom supported the democratic ideal, but only in so far as the populace was capable of good government. Before considering moderate conservatives of this kind, however, it will be instructive to consider the reasons that led a more extreme conservative thinker like Martin Heidegger to cling to his unqualified opposition to democracy in the postwar era, despite his experience of Nazism.

A few years after the creation of the Federal Republic, Heidegger republished a series of lectures he had delivered a few years before war broke out.[5] The central problem of modern politics, the lectures maintained, is not peculiarly German but extends to world civilization as a whole. To understand it, it is necessary to appreciate that the two superpowers which presided over a divided Germany – the USA and the USSR – are basically indistinguishable, since both reveal 'the same dreary technological frenzy, the same unrestricted organization of the average man'.[6] More particularly, both are prone to an ever deepening form of nihilism or, as Heidegger put it, a 'darkening of the world'.[7]

Heidegger's view of the true nature of Germany's postwar situation can now be stated. This is that Germany alone has avoided the universal nihilism which threatens the world because it is spiritually superior to all other modern nations. Like ancient Greece, it possesses a language which is 'the most spiritual of all languages'.[8] More generally, it is 'the most metaphysical' nation. German spiritual superiority, however, carries with it a duty, in the form of a 'historical mission'[9] to save mankind from the horrors of modern mass civilization in all its forms, including the democratic one.

From this standpoint, Heidegger dismissed the fuss which America and Britain in particular had made about Nazism as hypocritical, since it ignored the fact that Nazism is merely one of many manifestations of a ruthless modern technological culture. In fact, the 'manufacture of corpses in gas chambers and extermination camps' is as routine in the modern world as the processing of food in a 'motorized food-industry'. Genocide, indeed, suddenly appeared to be utterly banal, since the impersonal technological culture of modernity had rendered radical destruction of every kind totally normal.[10]

Heidegger's bleak picture of modern culture implied, then, that the Allied project of introducing democracy to West Germany would destroy Germany's spiritual superiority by imposing the massi-fication process which had destroyed the spiritual integrity of the Allies themselves. When he found that the democratization project appeared to be taking root, Heidegger despaired. In a well-known interview with *Der Spiegel* in 1966, he declared that 'Only a god can save us'.[11] In fact, Heidegger's real problem was not the lack of divine intervention: it was, rather, the fact that his conception of German national identity was so purely spiritual that it left no place for such pedestrian matters as the rule of law and institutions for limiting power. The result was that he veered between totalitarian sympa-thies and complete spiritual withdrawal, quite unable to envisage a stable basis for political moderation.

Heidegger's unqualified hostility to the new democratic order is in marked contrast to the struggle of the conservative historian, Friedrich Meinecke, to reach a positive accommodation with it. Like Heidegger, Meinecke regarded Nazism as only one aspect of a more general calamity which has afflicted Europe as a whole during the twentieth century. For him, this consisted in the advent of utopian ideologies that ignore the tragic core of human existence. What the tragic vision acknowledges is that 'the divine and demonic in man are indissolubly linked together...'.[12] Since utopian ideologies reject this, they cannot acknowledge the inescapable need for political power to restrain human beings: it has no place in their visions of the good society. The tragic vision, by contrast, places the inescapability of power at the centre of politics. Without the realism it provides, men are unprotected against utopian movements such as Nazism.[13]

Meinecke's invocation of the tragic vision had the attraction of offering Germans a theory of victimhood with which to ease feelings of guilt about Nazism: through no fault of their own, he implied, they had suffered an unfortunate historical fate. What was mainly striking, however, was his conclusion that previous nationalist excesses in German history did not mean that nationalism had to be entirely purged, as the Allies demanded. On the contrary, the principal task facing not only postwar Germany but the European world at large is that of achieving 'a truly healthy intermingling of the nationalist and socialist movements... free from nationalist excesses...'.[14] Until that happens, Germany should accept partition. Thereafter, Germany might properly resume the quest for national unity – but only, Meinecke added, 'as a member of a future federation... of the central and west European states. Such a United Nations of Europe', he optimistically observed, 'will naturally accept the hegemony of the victor powers'.[15]

The crucial question posed by Meinecke's sympathy for nationalism was to determine what kind of postwar Germany could adopt without sliding back into the excesses which had marked the past. His answer was that the relevant kind of nationalism one permeated by the tragic vision, which restrains excess by creating sensitivity to the inescapable place of power in life and the consequent need to avoid its abuse. But how was this abuse to be avoided? It was this question that provoked Meinecke's study of the cynical doctrine of *raison d'état* which he believed Machiavelli's treatment of power had encouraged.[16] A return to this cynicism could only be avoided, Meinecke maintained, by fusing power with a sense of high moral purpose, as the tragic vision seeks to do. The problem, however, was to explain how such a fusion could be achieved in the new Federal democracy. Meinecke proposed two solutions.

The first involved turning to religion in order to ensure that the Germans were constantly aware of 'a moral law derived from the Eternal and far above blood and race'.[17] As Meinecke acknowledged, however, religion was as much a source of division in Germany as of unity. In order to unite Catholics and Protestants, he dealt with this by defining the Christian message in extremely vague terms. It is, he wrote, about 'respect for the eternal and absolute;... recognition of the conscience as the "sun of our moral day"'. This strategy was in practice successful, in the sense that a compromise between Catholics and Protestants was in fact achieved, and played a crucial part in the postwar German reconstruction project.

Meinecke's second strategy, however, was more problematic. It consisted of preventing the future abuse of power by ensuring that those who exercised it were culturally enlightened. His aim, more precisely, was to purify the Germans of any remaining Nazi sympathies by reviving the golden age of Goethe. Ironically, as soon as Meinecke began to describe in more detail what this involved, a mildly authoritarian note began to creep into his thought. A mass of small Goethe

Communities, he suggested, should be created, with 'a *Handbook for Goethe Communities* indicating the right prose [for them to read],... and with all kinds of organizational hints'. Suddenly aware that his attempt to fuse power with spirituality might be moving in exactly the kind of direction he wished to oppose, Meinecke hastily added that 'I shall not sketch this further here, in order not to anticipate the free creative activity of individuals.'[18] He broke off too late, however, to avoid revealing his commitment to the bureaucratic belief that 'free creative activity' could be organized into existence.

Meinecke's aim, then, was to anchor the new German democracy in a form of nationalist realism that purified power by fusing it with religion and culture. It was a noble aspiration, but hardly entitled to the realist label. Ultimately, what it amounted to was 'an appeal to the executive statesman that he should always carry State and God together in his heart...'.[19] In effect, that is, Meinecke wanted to place the new democracy in the hands of political saints, without any indication that they could actually be found, or any institutional provision for rendering them accountable, if they could.

What seemed at first sight to be a major step towards a more viable compromise with the new democracy was provided by two émigré conservatives, Leo Strauss and Eric Voegelin, both of whom placed constitutionalism at the centre of their thought. In Strauss's case, however, the form of constitutionalism he favoured was the ancient, not the modern kind. The fatal flaw of modern constitutionalism, Strauss maintained, is that it is almost entirely about rights, and ignores the teaching of virtue and public service. Because the new German democracy is of this kind, it provides no protection against the return of dictatorship. As the ancients realized, the only way of preventing that is to educate a citizen elite in knowledge of the natural order, since this alone fosters the sense of piety which is the basis of all sound political order.[20]

Critics of Strauss question whether a 'natural order' actually exists, as well as taking issue with his elitism. The real problem presented by Strauss' political thought, however, lies elsewhere: it consists, more precisely, in his caricature of modern constitutionalism. In its modern form, constitutionalism is essentially a response to the most fundamental characteristic of the modern Western world, which is the appearance of social and political diversity following the collapse of a pre-modern consensus about fundamental values. In order to accommodate that diversity, thinkers like Hobbes emphasised the need for a formal or procedural constitutionalism. In doing so, they were not perversely turning their backs on virtue and the natural order in order to foster an egotistical concern with individual rights, as Strauss assumes. Rather, they were seeking to respond to the diversity with which neither ancient nor medieval thought had had to deal, and which could only be accommodated in a non-coercive way by a procedural approach.

Eric Voegelin, another eminent émigré, was also sympathetic to constitutionalism but agreed with Strauss that the modern form exposed the new Federal democracy to the return of dictatorship. In Voegelin's view, this is because it provides no remedy for the sense of alienation which inspired the radical ideologies of the interwar era and has continued unabated into the postwar decades. The source of this alienation he attributed to a modern, secularized version of the ancient Gnostic heresy, the essence of which is a vision of the established social order as a prison from which man's principal task is to escape. Despite the outward differences of the main ideologies, he maintains that they are all Gnostic in inspiration. Voegelin's account of the history of the heresy, and more especially of how it came to permeate nearly all contemporary western culture, is so sweeping that it leaves his thought open to the charge of vagueness at many crucial points. What is more relevant in the present context, however, is the fact that his desire to protect the new German democracy from subversion by Gnostic-inspired political movements had authoritarian implications which were more likely to subvert than save it. This becomes evident as soon as a crucial distinction he makes between two different kinds of representation is examined. One kind is what he termed 'elemental' representation, and the other, 'existential' representation.

By 'elemental' representation Voegelin referred to the formal system of popular elections on which modern western liberal democracies rely. Its weakness is that it leaves a society at the mercy of any Gnostic tendencies to which the masses are prone. By 'existential' representation, he referred to a system in which the ruler is representative in the deeper sense that the values he stands for reflect the society's whole way of life.[21] Voegelin's contention was that only a democracy based on the latter, existential kind of representation will be secure against extremist movements like Nazism because it permits power to be placed in the hands of an elite which is free from Gnostic tendencies. As Hans Kelsen, one of Voegelin's former tutors, was not slow to point out, however, the concept of existential representation could easily sanction exactly the kind of totalitarian system Voegelin opposed, since it permitted the Soviet government, for example, to claim to be the existential representative of society.[22] More generally, the concept of existential representation provided a means of subverting any liberal democracy simply by asserting that it was not genuinely representative. Voegelin would no doubt reply that this misrepresented his intention, which was to fight the continuing influence of Gnosticism on postwar German culture. The danger, however, was that this would require 'de-Gnostification' processes akin to the denazification ones that had risked reintroducing totalitarian forms of rule. Since Voegelin did not countenance this, his conservative critique of German democracy ended, like the previous ones, in political paralysis.

There was, however, one notable German thinker so anxious to embrace the new democracy that it seemed he might avoid the fate of the foregoing conservatives. He was Karl Jaspers, who came to the defence of democracy during the 1960s at a time when faith in it had been undermined, in particular, by the realization that many ex-Nazis continued to occupy key positions throughout the social order, even rising to the position of President (Lübke) and Chancellor (Kiesinger) at the end of 1966. The following year, Alexander and Margarethe Mitscherlich lamented the apparent West German 'inability to mourn' for the victims of Nazism, in a book of that title.[23] It was against this background that Jaspers published *Wohin treibt die Bundesrepublik?* (1966),[24] in which he rejected the influence of the British and American models on the constitution of the Federal Republic and attempted to purge the German political tradition, so to speak, by developing a distinctively German model based on Kant's republican ideal, the essence of which is that it makes politics inseparable from the moral self-education of democratic citizens.[25]

In what ways did Jaspers consider the Federal Republic should be restructured in order to implement his Kantian model of democracy? Three main changes, he wrote, are necessary. The first is it to replace the nationalist conception of German identity by a cosmopolitan one, grounded in membership of a universal community. The basis of this cosmopolitan identity is what Jaspers terms 'The Encompassing', which cannot be grasped through mystical insight but only through universal human communication.[26] Although inspiring, Jaspers' vision of a universal community was open to the charge of being nothing more than an abstract metaphysical vision. It was therefore somewhat unfair of him to castigate the Federal Republic for not measuring up to it.

Jaspers' second condition for democracy was more realistic. This consisted of rejecting the doctrine of popular sovereignty upon which the Allied model was based on the ground that it had paved the way for the kind of elective dictatorship which had destroyed the Weimar Republic.[27] Instead, democracy must be re-established on a Kantian commitment to the rule of reason, which provided the only secure basis for the rule of law. From this point of view, Jaspers believed that the 1949 Basic Law was an important step towards a genuinely democratic ideal. It failed, however, to satisfy the third condition for democracy.

Jaspers' third condition for a truly democratic society is the existence of a sense of individual moral responsibility, combined with a collective sense of political responsibility. In *The Question of German Guilt*, published shortly after the war, he explained that all Germans are *politically* liable for all crimes committed in the name of the Reich 'inasmuch as we let such a regime rise among us'. They are not *morally* liable, however, 'insofar as many of us in our deepest hearts opposed all this evil and have no morally guilty acts or inner motivations to admit'.[28] Unlike moral liability, political liability 'leaves the soul untouched'.[29]

The need for a strong sense of collective political responsibility, Jaspers believed, required the new Federal democracy to educate the German populace in 'the basic facts' of recent German history.[30] It also meant making the populace aware, he added, that in addition to moral and political guilt, there can also be metaphysical guilt. This consists in 'the lack of absolute solidarity with man as man', and originates in blindness to the Encompassing.[31]

One of the most powerful criticisms of Jaspers' analysis of German war guilt came from Hannah Arendt, who argued that it inevitably trivialized Nazi atrocities by treating the unspeakable as if it could be discussed in terms of ordinary moral concepts. Jaspers replied that by demonizing the Holocaust as Arendt had done in her classic study of *The Origins of Totalitarianism*, she had conferred upon it a satanic grandeur, and that in order to avoid this, what was necessary was to grasp the banal character of evil which he sought to emphasize.[32] Arendt was so impressed by this response that she subsequently made the theme of the 'banality of evil' the subtitle of her study of Eichmann's trial.

Arendt's criticism of Jaspers, however, had missed the principal problem created by his Kantian reformulation of democratic theory. This lies in his conclusion that 'without purification of the soul, there is no political freedom'.[33] What democracy requires, more precisely, is endless self-purification through sacrifice. The invention of the atom bomb, with the consequent risk of human extinction, led Jaspers to lay even greater stress on this need. The result was that his democratic ideal inevitably acquired an illiberal character, as was evident when he denounced any statesman who tolerates those who refuse to engage in self-purification.[34]

Despite his attempt to achieve a positive accommodation with the postwar reconstruction project, then, Jasper's identification of democratic citizenship with spiritual purification ended by creating the danger of authoritarianism already noted in other German conservative thinkers. To his credit, however, he had tried to make a positive contribution to the reconstruction project by rooting democracy in the German philosophical tradition, instead of dismissing it as merely an alien Allied imposition.

The Radical Critique of the New Democracy

In the immediate postwar decade, radical dissent was marginalized in West Germany partly by American domination and partly by fear of Russia, following the Berlin Occupation. During the 1960s, however, a more sympathetic mood developed as a result of increasing concern, already mentioned, about the continuation in office of an ex-Nazi elite. Against this background, radical criticism once again began to attract a wide hearing, more especially amongst the student generation. A new lease of life was acquired, in particular, by a work published two decades earlier by Adorno and Horkheimer, two of the most influential Frankfurt School theorists. This was *The Dialectic of Enlightenment*, in which they concluded that in the absence of revolutionary action, the fate of the West would be to move towards 'total integration' in 'an administered world'.[35] Following their return from exile in the USA, however, the authors had lost their revolutionary enthusiasm to such an extent that they 'acted as pro-American, democratic adult educators' who stored their earlier radical work 'in a box in the basement of the [Institute of Social Research] which the younger researchers were not supposed to open'.[36] Disaffected

German students therefore directed their attention instead to a member of the Frankfurt School who had remained in the USA but was determined to keep the radical message alive. He was Herbert Marcuse, whose *One Dimensional Man*, although initially published in the USA, became the best-selling radical tract of the 1960s.

In that work, Marcuse echoed Heidegger's contention that the great problem of the modern West is no longer capitalism but the all-pervasive dehumanization caused by a culture exclusively committed to technological efficiency. The fact that, in liberal societies, this culture had brought mass prosperity without destroying the rule of law did not prevent him from insisting – again like Heidegger – that it was nevertheless fundamentally indistinguishable from totalitarianism. 'The world of the concentration camps', Marcuse wrote, 'was not an exceptionally monstrous society . . . What we saw here was the image, and in a sense the quintessence, of the infernal society into which we are plunged every day.'[37] What was it, one must ask, that Marcuse found so monstrous and alienating about prosperity and the rule of law?

Marcuse's answer was almost unbelievably trivial. Behind a jargon which claimed to give his thought objectivity, the kind of features of modern society which he described as alienating included a notorious description of urban sex. 'Compare love-making in a meadow and in an automobile', he wrote,

> [or] on a lovers' walk outside the town walls and on a Manhattan street. In the former cases, the environment partakes of and invites libidinal cathexis and tends to be eroticized. Libido transcends beyond the immediate erotogenic zones – a process of nonrepressive sublimation. In contrast, a mechanized environment seems to block such self-transcendence of libido. Impelled in the striving to extend the field of erotic gratification, libido becomes less 'polymorphous,' less capable of eroticism beyond localized sexuality, and the *latter* is intensified.[38]

As this example reveals, Marcuse's concept of alienation amounted to little more than an aging German scholar's romantic fantasies about a lost rural world. If that criticism seems too dismissive, then consider instead the concept of 'liberation' Marcuse proposed in his most popular work, *A Critique of Pure Tolerance*. There, he explained that 'true' toleration involves not only 'extreme suspension of the right of free speech and free assembly', but also 'withdrawal of tolerance from regressive movements *before* they can become active; intolerance even toward thought, opinion and word, and finally, intolerance in the opposite direction, that is, towards the self-styled conservatives, to the political Right...'.[39] The new German democracy undoubtedly had major limitations, but Marcuse's alternative seemed to be far worse.

This was the view, in particular, of the most able of the younger generation of radical thinkers who read Marcuse. Rejecting Marcuse's criticism of the new democracy, Jürgen Habermas insisted instead on rooting his own thought in what he described as 'the deep, everyday experience we lived through after 1945: things got better with the reintroduction of democracy, and even simply of the rule of law'.[40] It is the quest for a more moderate position, in which Habermas played a fundamental part, that must now be considered.

The Quest for a Moderate Consensus: Legal Rights, the Social Market Ideal and 'Constitutional Patriotism'

In order to move beyond conservative dreams of spiritual renewal and radical theories of alienation, moderate German political thinkers sympathetic to the democratic reconstruction project had to find a way of constructing a consensus that would support it. Their main strategy for doing this consisted of trying to find a philosophically coherent way of combining the two ideals on which the Federal constitution was constructed, viz. those of the *Rechtsstaat* and *Sozialstaat*.

The *Rechtsstaat*, as Ernst-Wolfgang Böckenförde remarks, is a peculiarly German concept which has no equivalent in any other language.[41] Originating in early nineteenth-century German liberal thought, what characterizes it is the identification of the rule of law with the rational state.[42] The difficulty about applying the *Rechtsstaat* ideal to the Federal Republic, however, was that German thinkers did not agree on whether the objective, universally valid concept of reason it presupposed was philosophically defensible. Scepticism on this account was characteristic, in particular, of legal positivist theory, according to which the basis of a legal system is never reason but always sovereign authority. For Hans Kelsen, its leading representative, the legitimacy of a legal system is inseparable from the fact that it is actually efficacious, in the sense of being acknowledged by those subject to it. This efficacious legitimacy constitutes what he terms the *Grundnorm* (basic law), a concept which cannot be described as either rational or irrational, or moral or immoral, since it is impossible, he maintained, to get behind it, so to speak. Although Kelsen did not intend to shield the government from criticism, his rejection of any higher standard seemed, despite his denials, to deprive the new democracy of a stable normative foundation by making it indistinguishable from a mere power structure What made the normative issue even more problematic was that Kelsen denied intrinsic value to democracy, treating it as merely a method of decision-making. More precisely, he wrote, it is 'a *procedure*, a specific method of creating and applying the social order constituting the community, which is the criterion of that political system properly called democracy'.[43]

Postwar fears about the fragility of the new democracy, intensified in particular by concern about the continuing influence of former Nazis over the new democracy already noted, led legal positivism to be discredited. But where was a more satisfactory theoretical basis for the *Rechtsstaat* to be found? The most philosophically impressive answer was provided by Jürgen Habermas' revision of the concept of 'constitutional patriotism', a concept central to Left-liberal thinkers at large. Before examining Habermas' thought, however, it is necessary to consider the second ideal to which moderate defenders of the new West German democracy appealed.

The constitution of 1949 had proclaimed not only that the new democracy was a *Rechsstaat* but that it was also a *Sozialstaat* which guaranteed a material right to property, a right to work and various other social benefits. To spell out what implementing the ideal of a *Sozialstaat* involved, however, was no easier than clarifying what a *Rechsstaat* required. What was no less problematic, however, was the assumption quietly made in the constitution that the *Rechsstaat* ideal did not conflict with the *Sozialstaat* but could be harmoniously united with it. It was this assumption which the Christian Democratic and Christian Socialist parties took for granted when they tried, during the early postwar period, to steer a path between the conservative and radical extremes. But were they entitled, one must ask, to assume that *Rechsstaat* and *Sozialstaat* are indeed compatible, as the constitution assumed? What soon became clear was that, far from being compatible, there were potential sources of conflict between them which might jeopardize the future of the new democracy.

The tendency to play down these sources of conflict is evident, for example, in Alfred Müller-Armack, a leading defender of the widely admired 'social market economy' (a term he invented) and a member of the influential Ordo-liberal group of intellectuals. Only extensive state planning of the economy, he maintained, can secure social justice by erecting 'on the basis of a market economy a multiform and *complete* system of social protection'.[44] As Müller-Armack himself recognized, however, it was not at all clear how far planning could go before it threatened the survival of the free market. In response, he merely observed that the nature of the balance between public and private sectors could 'not be decided in advance'.[45] This left open the disturbing possibility that it might only be decided too late.

A similar optimism about the possibility of uniting *Rechsstaat* and *Sozialstaat* in an harmonious organic social order was displayed by Wilhelm Röpke, who exerted a significant influence on the economic policy of the new Germany despite the fact that he was Swiss.[46] For Röpke, the danger confronting the postwar world was of a new totalitarianism, created by the emergence of a mass of 'spiritually homeless and morally shipwrecked' individuals with no 'capacity for true religious faith and for cherishing cultural traditions ... '.[47] It was this nightmare, and not merely the problem of welfare and economic growth, which led Röpke to defend the social market economy as the only safe option open to postwar democracy. What he sought, more precisely, was a compromise between capitalism and collectivism that would permit 'a healthy balance between the individual and community ... '.[48] Those who committed themselves to what he termed this 'third road', he said, would recognize in the Papal Encyclical *Quadragesimo Anno* (1931) a clear outline of the Christian social and political ideas that they must adopt in order to implement it.[49]

How coherent was this optimistic attempt by social market theorists to develop a concept of German democracy that combined *Rechsstaat* and *Sozialstaat* in an organic social vision inspired by Christian sentiments? The answer must be: not very. In the first place, there was the prospect of the erosion of freedom by endless state expansion that has already been indicated. Secondly, there was the danger, completely unforeseen by thinkers like Röpke, that social market policies would lead to the growth of massive systems of patronage – a phenomenon which, by the end of the twentieth century, was to place a question mark over the future of the Christian Democratic defenders of social democracy not only in Germany but also in Italy and Belgium. In addition, there was the failure to foresee that democratic governments would not always plan in the public interest, as had been assumed, but would do so with an eye to winning electoral support. Yet another problem was that the acquisitive mentality sanctioned by the market ethos might actually foster the process of 'massification' Röpke feared, rather than preventing it. Still another was that Röpke's sympathy for the Catholic corporatist vision developed in the 1931 Papal Encyclical[50] was open to the charge of being unduly optimistic about the spontaneous sources of social cohesion in modern Western societies. Finally, social market doctrine took for granted a degree of social consensus that did not allow for the increasing diversity of postwar German society, reflected especially in the growth of feminist, multicultural and green movements.

When these objections to the West German 'social market' ideal so widely admired by other European democracies in the early postwar decades are taken as a whole, the only possible conclusion is the one drawn by Ralf Dahrendorf. The claim that the social market economy presented a viable 'third way' between capitalism and socialism, Dahrendorf has remarked, serves only to obscure the fact that the concept of the 'social market' is merely 'a concoction of seemingly incompatible ingredients...there is no "system" which could be called a "social market economy"; there is only a reality which has come about through special, though not necessarily unique, circumstances'.[51]

Dahrendorf penned this damning conclusion with the benefit of hindsight. By the early 1970s, however, it was already clear that the social market ideal had failed to stabilize the new democracy. An American study by Almond and Verba, for example, revealed that although most Germans were more or less satisfied with their present political system, they did not feel emotionally attached to it.[52] 'Order', Kurt Sontheimer observed around the same time, 'is still more important to Germans than democratic legitimacy and control'.[53] The implication is clear: it was necessary to look elsewhere for a coherent way of achieving the union of *Rechsstaat* and *Sozialstaat* at which the Federal constitution aimed. The key figure in this respect is Habermas, to whom it is now necessary to return.

Having rejected the legal positivist theory of the *Rechsstaat* developed by Kelsen, Habermas sought to replace it by one which provided a cast-iron normative basis. This could only be done, he believed, by developing an objective, universally valid concept of rationality with which to underpin the new theory. The first step in that direction, Habermas maintained, consists of rejecting the 'monological' concept of rationality that has dominated liberal thought as a result of the 'philosophy of consciousness' which the modern West has uncritically accepted since the time of Descartes. What the monological concept fails to grasp is that reason is not the possession of isolated individuals but is, on the contrary, an essentially shared or intersubjective phenomenon. Failure to grasp this not only condemns man to a solipsistic condition but also makes it impossible for democratic theory to incorporate the diversity of moral and political standpoints.

What is necessary, then, is to restate the *Rechsstaat* ideal in terms of a 'dialogical' or discursive concept of rationality. Being essentially social, rationality in this sense can only be fully developed through the experience of universal communication. This revised concept of rationality, Habermas emphasized, is not something plucked out of thin air: on the contrary, it is rooted in 'the structure of a rationality which is immanent in everyday communicative practice, and which brings the stubbornness of the life-forms into play against the functional demands of autonomized economic and administrative systems'.[54] It was by reformulating the defence of democracy in terms of this communicative concept of rationality that Habermas sought to protect it from the subjectivism to which Kelsen had left it exposed.

This, then, is the philosophical strategy by which Habermas has sought to give the *Rechsstaat* an objective rational foundation. Since his concept of communicative rationality is a procedural one, however, it left the problem of social cohesion untouched. In order to complete the construction of a new basis for a moderate democratic consensus, Habermas therefore proceeded to rework the *Sozialstaat* ideal, as well as the *Rechsstaat* one. As he himself put it, 'Democratic citizenship can only realize its integrative potential' if it offers 'social security and the reciprocal recognition of different cultural forms'.[55] His revision of the *Sozialstaat* has resulted in a form of socialism purged of all the utopian impulses previously associated with the Marxist tradition. The most that this revised form of socialism can offer, Habermas explains, are

> hopes and starting-points for the conquest of unhappiness and misery which are generated by the structure of social life . . . it can do nothing to overcome the fundamental perils of human

existence – such as guilt, loneliness, sickness and death. You could say that social theory offers no consolation, has no bearing on the individual's need for salvation.[56]

Despite the non-revolutionary nature of Habermas' socialism, he has nevertheless continued to describe it as radical on the ground that it is inspired by the 'outrageously strong claim' that 'there is a universal core of moral intuition in all times and in all societies'.[57] There was little about this claim, however, to prevent socialism of this kind appealing to progressive members of the middle class.

In accordance with the formalism of the communicative ideal of rationality in terms of which he theorized the *Rechsstaat*, Habermas stressed that the theory can never 'cash out the expression "socialism" in terms of a *concrete* form of life' but can at most 'indicate necessary conditions under which emancipated forms of life would be possible today'.[58] Theory, in other words, cannot shed much light on exactly what measures the *Sozialstaat* requires. In general, however, what is clear is that the new synthesis of *Rechtsstaat* and *Sozialstaat* rests on the concept of *Verfassungspatriotismus* ('constitutional patriotism') which stands at the centre of Habermas' search for a moderate consensus. Since this concept, as Jan-Werner Müller notes, was not 'one man's maverick idea' but was 'very much part of a West German liberal consensus that encompassed the editors of *Die Zeit*, writers [and] social scientists, as well as politicians'[59] who all found in it a concept of German political identity applicable both before and after unification in 1990, it is necessary to consider more closely what it involves.

The term constitutional patriotism was first used by Dolf Sternberger, one of the foremost defenders of postwar West German democracy, in the course of celebrating three decades of survival of the Federal Republic.[60] In Sternberger's thought, however, it was still linked to nationalist sentiment, albeit in a form wholly purged of all *volkisch* tendencies and shaped instead by an ideal of civil society in which a commitment to the rule of law was of a paramount significance. For Habermas, by contrast, the essence of constitutional patriotism is that it completely detaches political identity from nationalism in any guise, making it instead wholly dependent on free collective choice, as expressed in terms of constitutional forms and universal rights of individual participation. 'If we do not free ourselves from the diffuse notions about the nation-state', he wrote, we will be unable to continue unburdened on the very path that we have long since chosen: the path to a multicultural society, the path to a federal state with wide regional differences and strong federal power, and above all the path to a unified European state of many nationalities. A national identity which is not based predominantly on republican self-understanding and constitutional patriotism necessarily collides with the universalist rules of coexistence for human beings.[61]

Habermas not only radicalized Sternberger's concept of constitutional patriotism by purging it of any connection with nationalism. In addition, he purged it of any direct link with state power, or indeed with power of any kind, linking it instead to commitment to 'universalist rules of coexistence'. Sternberger, by contrast, had associated the ideal with substantive support for the state.

Finally, Habermas radicalized the concept yet further by linking it to the memory of the Holocaust, and to the consequent demand for a far greater change in the postwar German sense of historical identity than more conservative thinkers like Sternberger required. The only appropriate identity for Germans, Habermas maintains, is one which recognizes the radical discontinuity in German history symbolized by Auschwitz. 'Because of that horrible break in continuity,' he writes, 'the Germans have given up the possibility of constituting their identity on something other than universalist principles of state citizenship, in the light of which national traditions can ... only be critically and self-critically appropriated.'[62] What they have, whether they like it or not, is a 'post-traditional' identity which can exist 'only in the method of the public, discursive battle around the interpretation of a constitutional patriotism made concrete under historical circumstances'.[63]

How satisfactory, then, is Habermas' revised version of constitutional patriotism as a vehicle for developing the relationship between *Rechtsstaat* and *Sozialstaat*? The principal weaknesses have been ruthlessly exposed by German contemporaries. Niklas Luhmann, for example, has used systems theory to mount a radical attack on the very concept of the legitimation enterprise to which Habermas' thought is devoted. What Habermas has failed to appreciate, he maintains, is that no modern society can be legitimated by the search for an independently grounded authority, since the irreducible diversity of the autonomous subsystems in such societies precludes the possibility of identifying an impartial or independent standpoint for arbitration between them. In this respect, Luhmann is at one with Habermas' postmodern critics, who share Luhmann's vision of modern societies as constituted by a 'polycontextural' nature which inevitably dooms any claim to normative universality to being intrinsically contestable.[64] As Luhmann himself puts it, what Habermas' search for universally valid rational norms fails to appreciate is the fact that today, 'The theorist of cognition himself becomes a rat in the labyrinth and must consider from which position he observes the other rats.'[65]

In this situation, Luhmann maintains, the problem of social integration can only be dealt with by completely abandoning Habermas' legitimation enterprise and adopting instead a non-moralistic approach to politics which acknowledges all opinions as entitled to be heard, while simultaneously promoting throughout society a realistic spirit that acknowledges the need to allow the social system to evolve smoothly. To make legitimation depend, as Habermas does, on a rational consensus is simply to maintain a moralistic stance which refuses to acknowledge the irreducible nature of modern subsystem diversity.[66]

A somewhat similar critique of Habermas' legitimation enterprise has been developed by Claus Offe, who has accused him of perpetuating, despite Habermas' disclaimers, what Offe calls the classical Frankfurt tradition of 'emphasizing "superstructural" elements as the decisive level of societal dynamics'.[67] In less technical language, what Offe means is that Habermas assigns too much significance to rational deliberation. This criticism is supported, albeit from a different direction, by Hans-Georg Gadamer, for whom only tradition, and not the formal abstractions of reason, can provide the foundation for moral and political life.[68]

In response to these criticisms, Habermas has qualified his commitment to universal rational principles by giving more space to compromise and negotiation in his political theory. He continues to maintain, however, that only such principles can validate the democratic order ethically by permitting it to claim to be more than a sectionally based system which 'reflect[s] the moral intuitions of the average, male, middle-class member of a modern Western society'.[69] This does not, however, meet the most cogent criticism of his position, which is that it fails to take account of the part played by political construction in the constitution of democracy, in a sense which permits no appeal to a supra-political order of rationality of the kind he postulates. In this respect, he has failed to silence sceptics who maintain that his thought is at bottom an attempt to de-politicize politics by a flight into the ethical. This charge has been made in its most cogent form by conservative thinkers influenced by Carl Schmitt, for whom political unity has no rational foundation but is only created by the decision of a leader who rallies the masses by making them aware of the need to combine against a foe. Since this criticism is central to New Right theorists who became briefly influential during the 1990s, further consideration of it will be postponed until later in this chapter.

A second, very different critique of Habermas has focused on his concept of modernity, rather than on the rationalism of his legitimation project. Habermas' defect, Ulrich Beck has maintained, is his unduly optimistic view of modernity, as reflected in his inability to recognize that the Western world has now entered a phase of development in which Habermas' concern for social justice has been replaced by fear of artificially created global risks which, for the present at least, no institutions are able to remedy. As Beck puts it, 'the sources of danger are no longer ignorance but *knowledge*; not a deficient but a perfected mastery over nature; not that which eludes the human grasp but the system of norms and objective constraints established with the industrial epoch'.[70] Although Beck's work has helped to fuel the environmental concerns that gave birth to the Green movement,[71] sceptical commentators note that he has produced very little empirical evidence to support his speculations.[72] They also note that he ignores facts, such as a continuing increase in life expectancy in most parts of the world, which suggest that risk society may be an increasingly attractive one in which to live, rather than a source of human misery.[73]

The third body of criticism provoked by Habermas is concentrated on his ideal of constitutional patriotism. This mistakenly assumes, it is argued, that the achievement of mutual transparency by participants in the communicative process will ensure the elimination of conflict, and hence of politics itself. In addition, critics like Ralf Dahrendorf have claimed that the ideal is too formal or 'thin' to exercise any unifying power. As Dahrendorf put it, 'Constitutional patriotism remains a thing of the mind, not the heart. It does not satisfy the need of many to live by and pass on to future generations deep structures of life in society.'[74] By systematically rejecting the emotional bond provided by even moderate forms of nationalism, another thoughtful critic has observed, Habermas has run the risk of creating what is merely 'an anti-nationalist national "civil religion" centred on the Holocaust'.[75] Although such criticism may be too harsh, it is difficult to see how a 'thin' constitutional patriotism can unite a multicultural society, let alone overcome the irresistible tendency towards subjectivism identified by Arnold Gehlen as the most dangerous feature of modern civilization.[76]

Despite these criticisms, Habermas' achievement has been to provide the Federal Republic with a concept of democratic citizenship that helped to protect it against the excesses of nationalism, conservatism and radicalism alike. In his capacity as one of Germany's leading public intellectuals, this achievement went beyond the sphere of theory: it consisted, in the words of Jan-Werner Müller, of providing, along with other members of the small Left-liberal elite to which he belonged, 'a substitute for a broader critical public that was yet to develop'.[77] Habermas' achievement, in brief, must be seen in the context of the transitional generation to which he belongs – a generation faced with the task, that is, of emerging from the shadow of Nazism and assisting postwar Germany to work out a democratic alternative. Far from rendering this role superfluous, Müller suggests, unification has 'arguably given [it] another lease of public life', since with the addition of East Germany, the questions of democratisation and westernisation are 'back on the agenda'.[78] If Habermas' concept of communicative rationality is problematic, the message he taught, which was that diversity should be tolerated and that debate should replace the political elimination of opponents, remains relevant. What is true, nevertheless, is that since 1990, critics of the rationalist framework upon which his synthesis of *Rechsstaat* and *Sozialstaat* relied have tended to become more influential than they were before the wall went down. What must now be considered is the nature of the new challenges which have arisen to Habermas' version of the democratization project and, finally, the ways in which the new Berlin Republic has responded to the post-unification situation.

Responses to Unification

What was especially striking about the events of 1989, Joachim Fest observed, was neither their largely peaceful character nor the absence of social revolutionary fervour: it was the fact that, for the first time in history, a revolution had not been preceded by extensive theorizing.[79] In this respect, the East German revolution was quite unlike those in Poland, Czechoslovakia and Rumania. Perhaps the previous silence of both East and West German intellectuals, Fest wrote, helped to explain their subsequent silence in the face of the year's revolutionary events.[80] Once this initial silence was broken, however, the German intelligentsia resumed the debate about German identity, which was intensified still further by a succession of events during the following decade – in particular, the Gulf War, the Kosovo War and Daniel Goldhagen's book, *Germany's Willing Executioners*.[81] This was not, however, simply the story as before. In the course of 1989–90, an event of major consequence for the subsequent progress of German political thought had occurred: the Left had suddenly lost the position of moral superiority it had increasingly enjoyed after 1968. Now, it could no longer count on shaping the terms and outcome of political debate.

What placed the Left on the defensive was its misgivings about unification. One such misgiving was that of Gunter Grass, who commended cultural unification but rejected *political* unification on the ground that it would create 'a colossus, bedevilled by complexes and blocking its own path and the path to European unity'.[82] A second was that of Hans Magnus Enzensberger, who accepted political unification whilst simultaneously disparaging it on the ground that the Germans had finally acquired a 'normal' identity which was 'bordering on the ridiculous. They have become a nation of shopkeepers, incapable of a greatness that the world, in any case, is better off without.'[83] For Habermas, finally, only a qualified affirmation of political unification was possible: one, that is, which accepted it only in so far as it was compatible with constitutional patriotism.

This generally unenthusiastic response to unification meant that the Left was unable to present effective opposition to the revival of conservative thought which occurred during the 1990s. This did not suddenly emerge out of thin air: the ground had been prepared during the previous decade by a 1986 newspaper article in which Ernst Nolte had resumed Heidegger's earlier attempt to 'normalize' Nazi atrocities by denying their uniqueness. The Gulag Archipelago, Nolte claimed, was 'more original than Auschwitz', and 'class murder by the Bolsheviks' was 'logically and actually prior to race murder by the Nazis'.[84] What now favoured the normalization project, however, was the boost to conservative confidence given by President Reagan's visit to the Bitburg cemetery in 1985, to lay a wreath as a signal that

Nazi crimes had been forgiven. This new confidence was particularly evident in the intense debate between right- and left-wing intellectuals about German national identity – the so-called *Historikerstreit* ('historians' conflict') – triggered by Nolte's article. Despite the public support for 'normalization' of German history provided by other notable conservative intellectuals,[85] however, the liberal Left orthodoxy, led by Habermas, continued to be dominant until reunification suddenly placed the Left on the defensive.

Now the way was clear for more extreme conservative voices to be heard, and in particular for the renewed intellectual activity of members of the New Right.[86] The latter, some of whom were renegades from the Left,[87] were particularly anxious to win respectability by emphasising that the movement was not a resurgence of Nazism. To this end, they deployed five simple but effective strategies for keeping the Left on the defensive.

In the first place, they publicly disavowed the use of violence in any form, adopting instead the Left's own Gramscian strategy of cultural transformation through media penetration. Secondly, they also distinguished themselves from the Nazis by refusing to reject everything western as a matter of principle. As Rainer Zitelmann put it, the division of Germany over which Adenauer presided did not automatically have to be regarded as a betrayal of the nationalist cause: the western alignment of the Federal Republic could be seen either as 'a proven antidote to the re-emergence of a nation-state' or as 'a means of overcoming the division'.[88] If a European identity could be accepted by the New Right, however, the control exercised by the United States over German life since 1945 could not. The extent to which New Right bitterness towards the USA exceeded its hostility towards the USSR was succinctly conveyed by Dieter Stein, the editor of the New Right newspaper *Young Freedom*. The Soviets, he observed, had 'chopped off Nazi heads in Leipzig and then stopped', but the USA had systematically sought to deprive all Germans of their Germanness.[89] In the first statement of New Right doctrine, *Ties to the West* (1993),[90] contributors demanded that future German foreign policy should be shaped by a traditional regard for Germany's geopolitical situation, maintaining its independence by exploiting its position in the middle of Europe to balance East and West against each other.

Thirdly, members of the New Right extended their bid for respectability by casting themselves as the true liberals of the reunified

Germany. Under the Federal Republic, they claimed, Germany had been increasingly subjected to a leftwing orthodoxy so comprehensive and oppressive that it amounted to a new form of totalitarianism, as bad as the Nazi one to which the New Right claimed to be opposed. Indeed, Botho Strauss maintained, the emergence of neo-Nazis was actually caused by the liberal-democratic system of the Federal Republic, in so far as this had resulted in a deracinated mentality which was bound to produce barbarians.[91] At the international level, they polished their liberal image by claiming to defend cultural diversity against a universalist American liberalism which imposed a uniformly drab, massified pattern of life on the world at large. Race was not mentioned: cultural, not racial, diversity was the theme.

Fourthly, the New Right bid for respectability was still further consolidated by its claim that the memory of Auschwitz was not being rejected: what was being maintained was only that the uniqueness of Auschwitz had been greatly overemphasized by the dominant orthodoxy. In addition, New Right supporters added that there was no question of refusing to mourn for Nazi atrocities: what they claimed was that only a unified nation possessed the sense of collective identity necessary to engage in genuine mourning. What was also asserted, in the same connection, was that Germany had long ago paid its moral debt for the Holocaust by the deaths of seven million of its own citizens in the Second World War. As one New Right historian, Karlheinz Weissmann, put it, 'no people has done so much penance for the deeds that it carried out, or that were carried out in its name'.[92]

Finally, the New Right's bid for respectability crystallized in the claim that its members alone fully understood the meaning of political responsibility. With Habermas in particular in mind, the New Right maintained that the Left had systematically evaded responsibility by retreating into a utopian vision in which discourse could solve all conflicts. By encouraging this absurd idea, the Left had smothered West Germany beneath a universalistic rationalism completely disconnected from the concrete values of national life. As Rainer Zitelmann put it, the ideology of Habermas and his generation has been a 'fascism cudgel', enforcing a 'politically correct' version of history intended to destroy all German national pride.[93]

The great claim of the New Right, in short, was to 'normalize' Germany's national identity by restoring political responsibility and genuine freedom. But what exactly did national identity involve?

The New Right answer was somewhat vague, such clarity as it possessed owing much to the writings of two in particular of the circle of thinkers associated with the interwar 'conservative revolutionary' movement. They were Carl Schmitt[94] and Ernst Jünger.[95] The latter's return to postwar intellectual respectability was so complete that the Chancellor (Helmut Kohl) marked Jünger's 100th birthday (in 1995) by making a congratulatory visit to his home in a remote south German village. The efforts of two New Right thinkers in particular contributed significantly to the new lease of life enjoyed by these old theorists of nationalism. One was Martin Walser, the other Karl Heinz Bohrer.

Walser's contribution to New Right thought lay in his presentation of Germany as the victim nation of the modern European world, notable more for its division, pathetic impotence and humiliating situation of international dependency than for any potentially militant tendencies. 'People who relish being Englishmen, Frenchmen and Italians', he wrote during the 1980s, relish the fact that 'the German, cut in two, remains divided into two halves. The right to self-determination, which of all human rights is now seen as the highest everywhere – the Germans should not have it.'[96]

By exploiting Walser's victim nation theme, the New Right could pose as the defender of a country which it was merely helping to rise from the sick-bed to which America and the USSR had confined it ever since 1945. What helped the New Right even more was the fact that Walser did not restrict the theme of victimhood – or, more accurately, of inadequacy or deficiency (*Mangel*) – to the national level but extended it in his novels to include the individual lives of those who, like himself, comprised the petit bourgeois class. Like the German nation, these lacked self-confidence and were doomed to a life of inner division, social impotence and constant humiliation.[97] What gave this analysis a political dimension was Walser's assumption that the individual lives of many Germans could never possess the dignity referred to in Article 1 of the Constitution unless national reunification was achieved. Until then, the only prospect of authenticity lay in withdrawal into the private world of personal emotion. At the basis of that world lay the deepest emotion of all, which Walser described in his own case as the 'need for Germany'.[98] This appeal to purely subjective considerations was the most problematic aspect of his position. Since he believed, in addition, that the integrity of his own emotions gave him direct access to the life of the nation denied to other

German intellectuals, his brand of nationalism became indistinguishable from demagogy.

Walser's contribution to New Right thought, then, was a comprehensive portrayal of German history, politics and personal life in
terms of an unrelenting victimology, grounded in an irrationalist
commitment to personal emotion as the source of political truth.
The second intellectual associated with the New Right to be considered, Karl Heinz Bohrer, was also committed to an irrationalist
position. Since Bohrer's irrationalism was far more philosophically
sophisticated than Walser's, however, he provided more intellectually
demanding members of the New Right with an alternative, less
subjective way of defending nationalism than by simply appealing
to their emotional revelations.

In order to understand the path to irrationalism taken by Bohrer –
a very different one from Walser's – it is necessary to notice that his
philosophical starting point was not politics but aesthetics. More
specifically, Bohrer began with a sweeping rejection of modern
western culture on the ground that it has been shaped by a craving
for intellectual security in the form of complete objectivity, truth and
clarity.[99] In order to satisfy this craving, it aims to create an entirely
known, fully predictable and perfectly safe environment which is
totally subject to rules or laws of various kinds. The disastrous result
is that what Bohrer terms 'the aesthetic moment', which is the key to
human identity, has become wholly unintelligible. This is because
the aesthetic moment is a moment of 'suddenness' which cannot be
comprehended within the rationalist framework into which modern
western culture has straitjacketed human experience.

Bohrer's strategy for breaking out of the rationalist prison and
restoring the non-rational experience of suddenness to its proper
place in western culture has two parts. The first is a cultural revolution, the aim of which is to restore contact with the anti-rationalist
standpoint of such late eighteenth-century German romantic
thinkers as Kleist, on the ground that they were the first moderns to
appreciate the autonomy of aesthetic experience. Although his
philosophical position overlapped, as he himself noted, with that of
French postmodern thinkers like Derrida, who also wanted to
break with a rationalist culture that failed to acknowledge 'otherness', Bohrer dismissed this as an irrelevance: the real roots of
his own thought, he maintained, were in the indigenous German
tradition.[100]

The second part of Bohrer's strategy consists of extending his discovery of the autonomy of aesthetic experience by asserting the autonomy of political experience as well. The great misfortune of postwar Germany, he maintained, lies in its systematic flight from the political, the core of which is rationally ungrounded decision, into rationalist visions of a society governed entirely by norms and procedures. This immediately brought Bohrer close to Carl Schmitt, whose principal criticism of Weimar liberal democracy had focused on its inability to face up to the element of decision at the heart of political experience.

Applying his philosophy of suddenness to post-unification Germany, Bohrer insisted that Germany's greatest need was for a more positive, self-confident sense of national identity, of the kind enjoyed by other western European states such as Britain and France. Why was it, he asked, that they possessed the national self-confidence which Germany lacked? The answer, he maintained, lay in the universalist nationalism which had inspired the imperial aspirations of those countries. This, then, was what Germany needed to emulate: it too must develop a universalist nationalism, without which it would never possess a 'normal' national identity of the self-confident kind that characterized the British and French.

Ironically, Bohrer's demand for a universalist national identity appeared to coincide with the aspiration of Left-liberal thinkers like Habermas, whose ideal of constitutional patriotism was also universalist. The concept of universalism, however, was interpreted entirely differently by the New Right. Whereas the Left-liberal ideal of constitutional patriotism was universal because it had been purged of all specifically German characteristics, Bohrer stood this position on its head by insisting instead that what had to be universalized was a specifically German form of national identity.

The main problem presented by Bohrer's attempt to move from philosophical irrationalism to nationalist self-assertion is that he never explained why the *cultural* revolution needed to recapture the experience of 'suddenness' required a *political* revolution aimed at German unification. Since moments of suddenness, moreover, are confined to a small, aesthetically conscious élite, his philosophy offered the New Right no prospect of attracting mass support. His political marginality is, in fact, indicative of the relatively small impact of the New Right as a whole on the reunified state. Its period of influence, it has plausibly been maintained, was confined to a couple of years in the early 1990s.[101] Although it has not brought a marked shift to the Right in German politics, it may however have further undermined the Left-liberal Habermasian orthodoxy dominant during the decade prior to unification by fostering 'a new soft revisionism' that 'has begun putting question marks after what were once certainties'.[102] By 1998, for example, a question mark had been placed over the Holocaust memorial that was to have been built near the Branden-burg Gate.[103] Two years earlier, *Der Spiegel* had a cover story about revisionist interpretations of the war on the eastern front. Part of the story was about a new history of the war called *Stalin's War of Annihilation*, by Joachim Hoffmann. The message of the book was that the real cause of the Second World War was not Hitler but Stalin. Although *Der Spiegel* did not endorse the new interpretation, the attention given to it was a mark of changing times.[104]

What remains to be seen is whether the theme of the PhD thesis of another leading New Right intellectual, Rainer Zitelmann, makes much progress. This is that Hitler is best interpreted as a social revolutionary inspired by the American New Deal.[105] Although there is no doubt that Hitler was the agent of a social revolution, and that postwar German democracy might well have been impossible with-out the social equality he introduced, it is doubtful whether Nazism was an appropriate way of establishing the welfare state.

The Berlin Republic

In 1999, the Federal Government moved to Berlin, thereby marking the official beginning of the reunified state. Reflecting on the likely future of unification a decade earlier, the cautious judgement of Ralf Dahrendorf was that even sixty years would barely be enough to lay 'the social foundations which transform the constitution and the economy from fair-weather into all-weather institutions which can withstand the storms generated within and without'.[106] Bearing this in mind, I will conclude by considering with due caution the question which has been central ever since the adoption of the Basic Law in 1949: Is the new Germany likely to be able to maintain a 'normal' liberal-democratic political identity free from the ethnic nationalism that led it into two world wars, or is the old nationalism likely to reassert itself? Commentators may be divided into optimists and sceptics.

Grounds for optimism have not been hard to come by. All major intellectuals in Germany, Jan-Werner Müller remarks, now 'subscribe to the values of a liberal democratic Constitution'.[107] Offering broader grounds for optimism, another commentator concludes that 'Changes in patterns of value, in the character of the political system, and in prevailing political cultures have made citizens of Germany today very different from their (real or assumed) ancestry.' What has changed them most of all is the fact that the German state is now embedded in a world in which 'The mobility of labour, and the internationalization of culture, are posing serious challenges to any conception of the nation as a homogeneous ethnic and cultural entity.' It is only proper, accordingly, that 'Engagement with the admittedly fascinating course of German history should finally be wrenched away from emotionalized engagement with national identity building.'[108]

Despite such encouraging thoughts, sceptics query whether Germany's democratic identity has sufficiently deep roots to restrain restored national self-confidence, as well as survive a continuing rise in the level of unemployment and a declining rate of economic growth. In addition, East Germany's long experience of authoritarian rule, and the growth of extremist movements there, are likely to intensify problems caused by economic recession. The weakening of the pre-unification progressive consensus, moreover, has led Johannes Gross to argue that instability will increasingly become the norm to which the Berlin Republic has to adjust, if it is to survive.[109] In particular, Gross maintains, the basis of legitimacy will tend to become associated with the provision by the state of security, rather than welfare policies. In general, he concludes, the Berlin Republic is likely to be a more 'political' one than the Federal Republic, with conflict playing a greater part than consensus. Whether the response to a more political Republic will generate the statist solution favoured by admirers of Carl Schmitt, or will promote a demand for more participation, as republican admirers of Habermas hope, remains to be seen.

There may, in addition, be continuing difficulty in adjusting to cultural diversity. Following unification, it has been pointed out, there was no rush to abolish the *volkisch* concept of German nationality incorporated in the 1913 law on citizenship and retained by the Basic Law of 1949 when it extended citizenship to *Volksdeutche* (ethnic Germans).[110] Sceptics have also noted the special treatment of ethnic

German immigrants, of whom there were over a million from Eastern Europe and the Soviet Union in the three years from 1988 to 1991 alone.[111] Rogers Brubaker, for example, has commented that 'While politicians of all parties have invoked the limited "absorptive capacity" (*Aufnahmefähigkeit*) of Germany, especially with regard to Turks, it remains politically unacceptable to make the same argument about ethnic Germans.'[112] To the extent that the *volkisch* concept of national identity remains powerful in Germany, then, the ability of the Left-liberal ideal of constitutional patriotism to accommodate diversity will be severely tested.

So far as German commitment to the European Union is concerned, there is little to indicate any wavering. The sceptic, however, will retort that this commitment is perfectly compatible with the 'Mitteleuropa' strand in traditional German nationalist thought, according to which Germany's natural sphere of influence lies in middle Europe.[113]

Conclusion

There are, then, two poles in modern German political thought. At one is the idealistic universalism most strikingly represented by the philosophy of Kant and, more recently, by Habermas. At the other is the philosophy of power and nationalism represented by Treitschke and, more recently, by New Right theorists. Since 1945 the former, Kantian pole has exerted the main attraction. Whether it will continue to do so in the long term remains, as Dahrendorf noted, to be seen.

5

In the Shadow of *The Prince*:[1] Italian Political Thought Since Liberation

In order to ensure the future peace of the European world, the Anglo-American Allies were as deeply committed to replacing totalitarianism by liberal democracy in Italy as in Germany. On the British side, Churchill in particular 'was virtually unshakeable in his conviction that constitutional monarchy was the solution to every country's political problems',[2] while in the USA President Truman approved a memorandum from the Acting Secretary of State which stated that 'The time is now ripe when we should initiate action to raise Italian morale, make a stable representative government possible, and permit Italy to become a responsible participant in international affairs.'[3]

What seemed to bode particularly well for the reconstruction project in the Italian case was the fact that enthusiasm for democracy had been fostered there by the Resistance movement.[4] In addition, the only sources of internal opposition seemed to be relatively minor. In 1946, the monarchy was abolished by a democratic vote. Two years earlier, Palmiro Togliatti, the leader of the Italian Communist Party, had indicated his willingness to accept parliamentary democracy as part of a broader strategy of pursuing ultimate cultural hegemony by non-violent means. Although the Church continued to have misgivings about democracy, it was prepared to set these aside provided that the Christian Democratic Party won office. The Christian Democrats, in turn, were deeply conscious of Italian economic dependence on the USA and accepted that the Allied plans could not

126

be resisted. The dream of a glorious democratic future for Italy, in a word, seemed perfectly realizable.

Unfortunately, the dream ignored a massive fly in the democratic ointment that had temporarily been concealed by the sense of unity which the Resistance movement engendered. This was the fact that, beneath the surface, the Italian nation continued to be as deeply disunited as it had been when it was originally unified a century earlier. In the face of profound geographical and social divisions, accompanied by mainly local political allegiances, a pretence of national unity had only been sustained after 1876 by what is known as the *trasformismo* style of politics, in which political power was traded amongst members of the Italian elite in return for the mutual provision of benefits. In particular, northern aristocrats and business leaders who wished to retain political power united with southern estate owners who were prepared to use their influence over peasant voters in return for being left undisturbed by reforming measures. By the time of the First World War, general disillusion with this style had become a major reason for the contempt in which liberalism was held – a contempt which paved the way for fascism. Three decades later, the hope of finally escaping from *trasformismo* politics helped to inspire the Resistance dream of postwar national rebirth. The tension between dream and reality quickly became apparent, however, when the final defeat of fascism and the departure of the Nazi enemy exposed the continuing profound cleavages in Italian national life.

From that time until the present day, the challenge facing Italian thinkers and politicians alike has been to construct an alternative, less corrupt form of politics than the *trasformismo* one. In the event, success has not been notable: an unprincipled kind of conservatism, resting on an extensive restoration of the old order and involving many former supporters of fascism, dominated postwar Italian political history until 1992–94. At that time, the unexpected dissolution of the old elite once again reawakened hopes that Italy could rise above the widespread political corruption, organized crime and lack of respect for law which had characterized the postwar decades. Whether the end of the century really brought with it political improvement, or merely replaced one corrupt elite by a different but equally corrupt one, remains to be considered. Before doing so, however, the postwar search for alternatives to the tendency to reduce politics to 'a fierce struggle for spoils...moderated only by a careful concern to cut all parties and pressure groups in on all deals' must be considered.[5] These alternatives have taken five main forms, associated with liberal, radical Left, moderate social democratic, radical Right and postmodern thinkers respectively.

The Failure of Postwar Crocean Liberalism

The focal point for liberal opposition to Mussolini during the fascist era had been the writings of Benedetto Croce.[6] Once fascism had been defeated, however, Croce found it impossible to transform his philosophy from an inspiring oppositional one into a viable vision of reconstruction. There were a number of reasons for this, of which the first was his belief in the rationality of the historical process. Every fact, as Croce put it, 'has to fulfil a function in the development of the spirit, in social and human progress, if not as a direct creator of new values, at least as material and stimulus for the strengthening, deepening and widening of ancient values'. Despite Croce's insistence that this function 'cannot be known and judged by us' but only by future historians,[7] critics objected that if all events have a rational basis, then fascism too must have had one. In the aftermath of the Liberation, this was not a message liberals wished to hear. In addition, such a belief was repugnant even to a fellow liberal historicist like Guido de Ruggiero because it seemed to weaken the possibility of effective liberal resistance to any future totalitarian threat.[8] What was more attractive to liberals was Croce's assumption that the Italian liberal tradition was a progressive development to which fascism was wholly alien. Critics, however, had no difficulty in establishing that liberal history was more complex than this optimistic interpretation allowed. Indeed, they maintained, the roots of fascism lay in the Italian liberal tradition itself, since it had encouraged the unprincipled practice of *trasformismo* politics. Croce was thus open to the charge of whitewashing the liberal past in a way that displayed dangerous complacency.[9]

The most important limitations of Croce's liberalism came, however, from his concept of liberty itself. In the first place, it was highly elitist, since he identified freedom with a degree of aesthetic creativity which only a few possess. It must not be imagined, he explained, that the majority of men can cultivate what he termed a 'politics of genius' since this 'requires depth of feeling and a power of intellectual synthesis found only in the ranks of the elite, who are devoted to the ideal'.[10] As this indicates, Croce's liberalism was completely at odds with a postwar society characterized in particular by the increasing politicization of the Italian peasantry – a politicization dramatically evident in 1950, when the failure of government to reform the southern land system led to extensive attacks upon the established order.

A second problem was that Croce defined liberty in its most profound sense as 'wholly a question of the disposition of minds fired to fervour and love'.[11] Since liberty of this kind is essentially an inner spiritual condition, it is perfectly compatible with any kind of political regime: even under fascism, for example, a man may retain inner liberty. As critics have noted, Croce's inner concept of freedom made it difficult for him to defend his own record of opposition to fascism, since inner freedom is not in danger even in a totalitarian regime.

A third problem was that the inner nature of Croce's concept of freedom meant that he had no interest in constructing constitutional checks and balances which would prevent fascism occurring again. Such restraints on power appeared irrelevant because liberalism, as Croce understood it, did not view the state with suspicion but treated it as simply the means to a morally higher life. What freedom requires, as Croce put it, is 'that the citizen should be devoted and serviceable to the State, and ready if need be to give his life for it'.[12] Like Rousseau, who also identified inner (or moral) freedom with political freedom and rejected constitutional checks and balances, Croce appeared to be sacrificing individual liberty to unlimited political power.

Finally, fellow liberals regarded Croce's conception of freedom as electorally disastrous because it divorced freedom from social justice. Social justice, he maintained, could not be pursued until liberty in the formal sense of a concern for rights had been achieved. As Guido Calogero, the principal theorist of *liberalsocialismo* and a leading member of the Action Party, gleefully pointed out, this made it impossible for the Liberal Party (PLI), of which Croce was President from 1944 to 1948, to mount an effective political programme. Sadly, Croce made the Liberal Party's electoral plight even worse by insisting it was a special 'pre-party' which stood above ideological debate and therefore did not need to engage in active political campaigning.[13] The root of his difficulties in this respect, as the Marxist thinker, Antonio Gramsci, acutely remarked, was the fact that Croce's identification of freedom with inner liberty made him lukewarm about political parties of any kind, since joining one inevitably compromised personal integrity.[14]

Croce's postwar custody of the liberal cause, then, proved to be politically disastrous. Ironically, the greatest Italian liberal philosopher came to be regarded as a reactionary, bent on restoring the pre-1914 political world at a time when liberalism could only survive if it won a mass democratic base by incorporating an extensive programme of social reform. His yearning for a liberalism led by 'a new aristocracy, young and vigorous like that of other days'[15] was, as one commentator remarks, mere wishful thinking.[16] His political isolation, it may be added, was to be shared by other notable postwar liberal thinkers who adopted his elitist perspective. The poet Eugenio Montale, for example, who had been another leading liberal opponent of fascism, hoped that the end of fascism would herald the return of a pre-industrial age of social stratification and high culture – the world, that is, of 'my dead,/my trusty dogs, my old/serving women'.[17] When postwar Italy failed to satisfy his nostalgia in this respect, he followed in Croce's footsteps (after failing to become a senator in 1957) by declaring that he was above all parties, on the one hand, and then supporting the Italian economic and political establishment, on the other.

It remains to note that even liberals who tried to develop a less idealistic liberalism, more firmly rooted in recognition of Italian political problems, also found it difficult to avoid political marginalization. In *Christ Stopped at Eboli*,[18] for example, Carlo Levi placed the division between two very different civilizations of north and south – between, that is, 'Country and city, a pre-Christian civilization and one that is no longer Christian'[19] – at the centre of those problems, but could offer no remedy for this intractable situation. He only avoided political despair by clinging to the utopian ideal of an organic community, supposedly able to heal what he described as the modern 'break in man's unity' and concomitant 'tendency to fragmentize' which had given rise to fascism.[20] Ironically, Levi failed to realize that his 'organic' ideal could easily foster a style of politics impossible to reconcile with his liberal sentiments.

More generally, the highly diverse intellectuals who in 1948 founded the so-called Third Force attempted to forge a more viable liberal position by embracing an ideal of intellectual openness. Although this was theoretically suggestive, leading as it did to a shift of interest from Croce to thinkers such as de Tocqueville, the problem of practical relevance was never solved. Although many members of the Third Force found outlets for their ideas in journals such as *Tempo presente* (edited by Nicola Chiaromonte) and the centre-left weekly *Il Mondo* (published 1949–66), the nearest they got to a coherent theme was Giovanni Spadolini's ideal of 'the Italy of reason'.[21] Such an ideal, however, remained that of an intellectual elite whose political impotence was acknowledged by Mario Pannunzio in the final issue of *Il Mondo*. 'What reigns in Italy above all else', he wrote with resignation, 'is the deep-rooted and penetrating presence of a soft and priestly secret government that conquers friends and foes alike and tends to enervate all initiative and all resistance'.[22]

The Identity Crisis of the Radical Left

Against the background of liberal paralysis, the way seemed open for the communist Left, with its unique record of interwar opposition to fascism, central role in the Resistance and extensive national support, to fill the ideological vacuum Croce had inadvertently helped to create. In the event, however, American hostility to communism combined with the opposition of the Church and the Christian Democratic Party to exclude the Communist Party permanently from power, formally at least. What made this exclusion a matter for especially deep leftwing bitterness was the fact that Antonio Gramsci and Palmiro Togliatti, the two leading communist intellectuals, seemed to abet it by steering their party towards an accommodation with liberal democracy, in expectation that their moderation would make them acceptable partners in government. Instead, all they succeeded in doing was creating an acute identity crisis for Italian Marxists, who did not know whether to think of themselves as revolutionaries or democrats.

For Gramsci, the justification for rejecting Leninist revolutionary strategy was that the attempt to impose revolution from above would always inevitably end in dictatorship. His *Prison Notebooks*, which were widely read in Italy after being belatedly published there between 1948 and 1951, taught that the only way to avoid this was by a long process of mass cultural education prior to any attempt to introduce major political and economic change. Gramsci's doctrine involved, in particular, two heretical modifications of traditional Marxist thought, the first of which consisted in rehabilitating the concept of civil society – a concept rejected by Marx as an instrument of capitalist exploitation. Gramsci completely reversed this position by assigning civil society a position within the cultural superstructure, which he regarded as independent of the exploitative economic order in which Marx had located it.[23] Gramsci's second heretical modification consisted of restoring the intellectual to respectability, after classical Marxism had dismissed him as a mere mouthpiece for bourgeois ideology. More precisely, Gramsci defended 'organic' intellectuals.[24] Bourgeois intellectuals, caught up in a world of free-floating ideas, remained the object of his contempt: the organic ones he valued were those whose ideas remained firmly rooted in the social experience of the proletariat. The task of organic intellectuals – only to be pursued through the party, of course – is to engage in a long process of preparing the masses intellectually for Communist hegemony.

It was this revised version of Marxist doctrine that was taken over and made the official doctrine of the Italian Communist Party in 1946 by Togliatti, who for many years after Liberation was the general secretary. This meant in practice that instead of preaching revolution, the Italian communists worked peacefully not only with existing social democratic institutions but with capitalist ones as well, even working, indeed, with the monarchy. Against this background, there was no inconsistency in the 'historic compromise' made by the Communists with the Christian Democrats during the mid-1970s: they were merely pursuing the Machiavellian strategy incorporated into Communist thinking by Gramsci and Togliatti. Machiavellism backfired, however, by creating the crisis of Communist identity already referred to. The precise nature of the crisis lay in the fact that

> The distinction between democratic and socialist aims ... came to be lost in the minds of the party's audience. This created the problem of the 'two truths' – strategic and tactical – and a permanent state of confusion between the socialist state and the bourgeois state and between adjustments to national circumstances and patriotism.[25]

The identity crisis was so deep that it has persisted from 1946 to the present day. What made the paralysis of communist intellectuals even worse, however, was Gramsci's assumption that the Italian nation which they were supposed to prepare for revolution actually existed, when the reality was that the 'people' which they were to educate politically had as yet no common cultural identity. Their paralysis displayed itself in two main ways. One, exemplified by the former fascist, Galvano della Volpe, consisted of falling back on Marxist orthodoxy. This, however, was easily demolished by Norberto Bobbio, who pointed out that della Volpe was merely repeating the Marxist mistake of ignoring the need for constitutional restraints on power, regardless of the hands in which it was placed.[26]

The other manifestation of communist paralysis consisted of the fragmentation of the Left into an extraordinary variety of intellectually impressive but politically impotent visions of life developed by disillusioned literary figures. Looking back on forty years as a writer, for example, Italo Calvino attempted a brief overall characterization of the theme of all his work as a concern with 'lightness'. 'I have tried', he wrote, 'to remove weight, sometimes from people, sometimes from heavenly bodies, sometimes from cities; above all I have tried to remove weight from the structure of stories and from language.'[27] His pursuit of lightness, Calvino emphasized, did not 'mean escaping into dreams or into the irrational'. It was reflected, rather, in his resort to irony, fantasy and play. Admirable though this might be as a personal philosophy, its political inconsequence is obvious in Calvino's own summary of his position, which is that not politics but 'only laughter can offer us a revolutionary mutation of human consciousness'.[28]

Pier Paolo Pasolini turned instead to a quest for the innocence of natural man, identified with a romanticized vision of the peasantry and urban outcasts. In *Le ceneri di Gramsci* (1954) – a poem addressed to the dead Gramsci – Pasolini described his rejection of rationalism in all its forms and his adoption of a rival vision based instead on

> the heat of the instincts, of my aesthetic passions;
> drawn to a proletarian life
> from before your time, my religion
> is its gaiety, not its age-old struggle:
> its nature not its consciousness...[29]

Unfortunately, Pasolini's conception of rationalism was so comprehensive that it threatened to destroy civilization in any form, ending in a drop-out ethic which failed to get beyond a celebration of the gutter.

Other disillusioned Marxists, finally, faced a solitude and anguish softened in some cases by religion. This was a major source of comfort, for example, to Ignazio Silone who described, in his autobiographical contribution to Richard Crossman's anthology *The God that Failed*,[30] how his roots in the civilization of the south led him to realize the utter futility of political radicalism and to rediscover Christianity, albeit in a very unorthodox form. Silone's rediscovery of religion led him, more precisely, to the apolitical, utopian ideal of socialism he portrayed in *The Story of a Humble Christian* – a socialism, that is, entirely purged of any connection with power and inspired solely by a Christian sense of 'fraternity and ... instinctive devotion to the poor'.[31] Spiritual nobility, in brief, might console for the retreat into political impotence.

Outside the ranks of Marxism, radical intellectuals sought to develop a coherent identity by turning in yet other directions. Amongst them, Umberto Eco was particularly notable.[32] A radical Catholic and leading member of the avant-garde Gruppo 63, Eco has been described as standing 'at the intersection of democratic and revolutionary politics'[33] – a position mainly characterized by his attempt to democratize the radical cause by rescuing it from the elitist cultural perspective of Gramsci and Togliatti. The problem with Eco's democratized brand of radicalism, however, was that it continued to rely on a concept of 'the system' which linked him to radicals like Marcuse and the Red Brigades, with whom he disagreed. Although he maintained that his own concept of the system was rooted in the existing order and thus avoided the abstract character of theirs, his attempts to clarify it never overcame a tendency towards vagueness which left its political implications unclear. This vagueness was evident in 1995, for example, when Eco warned an audience of American students about the continuing survival of the 'system' of 'Ur-fascism', or 'eternal fascism', which he defined so loosely that it became little more than a blanket term for anything he disliked about life. [34]

Neither communist nor non-communist intellectuals, then, were able to provide effective ways of overcoming the identity crisis of the postwar Italian Left. In the case of the communists, what brought that crisis to a head was the 'historic compromise' with the Christian Democratic Party announced by Berlinguer, the Communist leader, in 1973.[35] It is against this background that the emergence of the Italian New Left must be seen.

Antonio Negri and the New Left

In the ethos of intense political alienation and developing economic recession which characterized the 1970s, terrorism – emanating from both Left and Right – became the most disturbing feature of the decade, culminating in a frightful explosion at Bologna railway station in August 1980. Two years earlier another terrorist atrocity had occurred when the leaders of the Red Brigades – a leftwing terrorist group – were put on trial: its members responded by murdering Aldo Moro, the Prime Minister. A year later the leading philosopher of the Italian New Left, Antonio Negri, was arrested and accused of being the brains behind Italian terrorism since 1971, despite the fact that the only thing of which he appeared guilty was legal opposition. A subsequent series of trials exposed in dramatic fashion the frailty of the postwar Italian constitutional tradition. In the present context, however, the main concern is to understand the line of thought which made Negri the object of government suspicion. This was most systematically developed in Negri's principal philosophical work, *The Savage Anomaly*, which he wrote while in prison in 1979.[36]

Although the work took the form of a study of Spinoza's philosophy, it was no mere piece of intellectual history: its aim was to draw on Spinoza in order to attack what Negri regarded as the unduly narrow, state-centred concept of *'constituted* power' which he maintained has restricted modern European political thought to what he dismissed as such politically superficial topics as the rule of law, constitutionalism and the party system.[37] In a critique of the modern western political tradition reminiscent of Foucault – Negri himself acknowledged that he had 'rinsed [his] clothes in the Seine'[38] – he proclaimed that even more radical political thinkers have failed to get beyond the modern western obsession with constituted power as a result of restricting their thought either to modifying it (as in the liberal case) or to abolishing it (as in the more ambitious Marxist kind of radicalism). In either case, Negri holds, their error consists in the perpetuation of a dualist way of thinking which contrasts the state, identified in juridical terms, with society conceived as the sphere of a separate productive process. To understand politics properly, this dualist approach must be replaced by a monistic one which grasps social reality as a single, unitary process in endless reconstruction – that is, as *'constituent* power'. Almost alone amongst modern thinkers, Negri maintains, Spinoza overcame dualism and grasped this monistic concept. Here, Negri ascribes to Spinoza a voluntarist doctrine alien to the restraints upon the human will implicit in Spinoza's concept of matter. What is more problematic, however, is the subsequent development of Negri's thought, in which he has sought to go far beyond Spinoza by developing a vision of impending global revolution based on the contemporary emergence of a new form of empire, marked above all by the advent of a revolutionary proletariat whose nature is completely incomprehensible to traditional Marxist theory, trapped as it is within the dualistic perspective of constituent power.[39]

What has created the new proletariat is new technologies which have made man's relationship to the means of production, which was central for Marx, irrelevant to the contemporary worker, whose total cultural dispossession is crystallized in an identity wholly constituted by new technologies of information, networking, spectacle and communication.[40] Far from producing a condition of impotent alienation, these technologies have empowered the new proletariat by conferring upon it the entrepreneurial initiative formerly restricted to the bourgeoisie, which has now been reduced to a superfluous existence.[41] In addition, the interdependence intrinsic to the new technologies has socialized the new proletariat. The result is that crisis is now 'coextensive with the postmodern totality of capitalist production'.[42] Rising to the heights of utopian optimism, Negri announced that no violence is necessary in order to exploit this crisis, since the self-confidence inspired in the new proletariat by its indispensable skills makes it unnecessary.[43] All that is required is what Negri terms a strategy of 'exodus', which is the peaceful withdrawal of labour from the work place.[44]

How plausible is Negri's revolutionary vision? The problem at the heart of his thought both before and after his imprisonment in 1979 is his crucial distinction between constituted and constituent power. More precisely, the concept of 'constituent power' which he offers as the radical alternative to constituted power caricatures much modern political thought by attributing to it a dualistic separation between the juridical order of the state and the productive order of society. In reality, liberal-democratic theorists like de Tocqueville were concerned to draw a crucial *distinction* between the juridical and the social order, not to make an absolute *separation* between them. They have insisted on making that distinction, not because of conceptual confusion, but due to a well-founded suspicion of power, regardless of whether it is placed in the hands of the old monarchy, for example, or in those of the new proletariat portrayed by Negri.

A further problem, relating more directly to Negri's theory of empire, is that the 'exodus' of the new proletariat predicted by Negri shows no sign of occurring. Negri can, of course, fall back on a concept of false consciousness in order to explain this, but that is merely a way of evading the fact that the new proletariat does not share his dream of revolution. In particular, his vision of a coming 'postmodern fascism', of which Berlusconi, the Italian Prime Minister, is identified as a forebear, is merely a desperate attempt to shore up revolutionary hopes in the face of a society which shows little taste for them.[45]

Finally, even leftwing commentators have expressed misgivings about the very existence of a new global proletariat, of the kind Negri maintains has been created by the IT era. Specifically, they have objected that all Negri's work on empire really does is point to a set of characteristics which generates no sense of group identity amongst the highly variegated people who display them.[46] Once his optimism is discounted, it is easy to sympathize with the assessment of the position of the Italian communist Left by Mario Tronti, one of its more sceptical members. In the introduction to a book which appeared in 1992, Tronti gloomily remarked that 'We are trapped in the present, not only unable to escape it but finding it difficult to move about in it with the grit of ideas – that is, with the weapons of criticism.'[47]

Neither liberal nor leftwing thinkers have succeeded, then, in constructing a model upon which a viable Italian political identity can be built. The situation on the Right, however, has not been much better, as a glance at some conservative thinkers confirms.

Conservative Responses to Postwar Italian Democracy

The difficulty of constructing a principled form of conservatism which avoided both the impotence of the Left, on the one hand, and the mere pursuit of power which marked Christian Democratic practice, on the other, is illustrated by the work of several of the best known thinkers. The problems created by turning to Catholic theology are evident, for example, in the writings of Augusto Del Noce, for whom the root of Italy's postwar political problems lay in the increasing influence of modern atheistic secularism, which he regarded as essentially self-destructive. In particular, Del Noce lamented the subordination of the state to capitalism, which marked in his eyes the final triumph of unrestrained egoism which modern atheism inevitably ushers in.[48] The difficulty about trying to base conservatism on traditional Catholic theology, however, was that it did not explain how a more secular society like Britain managed to avoid corruption on the Italian scale. In addition, Del Noce's Catholic theology assumed the existence of a divine plan which ruled the universe, including the social and political order. The problem, however, was to transfer this belief to the political sphere without adopting the authoritarian position occupied by the Church in the religious one. Del Noce, it need hardly be said, had no answer to that problem.

For those seeking a more modern, wholly secular conservative vision which nevertheless preserved traditional Catholic pessimism about human perfectibility, Ugo Betti offered a Nietzschean mode of thought which abandoned religious orthodoxy at the expense of introducing profound instability into the conservative commitment. For Betti, the eternal reality of life is the unrelieved story of violence, domination and guilt – a predicament for which no individual is ever responsible, and from which none can ever escape, caught up as all men are in the intractable, impersonal structures of an amoral social existence. From this existence democracy brings no release, and only the naïve would therefore ever have dreamt that the postwar Italian republican was likely to mark a significant break with the prewar fascist system. What was problematic about Betti's critique of democracy was the extreme spiritual idealism which inspired it – an idealism which might on occasion just as easily lead him to embrace revolutionary politics as conservatism. This was evident, for example, in his admiration for Amos, the revolutionary leader portrayed in Betti's play *La regina e gli insorti* (1949). The yearning for spiritual purity which inspired that admiration subverted the conservative aspects of Betti's thought still further by leading him to dismiss the stabilizing impact of postwar prosperity as nothing more than a loss of moral integrity. While conservatism of Betti's kind claims a lofty spiritual inspiration, it is an intrinsically treacherous ally since it has no place for the cardinal conservative virtues of moderation, compromise, prudence and balance.

For conservatives to whom neither Catholic orthodoxy nor Nietzschean pessimism offered a viable perspective, there remained the sceptical vision of history eloquently presented by the Sicilian aristocrat Tomasi di Lampedusa in his posthumously published novel *The Leopard* (1958). Echoing the elitist tradition of Italian political theory developed by Mosca and Pareto, Lampedusa rejected democratic idealism on the ground that dreams of reform only ever transfer power from one privileged group to another. On closer inspection, however, Lampedusa's conservatism proved to be as ambiguous and unstable as Betti's, although the source of the ambiguity in this case was no longer spiritual idealism. Specifically, it lay in Lampedusa's unsuccessful attempt to combine a fatalistic historical overview of Italy since unification, on the one hand, with his unrelenting insight into the personal and political folly of the aristocratic elite represented by *The Leopard*'s protagonist, Fabrizio, on the other. So sustained was Lampedusa's insight into Fabrizio's undoing, indeed, that he was hailed by Louis Aragon as a supporter of the Left, rather than as a reactionary. In an acute critical comment, the source of Lampedusa's ambiguity in this respect is traced by Gatt-Rutter to his identification of the blindness at the heart of Fabrizio's responses to the new Italy – a blindness reminiscent (albeit of a different kind) of that which afflicted Lear. 'The crumbling of his estate and class', Gatt-Rutter remarks, is made by Fabrizio

> to appear to himself and the reader . . . as part of the deterministic, naturalistic rise and fall of civilisations, while all along he makes or avoids decisions which, within their measure of freedom (and, for a Sicilian Prince in 1860, it is a considerable one), help to determine the specific features of a political system. He *chooses* to fulfil the economic determinism advocated by the new capitalism hegemony . . .[49]

Religion, idealism and historical fatalism failed, then, to yield an intellectually and morally coherent conservative identity. Perhaps the closest any thinker came to achieving that was one who rejected general visions of the human condition and relied instead on the lucidity born of scholarly research, not into history at large, but into the origins of Italian fascism.[50] Excessive postwar complacency, De Felice claimed, meant that Italians had completely failed to examine seriously the nature of their fascist past. Instead, they had constructed two myths which veiled it in a flattering fog. One was the Marxist myth, which enjoyed an almost unquestioned dominance in both the academic and the everyday world. The essence of this myth was that it absolved the bulk of Italians from responsibility for the fascist dictatorship by attributing it to violent imposition 'from above' by a small group acting in the interests of capitalism. In opposition to this view, De Felice focused attention on two unpalatable realities. The first was that Mussolini had enjoyed extensive popular support, at least until the racial laws were passed in the late 1930s. This popularity was perfectly understandable, he observed, as soon as it was recognized that fascism, far from being a wholly negative development, had a number of positive policies to its credit, including a welfare system and an attempt to control the Mafia. De Felice's second contention was that fascism was not a reactionary movement, as Marxism maintained, but contained an important revolutionary strand drawn, in particular, from the syndicalist tradition upon which Italian socialism was based.

Having antagonized the Italian Left by demolishing the Marxist myth, De Felice proceeded to earn even greater hatred by demolishing a second myth. This flattered post-Liberation Italy by projecting the history of the Resistance movement of 1943 back into the interwar period. De Felice's research on the popularity of fascism in interwar Italy, however, made it easy for him to show that anti-fascism in the same period had been at best somewhat feeble and badly coordinated.[51] Subsequent research has confirmed De Felice's view.[52] Conservative scepticism of this kind, however, is an affair of scholars, and was therefore without much practical significance. It offered no indication, moreover, of what a viable conservative compromise with postwar Italian democracy might involve. For that, it is necessary to turn to the disparate forms of 'realist' political theory developed by Norberto Bobbio and Danilo Zolo.

Constitutionalism, Social Democracy and 'Democratic Realism'

A notable feature of postwar Italian politics has been the absence of any significant place for a style of politics committed to constitutional rules: these have generally been valued only in so far as they happen to serve the purposes of the thinkers and politicians concerned. The life-long enterprise of Norberto Bobbio has been to defend a principled, constitutional form of 'real' democracy against 'ideal' democracy. Ideal democracy, Bobbio writes, means the sovereignty of the people, which has never existed, and never will. What actually exists, he maintains, is real democracy, which is a plurality of economic, corporative, and political groups in a continuous competition with one another – a competition that is never savage because it is regulated by norms that provide for pre-established and unanimously accepted procedures for the resolution of conflicts without recourse to the use of reciprocal force. The majority of these conflicts are resolved by negotiation among the parties and by agreements founded on continually renewable compromises. Democratic society is thus a pluralistic society and a competitive society, animated by the spirit of continual negotiation.[53]

Whether the 'real' democracy described here is in fact very real is questionable: to assume unanimous acceptance of procedures, for example, and to ignore socially and politically excluded groups for whom the institutions of 'real' democracy possess no legitimacy, is to display a large dose of idealism. In fairness, however, it must be added that Bobbio never intended his 'real' model of democracy – derived partly from Kelsen and Schumpeter, and partly from Popper[54] – to be more than a minimal definition. In order to understand what he believed an adequate model for postwar Italy required, it is necessary to consider the sweeping overview of the contemporary situation of the European world in the light of which he interpreted Italian problems.

Before the war ended, Bobbio had argued that what characterizes the modern West is a spiritual crisis created by the lack of a generally acknowledged set of authoritative limits.[55] The consequent danger is that political life will constantly veer between collectivism and individualism. Like Mounier, Bobbio maintained that stability could only be achieved by the middle way provided by personalist philosophy.[56] It was on this basis that he sought, during the postwar decades, to combine liberalism and socialism in a way which combined protection of individual rights with social welfare within a constitutional framework.

Two features made Bobbio's model unusual. One was his emphasis on the concept of civil society, with which postwar Italian intellectuals were almost totally unfamiliar, he observed, because they instinctively turned to the state as the main agent of reconstruction.[57] The other was his intensely sceptical view of politics, expressed in particular in his rejection of the Left's desire for participatory politics in favour of the elite theories of Mosca and Pareto.[58] Participatory democracy,

Bobbio maintained, is wholly incapable of producing a sense of national (as opposed to local) political identity.[59] Placing his own scepticism in historical context, Bobbio attributed it to a mode of thinking characteristic of 'a generation of people who lost their hopes...shortly after the end of the war, and have never recovered them except for occasional moments'.[60]

What then is to be made of Bobbio's claim to offer a realistic social democratic compromise? One of the most instructive critics of his political thought is Danilo Zolo, according to whom Bobbio's main defect is his failure to take adequate account of the social complexity that is the principal feature of contemporary western life. Instead, Bobbio relies upon an implausible appeal to the electorate not to ask too much from 'actually existing democracy', but simply to accept it as it is.[61] Far from accepting democracy as it is, Zolo responds, they will reject it, on the ground that constitutionalism, the rule of law and the other procedural mechanisms of democracy are unable to cope with the complexities of the information society and deliver the policies they expect.

A genuinely realistic theory of democracy, Zolo maintains, cannot be based on constitutionalism but only on what he terms 'a liberalized systemic standpoint'[62] – a form of functionalism, that is, which echoes the work of Luhmann. What this recognizes is that 'In modern societies the specific function of the political system is that of *regulating selectively the distribution of social risks, and so reducing fear, through the competitive allocation of security values*'.[63] Zolo's 'politics of fear' requires, in particular, that we abandon the moralistic tendency of contemporary English and American political philosophy, with its assumption that political impartiality is possible, and accept instead that politics is limited to 'the mediation of conflicts, the guarantee of security and the protection of civil rights'.[64]

Once moralism has been replaced by the politics of fear, Zolo holds, it is possible to take the crucial step in democratic reconstruction. This consists of drawing 'a clear distinction... between those democratic promises that had no chance of being kept and those that ought to have been kept – and should still be kept today – even within a rigorously realistic conception of democracy'.[65] Such a distinction cannot be drawn, however, until the need is acknowledged to protect social complexity by preventing the functional predominance of any particular subsystem, including the political one. Democratic realism, in other words, is about balance, and to protect balance is in fact 'the crucial "promise" which democracy must keep if it intends to distinguish itself in any other than wholly formal terms from despotic or totalitarian regimes'.[66]

Is Zolo justified in claiming that his own 'realist' version of democratic theory is more coherent than Bobbio's social democratic one? It hardly seems so. In the first place, although Zolo regards the essential 'democratic promise' as the protection of social complexity, there is no necessary connection between protecting social complexity and securing individual freedom. On the contrary, Zolo's functionalist defence of complexity is perfectly compatible with the violation of individual rights by an authoritarian political regime, provided it pursues an overall balance amongst subsystems. As Zolo recognizes, the 'Singapore model' of Lee Kuan Yew accords fully with his ideal.

A further difficulty concerns the crucial distinction Zolo draws between democratic promises which should be abandoned as inherently unrealizable and the 'realistic' ones he believes democracies should strive to implement. What is problematic is Zolo's belief that this distinction can be made in a way that does not provoke political contestation. Although he rejects Anglo-American belief in the possibility of an impartial political standpoint, in other words, he inconsistently incorporates an equivalent of it into his own thought. Similarly, his characterization of the political system as a structure which performs the function of 'reducing fear through the selective regulation of social risks' appears to assume that *which* risks are to be 'selectively regulated' is self-evident, as well as the means for regulating them. Since the answers are in fact not self-evident, and since Zolo rejects democratic debate as too messy to be acceptable, an authoritarian solution seems unavoidable.[67]

Finally, Zolo assumes that an important attraction of democratic realism in the Italian context is that it requires no civic virtue. Such realism, however, is perfectly compatible with the corrupt practices of postwar Italian politics unless it is tempered by a concern for the rule of law and for political accountability. Zolo's indifference to these concerns is not so much a step from idealism into realism as a removal of checks on the possible emergence of a corrupt dictatorship.

There is, however, a political position which claims to offer a more coherent account of democratic realism than either Bobbio or Zolo succeeds in doing. According to this position, true realism, in the contemporary Italian context, means accepting that only a strong executive, modelled perhaps on the French Fifth Republic, can govern a country faced by economic problems, internal divisions and organized crime. This is the contention of certain sections of the extreme Right, which must now be considered.

The Extreme Right

In 1995, the Italian Social Movement (MSI) which had been created in 1946 by supporters of Mussolini was replaced by a new rightwing party called the National Alliance. A major concern of the new party was to make itself more respectable by emphasizing its democratic commitment and dissociating itself from the fascist era. The reference to the need for 'political continuity' with fascism found in the MSI constitution, for example, was dropped, as was any reference to a corporatist 'third way'. This bid for respectability proved sufficiently successful to permit Gianfranco Fini, the leader of the new National Alliance party, to sweep to victory in the general election of the previous year (1994) as a member of an electoral alliance formed with Silvio Berlusconi, the leader of the new Forza Italia party. Their mutual aim was to stop the Communist Party from taking over as the principal power in Italian politics, following the demise of the Christian Democratic and Socialist parties during 1992–94 due to public outrage about corruption.

Whether the replacement of the MSI by the National Alliance really changed very much is debatable. It was reported, for example, that Francesco Storace, Mr. Fini's spokesman at the 1995 party congress, 'felt sufficiently comfortable with his heritage to greet journalists ... with an ironic fascist salute'.[68] A year earlier, Fini himself had described Mussolini, in a remark which received worldwide attention, as 'the greatest statesman of the century',[69] on the ground that he had seen clearly that strong leadership is the key to national unity. In Fini's view, it should be added, this insight was perfectly compatible with a commitment to liberty. In this respect he was not being hypocritical: Croce, after all, was originally a defender of Mussolini because he shared the 'authoritarian liberal' standpoint reflected in certain aspects of Fini's 'postfascist' position.[70]

What is mainly relevant in the present context, however, is that the best-selling author at the National Alliance congress bookstall was Julius Evola.[71] Evola had been associated with both the fascist and the Nazi movements, although it must immediately be added that true believers in both camps always regarded him as an outsider. Since Evola, more generally, is the only intellectual representative of the postwar Italian extreme Right to command a degree of international respect, the teaching which drew him to fascism and Nazism, despite the fact that he himself came to despise them, is of some interest.[72]

The core of Evola's thought is an ideal of personal spiritual liberation through *askesis*, by which he means the disciplined pursuit of a path, or 'way', to insight into the objective, unchanging principles of cosmic order.[73] The Western world is now spiritually lost, he maintains, because it confuses *askesis* with morality, religion or metaphysics, whereas it can best be understood through the Buddhist doctrine of an 'awakening' to spiritual truth. Evola holds, in other words, a traditional view of a rational universe opposed not only to the voluntarist strand in fascist doctrine but also to the Nietzschean stress on the will to power characteristic of leading members of the Continental New Right like his French admirer, Alain de Benoist.[74] The rationalist nature of this vision meant that he also rejected the biological racialism which inspired the Nazi movement, although his belief in the superiority of Aryan spirituality might be mistaken for racism.[75]

Even if the various unsavoury charges levelled against Evola are discounted, his conception of spirituality presents problems. The first is his assumption that in the ideal society the bulk of mankind will voluntarily accept elite leadership and hierarchy. Should that acquiescence not materialize, then Evola's ideal society would have to rely upon coercion, a possibility which he systematically refuses to consider.

The second problem concerns Evola's identification of *askesis* with Tradition (always capitalized),[76] which he regards as the objective embodiment of cosmic truth.[77] The difficulty, more precisely, is that Tradition in Evola's peculiar sense is 'a metahistorical reality' which has nothing to do with the past, in principle at least.[78] By making Tradition 'metahistorical', Evola can read into it whatever interpretation of cosmic truth suits his purpose.[79] Ironically, the abstract, unhistorical nature of Tradition means that his thought mirrors the abstract democratic theorizing to which his doctrine is opposed.

Finally, what makes Evola's political thought globally provocative is his belief that the superiority of Aryan spirituality entitles the Aryan race to preside over a universal empire. Although he insisted that ethnic and cultural diversity should be respected in the Aryan empire, they remain at the mercy of the imperial elite, since the elite alone understands the universally valid principles of cosmic order. The main point, however, is that Evola's support for European integration must be seen in the context of his imperial vision: integration is not desirable because it creates a power bloc capable of resisting American and Soviet influence, or a supra-national economy capable of enhancing European prosperity, but because it is a first step towards a universal Aryan empire. Since this almost inevitably made the ideal of European integration a formula for world war, it was hardly the most convincing case the postwar decades produced.

Did Evola believe, it may be asked, that the extreme Right should promote political regeneration by revolutionary action in the postwar democratic world? The answer seems to be no, since members of the spiritual elite 'do not belong to this world' but merely serve to ensure that, at the cultural level, 'Tradition is present despite all'.[80] He has nevertheless been suspected of sympathizing with the New Right demand that the elite should, in Gramscian fashion, prepare the way for an eventual coup. Whether Evola himself would have countenanced violence is doubtful, since he did not think it could create spiritual liberation, but his fusion of spiritual idealism and elitism with a vision of European unity will continue to provide the extreme Right with a suggestive body of thought. In practice, however, it was a wholly unspiritual, more populist form of centre-right conservatism that was to unite Italy politically towards the end of the twentieth century. Before considering this, however, it is necessary to consider the radical challenge to ideological visions of every kind that has come from the Italian version of postmodern political thought developed by Gianni Vattimo.

Postmodern Pluralism

For Vattimo, all the established categories of Italian and, more generally, modern western political thought have been rendered irrelevant by their inability to accommodate the human condition as it has now come to be experienced. Briefly put, what defines this condition is that there are no facts, only interpretations – 'and of course this too', Vattimo adds, 'is an interpretation'.[81] Elaborating on this theme, he echoes other postmodern thinkers when he explains that what has happened is that the absolute standpoint formerly provided by metaphysics has been replaced by a plurality of perspectives, all equally valid. 'If the postmodern subject looks into itself in search of a primary certainty,' he writes, 'in place of the security of the Cartesian *cogito* it finds [only] the intermittencies of the Proustian heart, stories from the media, [and] *mythologies* evinced by psychoanalysis.'[82]

What kind of philosophy, then, is appropriate to the radical pluralism of the postmodern era? Vattimo's answer is that it is a philosophy based on a new, 'weak' concept of rationality that abandons the search for a transcendental standpoint and adopts instead a hermeneutic perspective, in which man is viewed as a participant rather than a Cartesian spectator. What characterizes this hermeneutic perspective is, in particular, openness to the diversity of existence and, above all, a refusal to follow metaphyics in claiming to describe: it only ever *interprets*. It also accepts the inescapable plurality of possible interpretations, as well as their historical contingency. But what exactly does this new, weak rationality imply for political philosophy?

At first sight, the answer seems to be relativism, especially as Vattimo 'historicizes' postmodernism itself by insisting that hermeneutics is only appropriate to the modern western period marked by the disintegration of metaphysics. Vattimo emphatically rejects the charge of relativism, however, on the ground that hermeneutics brings with it the rediscovery of religion, in which he finds a basis for ethics that escapes postmodern deconstruction. In a book on religion coedited with Derrida, Vattimo insists he is not trying to solve the problem of relativism by an irrational leap into faith.[83] He claims, rather, that the western tradition has always been grounded in religion, but that this was concealed from sight by the mistaken belief that philosophy enables man to rise above his religious roots.[84] Now that postmodernism has demolished the conception of rationality which created this illusion, the religious roots of western experience are again visible. To discover religion, then, is not to embrace irrationalism: in the language of Heidegger, it is simply to achieve insight into man's condition of *Dasein* – his rootedness in the world, that is, which is prior to so-called philosophical reason, and is never transcended by it.

The difficulty with Vattimo's announcement of the 'return of the religious'[85] is that it creates confusion about the meaning of religion. More precisely, Vattimo's postmodern concept of religion has no place for the traditional concept of God, in the sense of an independent being, since he maintains that only interpretations exist, not facts. What is even more confusing is that he assigns the Christian doctrine of the Incarnation a vital place in a non-relativist ethical system, despite the fact that it rests on revelation.[86] It seems, then, that if Vattimo manages to avoid relativism, it is through faith, rather than through a coherent post-metaphysical philosophy.

So far as politics is concerned, however, Vattimo's use of religion is not crucial since he also defends a non-foundational postmodern 'ethics of interpretation' on the basis of two arguments completely independent of it. One is philosophical, the other sociological. According to the philosophical argument, the end of metaphysics encourages a general spirit of humility and moderation because no place is left for arrogant appeals to absolute values. In particular, sympathy for otherness creates solidarity, in the form of a sense of mutual responsibility and charity. As Vattimo puts it,

> Thinking that no longer understands itself as the recognition of and acceptance of an objective authoritarian foundation will develop a new sense of responsibility as ready and able, literally, to respond to others whom, insofar as it is not founded on the eternal structure of Being, it knows to be its 'provenance'... Is it chance that some philosophers... speak today about a principle of charity?[87]

Unfortunately, far from creating charity and solidarity, the post-modern discovery of diversity may unleash profound social conflicts previously contained by the metanarratives which postmodernism dismisses as exploitative ideological structures. Although Vattimo's second, sociological argument is intended to provide empirical grounds for his optimism, misgivings remain. According to this argument, the mass media create a tolerant pluralist ethos by forcing members of mass society to encounter a multiplicity of world views, thereby making it impossible for them to cling fanatically to absolute values.[88] As Vattimo writes in *Beyond Interpretation*,

> it may be that the epoch of the end of metaphysics to which the ethics of hermeneutics means to correspond is distinguished not only by the dissolution of the principle of reality into the Babel of interpretations, but also and indelibly by the dissolution of funda-mentalisms of every kind; it is not hard to see them as neurotic defences of identity...[89]

Once again, this passage is open to the charge of unwarranted optimism, partly on the ground that the toleration created by 'media pluralism' does not, on crucial issues such as race, run very deep for large sections of the electorate, and partly on the ground that Vattimo's emphasis on the liberalizing impact of the media ignores the fact that they may equally well be exploited for political purposes, as Berlusconi's successful promotion of his Forza Italia party makes clear.

Vattimo's 'weak rationality', then, has not yielded the non-foundational 'ethics of interpretation' at which his hermeneutic philosophy aimed. His belief that the end of metaphysics spontaneously fosters an ideal of solidarity capable of integrating postmodern pluralism without state action relies on an optimism unsupported by convincing argument. Above all, his belief in the moderating and integrating impact of the media threatens at times to make him look like the intellectual spokesman for Silvio Berlusconi, the controversial Italian Prime Minister who controls much of the Italian media. Vattimo is illuminating, nevertheless, when he 'deconstructs' surviving metaphysical elements in other contemporary philosophers. In Derrida's case, for example, he identifies a residual 'objectivist' urge to escape from 'the essentially metaphorical character of every language' into a 'proper', fully rational discourse which, for hermen-eutic philosophy, cannot exist.[90] In Habermas' 'ethics of communi-cation', likewise, Vattimo identifies surviving metaphysical or 'objectivist' yearnings, referring in particular to Habermas' failure to recognize that the end of metaphysics does not bring communicative transparency and harmony but merely exposes the diversity and opacity at the heart of human existence.[91] Although Vattimo's optimism has prevented him, then, from offering a viable model of integration for Italy, he has at least ensured a community of intel-lectual misery by effectively spiking the claim of leading French and German thinkers to have done so for their own countries.

The New Italian Republic

During 1992–94, what has been described as a 'political earthquake' occurred in Italy, the result of which was that the postwar party system unexpectedly collapsed.[92] This not only destroyed the authority and prestige of an entire ruling class but also called into question the principal conceptions of unity which had dominated the previous half century.[93] In brief, the Christian Democrat and Socialist parties which had effectively monopolized postwar office were swept away. On the Left, the Communist Party, which initially looked as if it would be the beneficiary of the power vacuum, disintegrated. The principal beneficiaries of this situation were three new groups on the Right. These were Forza Italia, the Northern League and the National Alliance (which had previously existed as the MSI, the fascist successor party).

Initially, the new groups reawakened old hopes of a reborn, less corrupt democratic republic rising from the ashes. Soon, however, the career of Silvio Berlusconi, who became Prime Minister for a second time in 2001, created doubts about how much had really changed since the days of Machiavelli. Berlusconi had already been found guilty three times of financial corruption, faced charges of collusion with the Mafia, and had intertwined his public and private interests by controlling over 90 per cent of Italian television.[94] The defence offered by his old friend, Fedele Confalonieri, the chairman of Berlusconi's television network, was not very flattering for Italians at large. 'Italy', Confalonieri observed, 'is not a normal country. Even an anomaly like Mr. Berlusconi must be understood in the context of the country. He has done nothing worse than any businessman in Italy.'[95] Berlusconi himself saw the secret of his success slightly differently, however. Using the football metaphors of which he is fond, he remarked that 'I heard that the game was getting dangerous, and that it was all being played in the two penalty areas, with the midfield being left desolately empty...And so we decided to fill that immense space.'[96] What Berlusconi left out of this succinct formulation was the style of politics by means of which he occupied the pitch.

The most striking characteristic of this style was Berlusconi's complete abandonment of the concern with civic virtue which had previously been central to the otherwise disparate conceptions of national unity advocated by many Italian political thinkers from Machiavelli to Croce and Gramsci. In place of civic virtue, Berlusconi combined control of the media with an anti-state mix of promises of economic prosperity through free enterprise, appeals to individual initiative and support for family values. His expertise in advertising was such that he was able to defeat the Communist challenge of the early 1990s by creating a new centre-right party, Forza Italia, within a period of three months. In particular, by combining his media skills with his grasp of the old clientelistic system of politics, he was able to ally with two profoundly opposed politicians, Umberto Bossi, leader of the Northern League, and Gianfranco Fini, leader of the National Alliance, whose support lay mainly in the south. The coalition preserved Italian unity, but by means not foreseen by any of the political models Italian political thinkers had explored in the decades after 1944. Despite this, some took an optimistic view of the new republic. Norberto Bobbio, for example, observed that the post-1994 political order could be seen as a shift towards what he called 'real' democracy because it marked the belated emergence of Italy from the misleading antifascist mythology of the Resistance, a mythology which had lumbered the postwar democratic Republic with an unrealistic theory of legitimation from the outset.[97] What Bobbio's realist interpretation ignored, however, was the fact that Berlusconi's personalist, media-based style of politics entirely lacked the constitutionalist commitment on which Bobbio himself had always taken his stand.

A different source of optimism was provided by the work of John Rawls, which suggested that a secular consumer culture can survive perfectly well provided it displays a concern for social justice. Rawls' *A Theory of Justice* had been translated into Italian in 1982.[98] Two years earlier, a leading Italian Rawls scholar, Salvatore Veca, published a collection of essays in which he drew heavily on Rawls to defend a democratic ideal based on the ideas of contract, universally valid procedural rules of justice, a commitment to political pluralism, and substantive political programmes based on rational choice theory.[99] The problem about applying Rawlsian theory to Italy, however, is that underlying it is a deep-seated American tradition of civil association which is completely lacking in the political history of modern Italy. In particular, Rawls' concern with universal principles of justice as the foundation of a liberal society is at odds with many deeply established features of Italian life, as Paul Ginsborg noted at the end of his study of contemporary Italy. Above all, Ginsborg wrote, the sensibility of government to civil society remains low:

> the need to take seriously the relationship between families and the state, the abandonment of clientelistic and familistic cultures, the bridging of the gap between formal democratic culture and everyday life, these seem all to be far down the agenda of government, if they are present at all.[100]

The foundations for a moderate liberal-democratic position, then, still seemed to elude Italy. On the other hand, under the new republic the extreme Right had, outwardly at least, opted for a show of respectability. But what of the radical Left? At the risk of some exaggeration, Norberto Bobbio has summed up the situation with admirable lucidity. Although 'neither theoretical Marxism nor militant Marxism is totally dead',[101] he remarked, 'the radical Left movements, abandoning the factory to the robots and "class" to the sociologists, [have] pursued other goals – in particular, defense of the environment and universal peace ... The ecologist and the pacifist are the figures who represent radical thought today. The ethical principle that animates them is nonviolence.'[102]

What remains to be considered is whether Italy's membership of the European Union has added significantly to the themes which political thought must take into account. This question can most conveniently be considered in the conclusion.

Conclusion

Ever since the Risorgimento, the fundamental problem for Italian politics has been the creation of a national identity. During the decades since 1945, that problem has in one sense been solved. The solution, however, did not consist of a belated achievement of an ideal of civil association in the face of continuing family and clientelistic ties, the division between north and south, and a long tradition of corruption and even criminality in state administration. It consisted, rather, in social integration achieved by a combination of economic prosperity and exposure to the mass-media. If the outcome has been in many respects a comfortable one, what is still lacking, as Paul Ginsborg observes, is 'a public sphere in which Italian citizens could more easily espy some of democracy's virtues and not just its vices, and with which they could perhaps come to identify'.[103] Without progress on that fundamental front, there is little likelihood of reforming the most disturbing aspect of the Italian state, which is a system of justice that has few parallels in the rest of Europe. That system, Perry Anderson has noted, is a 'mixture of a Fascist derived legal code, arbitrary emergency powers, and chaotic procedural and carceral conditions ... There is no habeas corpus in Italy, where anyone can be clapped in jail without charges for over three years.'

In addition, there is 'no separation of careers, and little of functions, between prosecutors and judges', while 'the average length [of a trial] is ten years, and the backlog of cases in the courts is now [viz. 2002] some three million'.[104]

Is it possible that membership of the European Union will impose on Italy constraints that facilitate improved state administration and even promote the growth of a public realm? The effects of external constraints, it has been remarked, have certainly in the past gone 'beyond mere economic advantage. As European legislation developed . . . it enriched Italian democracy in many ways – in the area of equal opportunities, with regard to the environment, on the issues of justice and human rights'.[105] Despite these beneficial consequences of European involvement, however, at least two considerations suggest the need for scepticism about how much impetus it can give to necessary reforms.[106] One is that the enthusiasm shown by Italian politicians for European involvement, especially since Andreotti's Presidency of the Community in 1990, has (in the past at least) been counteracted by their tendency to treat European issues as a side-show which distracts from their primary commitment to municipal involvements. A well-known illustration of Italian parochialism was the relatively rapid resignation of the Christian Democrat Franco Maria Malfatti from the Presidency of the Commission after reluctantly accepting the post in 1970. In March 1972 Malfatti resigned in order to resume his career at Rome.[107]

The other source of scepticism about the beneficial impact of the European Union on Italian democracy is that even a more active involvement in it would not alter the need for domestic reform, since national authority remains vital for the allocation and administration of such crucial functions as welfare provision. In this respect, indeed, the danger is that a European political identity may simply act as a pretext for prolonging the Italian tradition of accepting centralized, bureacratic government, if it promises to remove responsibility whilst simultaneously delivering prosperity. It has been rare indeed, Ginsborg remarks, 'to hear serious discussion about the possible bureaucratic tyrannies of the European Commission, of its sometimes absurd and damaging insistence on standardization, [and] of the very serious democratic deficit that existed in the structures of the Community . . .'.[108] Perhaps pessimism on this issue, however, as indeed on many others, may be alleviated a little by recalling Byron's optimistic observation about Italy at a time when things seem to have been considerably worse than they are at present. In Italy, he remarked, 'there is no law or government at all; and it is wonderful how well things go without them'.[109] It is, needless to say, not a thought which would have met with Machiavelli's approval.

6

Political Thought in East-Central Europe: From Empires to the European Union

For the nations of central and eastern Europe, liberation from Nazism at the end of the Second World War brought only subjection to yet another system of imperial rule, in accordance with a fate which had shaped the lives of most of their inhabitants for at least two centuries. At the end of the First World War, the liberal victors had hoped to break this pattern by a peace settlement that replaced imperialism by democratic nation-states. The democratic dream soon foundered, however, as the new states succumbed (with the exception of Czechoslovakia) to various forms of dictatorship. If this was disappointing, it was hardly surprising: what the proponents of democratization had ignored in 1919 was the fact that the long history of dictatorship in eastern Europe could not be attributed entirely to external factors. On the contrary, there were major internal obstacles to the creation of a more humane and liberal system of government. Since these continued in existence down to the velvet revolutions of 1989 and beyond, it is necessary to note their existence at the outset in order to appreciate the political constraints to which this part of the European world is subject.

A principal obstacle to liberal-democratic idealism was an authoritarian political tradition that persisted even when the outward forms of parliamentary government had been adopted.[1] Another consisted of social divisions made more divisive by the fact that they sometimes coincided with religious ones. These divisions were further intensified by the ethnic concept of nationality upon which the new states had been constructed in 1919, which created the risk of legitimizing programmes of national purification wherever ethnic minorities existed. Even when an eastern European government pursued liberal policies, as Thomas Masaryk's did in interwar Czechoslovakia, minorities remained alienated from the state because the political elite continued to be largely confined to the Czech majority. Only his unduly optimistic belief that 'we are entitled to expect that the tension between States and races will decrease'[2] permitted Masaryk to avoid acknowledging the intractability of a problem that would lead Slovakia to secede not long after the velvet revolution and would eventually tear Yugoslavia apart. If the general situation of minorities has improved in eastern Europe since 1945, it would nevertheless be premature to attribute this to moral and political enlightenment: Poland, for example, has no large minority left because the Jews, Ukrainians and Belorussians were either massacred or expelled during and after the Second World War.[3]

The final obstacle to liberal-democratic reformism which will be noticed is one which has distinguished the eastern European political tradition more decisively from the western than any other. This is the absence of an autonomous tradition of civil association. Even though some parts of eastern Europe (notably Bohemia and Moravia) have experienced it in some degree, the state always retained the upper hand. When the absence of civil society is combined with the other obstacles just mentioned, eastern Europe may be regarded as 'a transitional zone between the Western tradition of the division of power and the Eastern tradition of concentration of power', the latter finding its fullest expression in Russia.[4]

It is against this background, then, that political thought in the 'other' Europe must be seen. Attention will be concentrated on thinkers from Poland, Czechoslovakia and Hungary because they have made the most significant theoretical contribution to postwar political debate in eastern Europe at large. Since the end of the Second World War, three phases may be distinguished in that debate. In the first, which extended from roughly 1950 to the 1980s, mainly émigré thinkers developed a sustained critique of totalitarianism. In the second, partially overlapping phase, which extended from roughly 1968 to 1989, a growing sense of the instability of the totalitarian system led to speculation about the possibility of some accommodation between one-party states and a limited form of civil society. Finally, a third phase followed the unexpected collapse of Soviet rule in 1989, after which the concern has been partly to find a viable form of democratization for the post-communist states and partly to gain entry to the European Union.

The Critique of Totalitarianism

In his novel *1984*, George Orwell had portrayed Winston Smith as spiritually broken by the totalitarian regime under which he lived. A few years after Orwell's book appeared the Polish exile, Czeslaw Miłosz, painted an even more pessimistic picture. In *The Captive Mind* (1953), he maintained that intellectuals like Smith did not need to be physically terrorized in order to be made to conform. Because capitalist societies pay little attention to them, they are prone to feelings of isolation, whereas the Communist system offers the recognition they crave, gives them secure jobs, encourages them to write, compose or paint, and even permits them to travel to non-communist states – provided they unfailingly conform to the Party's view of the objective requirements of dialectical materialism.[5] The totalitarian lie is therefore easily swallowed. The price paid, however, is internal paralysis and profound apathy.[6]

Although Miłosz's study was a salutary corrective to Orwell's failure to appreciate the positive attraction totalitarianism might exert, the precise nature of his own position was vague, mainly because he tended to define totalitarianism in psychological rather than political terms. He equated it, more specifically, with intense pressure to conform. Since pressure to conform is found in both liberal-democratic and totalitarian regimes, however, this obscured the differences between them. Miłosz himself, indeed, continued to feel almost as threatened by conformist pressure after he fled to the West as he had done in Poland. 'Let me not forget', he wrote, 'that I stand in daily risk of losing [my freedom] once more. For in the West also one experiences the pressure to conform.'[7] Miłosz's psychological approach to totalitarianism, in a word, led him to minimize the significance of the fact that in the West he was protected by the rule of law.

For nearly two decades, there was little need for eastern European political thinkers to give more theoretical precision to the concept, mainly because it was felt to be increasingly irrelevant after the period of de-Stalinization (1956–68). After the brutal suppression of the Prague uprising of 1968, however, interest in it revived to such an extent that it became, in the words of Jacques Rupnik, the 'common denominator' of political theorizing for dissident eastern European intellectuals.[8] As Rupnik notes, the revival was not merely a return to the 'classic' concept of totalitarianism developed by Hannah Arendt, and thereafter by a succession of American political scientists during the 1950s. It involved, rather, 'a completely new attempt to redefine [the concept] in the light of the system's evolution and the new methods of Communist rule'.[9] More specifically, the task of redefinition had to take account of the decline of two features fundamental to the classic theory. One was the demand for ideological commitment, in place of which post-Stalinist regimes were content with a more ritualistic conformity. The other was the use of terror, for which less brutal means of control had been substituted.

Faced by these developments, a possible response was to conclude that the concept of totalitarianism was in the process of becoming superfluous. This was the view of two Polish commentators, Jerzy Wiatr and Jadwiga Staniszkis,[10] of the situation in their own country at least. What was necessary, they maintained (albeit for somewhat different reasons), was a 'post totalitarian' theory of the authoritarian state, characterized by some degree of social pluralism and the peripheral role of ideology. The premature nature of their optimism was made clear, however, by the suppression of the Polish Solidarity movement in December 1981.

The way was now open for defenders of the concept of totalitarianism to argue for its continuing relevance, albeit in a suitably modified form. This was the response of the Czech émigré Zděnek Mlynář, for example, who claimed that far from totalitarianism being on the decline, what had happened was that more effective techniques of social control had replaced the old Stalinist ones. The essence of the new totalitarianism, he maintained, lay in cybernetics – in the ability of the regime, that is, to destroy individuality by monopolizing all the principal means of acquiring and distributing information.[11] Although Mlynář's message was not entirely novel - cybernetic theory was merely a restatement in contemporary terms of the totalitarian reshaping of memory and perception previously described by Orwell – it provided a useful antidote to a misplaced eastern European optimism, as well as to the western tendency to equate détente with a process of genuine liberalization. A similar warning against false optimism was provided by Václav Havel, the Czech playwright and future president, when he spoke of a new form of totalitarianism in which oppression had not disappeared but simply been internalized. It is not true, he wrote, 'to say that our country is free of warfare and murder. The war and the killing merely assume a different form: they have been shifted from the sphere of observable social events to the twilight of an unobservable inner destruction.'[12]

The scepticism of Mlynář and Havel was complemented by that of the Czech philosopher Milan Šimečka,[13] on whom Orwell had had a profound effect.[14] The Communist system had only abandoned terror, he wrote, because it had discovered a new, 'post-terrorist' technique of control in the fact that 'all citizens are its employees and it is no problem to shift them up or down a scale of incentives... [This] has worked well because it was brought into play only when existing socialism... most resembled a consumer society, i.e. when it had something to reward or punish with'.[15] As Rupnik remarked, 'Within this system, police repression is replaced by the personnel office.'[16]

The revised model of totalitarianism which emerged from the dissident debate was well summarized in the course of an interview with the Polish writer, Adam Michnik, during the late 1980s. The Polish regime, Michnik agreed with his interviewer, was 'totalitarian in the revised sense that it is mobilized constantly to prevent the formation of a civil society independent of the party-dominated political order'.[17] Simply to revise the concept of totalitarianism in the light of new realities, however, was not the only challenge confronting dissident eastern European intellectuals. In addition, they had to defend their efforts against the charge which had previously led western European political thinkers to abandon the concept of totalitarianism. This was that it was an almost entirely ideological construct, and was therefore worthless for purposes of objective political analysis. How successful, one must ask, was the defence they mounted?

The Hungarian political theorist, Aurel Kolnai, responded by attempting to give greater precision to the psychological approach which had left Miłosz's work open to the charge of vagueness. More specifically, he identified the source of totalitarianism with a utopian 'cast of mind' which he believed western political scientists have mistakenly tried to analyze in terms of a commitment to values that are unrealizable in practice. In reality, he held, this cast of mind has two main characteristics. One is that it does not pursue values of *any* kind but is constituted, rather, by a yearning for perfection or purity. The other is that it involves a 'self-enclosed' or insulated mind which systematically disconnects the ideal society from all experience of the existing order, making the utopian goal not merely impractical, but *logically impossible* to achieve. In short, the source of totalitarianism is 'the tendency to judge the real world of our experience against a self-enclosed and perfect blueprint'.[18]

The danger with Kolnai's refinement of the psychological approach was that it risked postulating a model of totalitarianism so completely detached from the concrete realities of history that it shed little light on actual attempts to implement it. In particular, as Kolnai himself acknowledged, his analysis not only failed to explain why totalitarianism had occurred on such a vast scale in the twentieth century, but also why certain countries had been more prone to it than others.[19] It failed, in addition, to indicate whether the structure of the regimes which embodied the utopian impulse made them likely to survive or collapse. Despite his abstract, wholly unhistorical approach, however, Kolnai's psychological analysis, like Miłosz's, provided a timely reminder that totalitarianism had deeper roots in human nature than western liberal thinkers generally cared to acknowledge.

More philosophical attempts to defend the analytical value of the concept of totalitarianism were made by thinkers who introduced the idea of the totalitarian lie. This was invoked by Václav Havel, for example, to describe the situation which had developed by 1980: the lie simply involves accepting life within the totalitarian state, since 'In so doing one confirms the system, gives it meaning, creates it . . . and merges with it.'[20] In this form, Havel argued, the lie remains vital to the regime even when it no longer demands active ideological commitment. The only possibility open to those in this situation is to live the lie outwardly, but without inward commitment to it. Although Havel's concept of the lie testified to his personal integrity, the theoretical problem was that he linked it to a romantic standpoint which was both anti-political and anti-modern, being permeated by hostility towards 'the automatism of technological civilization and the industrial-consumer society'.[21] His quarrel, in other words, appeared not only to be with communism but with western industrial democracy at large.

The value of the lie as a tool for political analysis became even more questionable when Havel's fellow countryman, the pseudo-nymous Pietr Fidelius, characterized its essence, in its totalitarian form, as the attempt to create the illusion of intelligibility by imposing a 'violent unification of the truth' on the inescapable divisions, ambivalences and conflicts which always mark the human condition.[22] The problem was that this characterization was so general that it no longer had any specific connection with the Soviet empire but could be found throughout human history: a 'violent unification of the truth' has been a prominent feature, for example, of many great religious movements in the past.

The most philosophically ambitious attempt to give precision to the concept of the lie was made by the Hungarian philosopher, Leszek Kolakowski, who adopted a functional approach. Although Kolakowski acknowledged that the lie is commonplace in politics, its 'normal' use 'leaves the distinction between truth and falsity intact'.[23] The totalitarian use of the lie, by contrast, aims at destroying all privacy by the total mental and moral expropriation of the populace. The most vital part of this expropriation is 'the total possession and control of human memory', since memory is the key to any identity beyond the state.[24] Tony Judt, however, has observed that it is simply not true, as Kolakowski, Havel and others maintain, that only totalitarian regimes distort national memory by replacing the facts of history by an ideological lie. On the contrary, Judt writes,

> the very events of 1989 themselves may be about to enter the no-man's land of mythical and preferable pasts. It will be hard to claim that any of the liberations of Eastern Europe, even those of Poland or Hungary, would have been possible without at least the benign neglect of the Soviet Union; indeed there is some reason to believe that in Czechoslovakia, and perhaps Berlin, the Soviets played an active part in bringing down their own regimes. This is not a very appealing or heroic version of a crucial historical turning point; it is as though Louis XVI had engineered the fall of the Bastille.[25]

No less problematic is the fact that Kolakowski's concept of the totalitarian lie presupposed that he himself occupied a non-ideological standpoint – an assumption retained from his Marxist past. Having broken free from his early Marxist faith, however, the real basis of his new position was not so much the claim to transcend ideology as to destroy its absolutist pretensions by what he called his 'jester's philosophy' – a philosophy, that is, whose essence is precisely the rejection of all absolutes.[26] From this standpoint the concept of the totalitarian lie became redundant, being replaced by the more straight forward task of defending what was, in effect, an ideal of moderation.

For Michael Polanyi, a more profitable way of defending the concept of totalitarianism was inspired neither by psychological nor philosophical considerations but by economic theory. His starting point, more specifically, was dissatisfaction with Hayek's concept of the road to serfdom, on the ground that it rested on a naïve equation of totalitarianism with central planning. What was wrong with this equation, Polanyi maintained, was that it assumed that totalitarian regimes actually *can* plan the economy.[27] Hayek's error, in other words, was that he had been duped by totalitarianism's own propaganda. In the process he had fallen foul, like many others, of 'the common practice of ritual magic', according to which 'by sprinkling water you make the rain come down'. Just as 'the absence of practical results does not disturb those who believe in magic,...the same is true for those who believe in economic planning'.[28] If the rain actually comes, it is not because of the witch doctors' efforts.

In order to understand why a modern economy cannot be efficiently planned, Polanyi used the example of a large jigsaw puzzle. Suppose that solving the puzzle is very urgent but would take one person several weeks. The answer seems to be to engage a team of helpers – but how is the team to be organized? Giving a copy of the puzzle to each member of the team as part of a centrally directed plan to complete his version, and then adding up the results after a certain period, would have no obvious advantage. 'The only way to get the job finished quickly', Polanyi maintained,

> would be to get as many helpers as could conveniently work at one and the same set and let them loose on it, each to follow his own initiative. Each helper would then watch the situation as it was affected by the progress made by all the others and would set himself new problems in accordance with the latest outline of the completed part of the puzzle. The tasks undertaken by each would closely dovetail into those performed by the others.[29]

Whether this example establishes a conclusive case against central planning is arguable, since the possibility of finding a genius at super-fast jigsaw puzzle-solving seems still to be open. However that may be, it should be noted that Polanyi did not claim that unplanned order was perfect. 'If somebody insists that you need an engine to pull a train', he remarked, 'he must not be taken to deny that the efficiency of engines is very limited.'[30] What ultimately made his defence of economic freedom problematic, however, was his attempt to locate it within an overall vision of liberal democracy in which 'Freedom of the individual to do as he pleases, so long as he respects the other fellow's right to do likewise, plays only a minor part.' A free society, he continued, 'is not an Open Society', but one fully dedicated to supporting a distinctive set of beliefs about the conditions for maintaining a scientific view of the world.[31] Ironically, the danger with this vision of liberalism was that it ran the risk of introducing into Polanyi's liberalism authoritarian elements of precisely the kind he rejected in the totalitarian regimes.

Some of the most controversial analyses of totalitarianism came, however, from yet another quarter. Just as the interpretation of Nazi totalitarianism provoked an *Historikerstreit* in postwar West Germany, so the interpretation of Communist totalitarianism provoked one in east-central Europe. The key issue in this debate was whether the main causes of totalitarianism could be attributed to endogenous features of east-central European history, or whether an external cause – viz. Russia – could be made to bear most of the responsibility. According to one group of historians, it was a mistake to demonize Russia because important contributions to totalitarianism had been made by, for example, the legalistic and bureaucratic heritage of the Habsburg empire; by the cultural and social dislocation caused by two world wars; by revolution and the Nazi occupation; and by the existence of anti-semitic traditions exploited by both Nazi and Soviet totalitarianisms.[32] From this point of view, in short, the Soviet occupation was not the principal cause of totalitarianism but merely perpetuated features of east-central Europe's history which were not of Russia's making.

Less sceptical dissident thinkers, by contrast, were more inclined to construct their history in a way which ascribed complete responsibility for totalitarianism to Russia. Among those particularly anxious to demonize Russia in this way were thinkers who wanted to establish the existence of a central European cultural and political identity much more akin to the western European than the Slav one. Their reason for wanting to do so commands sympathy: what they objected to was the western European tendency, after Yalta, to think of 'Eastern Europe' in monolithic terms which complacently consigned all the countries within it to the sphere of rightful Russian influence, if not rule.[33]

Amongst dissident intellectuals who turned to history in order to establish the existence of a distinct central European identity, one of the most ambitious was the Hungarian political theorist, István Bibó, who sought to find in the history of his own nation in particular what an admiring fellow-countryman has termed 'an untainted democratic tradition'[34] that could be synthesized with progressive western European political thought.[35] More generally, Bibó found in modern history three distinct models of political development, characteristic of Western, Central, and Eastern nations respectively – the essence of the Central model being that it displayed impeccably liberal and democratic characteristics that made it more akin to the West than to the East (i.e. Russia) whose political tradition was wholly alien to it. Bibó's attempt to establish a distinct central European identity, however, attracted less attention than that of Czech dissidents, who were equally determined to demolish the crude western belief that, in the words of Vacláv Racek, 'the world behind the Iron Curtain is governed by a strange monolithic dictatorship of an Asiatic type'.[36]

Unlike Bibó, Czech dissidents were more concerned to establish the spiritual than the political basis of their putative central European identity. They wished, indeed, to elevate central Europe to a position of spiritual superiority over western Europe partly by maintaining that despite their cultural distinctness, they were just as much a part of Europe as the western states, and partly by claiming that they alone understood the nature of the general spiritual crisis which has (they said) exposed the whole of the postwar European world to totalitarianism. If the western democracies have so far managed to avoid totalitarianism, Miloš Kořan claimed, that is due not to political wisdom but is 'only thanks to the residual influence of transcendent [i.e. Christian] values from a pre-modern age'.[37]

This ambitious attempt to use history to establish a purified central European identity, free from any internal tendencies towards totalitarianism, was pursued in an especially dramatic way by an internationally esteemed Czech writer, Milan Kundera. In 1984, Kundera voiced the bitterness of many dissident intellectuals when he accused western European states of betraying central Europe by pursuing an ideal of European unity which consigned the latter to permanent membership of the Soviet bloc. In order to establish that this was in fact a betrayal, Kundera argued that, in the modern period, a common culture had given western and central European nations a common identity. Since the Second World War, however, the tragedy of western Europe is that a mass materialist culture has destroyed its sense of European cultural unity. Central Europe, by contrast, has retained that sense, despite the brutal attempts of Russia to destroy it. Central Europe is therefore now not only spiritually superior to western Europe but is also the only source of the moral inspiration necessary to prevent the western states from succumbing to totalitarianism. More generally, indeed, it is only the spiritual purity of central Europe that can provide a stable foundation for the unification of Europe to which the western states aspire.[38]

Although it is easy to sympathize with Kundera's bitterness over western European indifference to the fate of the central European states after Yalta, his exalted view of their spirituality proved wholly unacceptable even to some fellow central European intellectuals. Josef Hradec, for example, rejected Kundera's secular interpretation of central European identity out of hand, on the ground that it ignored the vital part played by religion in central European life. In addition, Hradec noted, Kundera had completely ignored the long and bitter history of rivalry amongst central European nations, all of which behaved like vultures towards each other whenever one suffered misfortune, as Czechoslovakia did in 1938, for example. On this point, Hradec's historical scepticism was supported by Timothy Garton Ash, who remarked that central European history does not reveal unity of any kind but only 'a territory where peoples, cultures, languages are fantastically intertwined, where every place has several names and men change their citizenship as often as their shoes'. Every attempt to distil some common 'essence' of central European history, Ash concluded, 'is either absurdly reductionist or invincibly vague'.[39]

Hradec's final objection, however, returned to the sensitive issue of Russia's role in creating and maintaining the totalitarian system. According to Kundera, central European nations were the passive victims of Russian imperialism. Hradec, by contrast, claimed that Kundera was simply incorrect when he claimed, for example, that the central European nations woke up one day shortly after the Second World War to find themselves enslaved by a foreign power. The truth is that 'our situation is not entirely the work of a usurping totalitarian power. The bed was already made by the romantic consciousness of a "Slav mutuality" in our country. And when the Russians perfidiously entered the bed, we got what we had asked for.'[40]

In similar vein, Milan Šimečka reminded Kundera that 'it was not the Russians who put paid to Czech culture which seemed to be evolving so promisingly...in the 1960s. It was our lot:...I saw with my own eyes how avidly our colleagues in culture, education and science set about the task of "cleaning up" culture.'[41] Above all, Šimečka maintained, Kundera was wrong to carry the demonization of Russia so far that he excluded it completely from western civilization. Šimečka's own position, however, was not much more coherent: going to the opposite extreme to Kundera, Šimečka maintained that Lenin himself was 'particularly un-Russian', on the ground that 'His ideological accent was that of Paris, London and Zurich.'[42] Suffice to note at this point that agreement by central European thinkers about what a central European identity involved was hardly likely to be achieved if they could not even agree about who the Russians were, from whom they wished to distance themselves.

The most serious difficulty about Kundera's argument, however, was one that neither Hradec nor Šimečka noticed, perhaps because they themselves failed to avoid it. This was a tendency to flee from political reality into a vague spiritual idealism. Kundera's flight was evident, above all, in his admiration for Franz Werfel's proposal, in 1937, for a 'World Academy of Poets and Thinkers' as the best means of dealing 'not only [with] Hitlerism but also [with] the totalitarian threat in general' in a way 'free of politics and propaganda'.[43] Although Kundera noted that Werfel had been ridiculed at the time, he shared Werfel's yearning for an escape from politics into a world ruled by artists and intellectuals. Unfortunately, Hitler considered himself amply qualified to hold his own in such circles.

The vain hope of overcoming totalitarianism by a flight from politics, it must be added, was not confined to dissident central European intellectuals like Kundera. As another Czech émigré, Václav Bělohradský, noted in an acute analysis of the western hopes that inspired détente during the 1960s, western liberal intellectuals also indulged in a similar flight when they based their faith in East–West dialogue on the idea of an inevitable convergence of all societies 'towards a single type of society, characterised by high technology and rational organisation, but completely neutral with respect to values and ideologies'.[44] The result was a western 'retreat of the political into the technical', to be presided over by managers who would replace politicians in a world in which everything would be subordinated to science and economic growth. In this world, the nasty features of Soviet totalitarianism would automatically disappear, since it was assumed that 'real power ... will shift from the hands of the communists to the hands of a supposedly "neutral" managerial class'.

This naive optimism, Bělohradský observed, concealed the fact that western European states had forgotten that liberal democracy is not simply a functional system for promoting science and growth but rests on moral and religious values. As a result of forgetting that this was the source of their own legitimacy, liberals in those states would be all too ready to support authoritarian regimes in eastern Europe, on the sole proviso that they professed sympathy for science and growth. It was hardly necessary for Bělohradský to add that the western states would also cease to be committed to the defence of limited government within their own frontiers.

Does a coherent theory of totalitarianism emerge from the wide-ranging dissident literature on the concept? What it plausibly suggests is that totalitarianism has far deeper roots than western liberal intellectuals have generally recognized, appealing as it does to aspects of human nature that liberalism fails to acknowledge. Overall, however, the answer must be that Jacques Rupnik was right to conclude that what the literature yields is not a 'scientific' or objective concept but 'a "subjective" notion which, like "democracy" or "liberty", rests on a value judgement ... [made by] those who employ it'.[45]

What must now be considered is the ways in which dissident intellectuals translated the theoretical critique of totalitarianism into strategies for practical resistance during the two decades before 1989.

Alternatives to Totalitarianism

By the mid-1970s, a new optimism about the possibility of securing significant changes in the totalitarian system had developed amongst Polish dissident intellectuals in particular. The new mood was well illustrated in 1976 by Adam Michnik, whose prophetic outline of 'A New Evolutionism' sketched a resistance strategy that was to be deployed by the Polish Solidarity movement with brief but spectacular success. Banking on the reluctance of the Soviet Union to go to war with Poland, whilst also insisting that it would be folly for Poland to challenge Communist political hegemony, Michnik aimed to create an independent civil society existing side by side with totalitarian power. 'Such a programme', he explained, 'should give directives to the people on how to behave, not to the powers on how to reform themselves.'[46]

The gradualist resistance techniques Michnik proposed involved rejecting an underground of any kind. What proved to be his most inspired insight, however, was his prediction that a large number of Polish Communist Party members were pragmatists who could be counted on for passive sympathy, even though they would never be political allies.[47] For the hard core of the democratic opposition it was necessary to rely on the intelligentsia, whose duty was 'to formulate alternative programs and defend the basic principles'.[48] Echoing dissident opposition to the 'totalitarian lie' already noticed, Michnik insisted that, above all, the democratic opposition 'should renounce material profit and official esteem ... so that we can expect the truth from them'.[49]

As Z. A. Pelczynski has remarked, Michnik's resistance strategy gave a new lease of life to an 'upside-down, neo-Gramscian version of Gramsci' – a version, that is, which renounced any form of violent revolution and did not aim to take over the state, but nevertheless followed Gramscian strategy in pursuing a long process of public education for resistance.[50] The kind of social order which Michnik and other dissidents hoped to put in place of the existing one also shared Gramsci's utopian faith in the possibility of creating a social order free from conflict. In other respects, however, the ideal of dissident eastern European thinkers followed different lines.

When trying to clarify their goal, dissident thinkers did not generally turn to western parliamentary democracy for a model. The sentiments of Václav Havel, whose hatred of western technological civilization has already been noted, were typical: he dismissed the parliamentary system out of hand on the ground that it merely perpetuated the slavish mentality he abhorred. More attractive was the idea of a third way. Although this was differently conceived by Polish, Czech and Hungarian dissidents, it was generally associated with the ideal of personal authenticity supported by, for example, Husserl's student Jan Patočka, whose central concern was to reformulate the Platonic ideal of 'care of the soul'.[51] It was this ideal which led Patočka to become spokesman for Charter 77, the Czech human rights movement created in January 1977, a commitment for which he died after eight hours of police interrogation.[52] Ideally, Patočka maintained, provision for care of the soul should always be organically connected to the social order, as it was in the case of the

Greek polis, which was the first civilization to incorporate the free intellectual inquiry vital for it.[53] In times of crisis, however, the organic order may be destroyed, in which case philosophy has to assume the task of 'care' no longer provided for in the public realm.

In the modern period, the only kind of philosophy which can perform this task is phenomenology, since only this can challenge the tendency of the dominant scientific perspective to support a materialist outlook that reduces the entire universe to a meaningless collection of facts. The result is spiritual alienation, in the face of which men are prone to abandon responsibility, retreat inwardly, and seek consolation for their thwarted spirituality in orgiastic eruptions of the kind displayed in the modern western revolutionary tradition that has inspired the totalitarian regimes. Worse still, this irresponsible, escapist impulse encourages men to indulge in a nihilistic cult of war, both within the state and between states. What makes unending war the fate of western modernity, however, is above all the technological mentality which has shaped its view of the universe since at least the seventeenth century. The significance of the First World War, Patočka writes, lies precisely in the fact that it demonstrated

> that the transformation of the world into a laboratory for releasing reserves of energy accumulated over billions of years can be achieved only by means of wars...it swept aside all the 'conventions' that inhibited this release of energy...Why must the energetic transformation of the world take on the form of war? Because war...is the most intensive means for the rapid release of accumulated energies. Conflict is the great instrument which, mythologically speaking, Force uses in its transition from potency to actuality. In this process, humans as well as individual peoples serve merely as tools.[54]

Drawing on the thought of Husserl, Heidegger and Jünger in particular, Patočka maintained that the only antidote to this nihilism is the recovery of meaning and responsibility by a phenomenological analysis that sweeps aside the impersonal scientific perspective and replaces it with an ethic of human authenticity. Echoing Ernest Jünger, Patočka associated authenticity with the heroic spirit of sacrifice shown by soldiers in the trenches – a spirit which displayed the sense of solidarity he sought to awaken amongst his fellow countrymen in face of the totalitarian oppressor. It is in this way, then, that phenomenology provides for 'care of the soul' in an age of spiritual nihilism. Other European thinkers, it may be added, also turned, like Patočka, to phenomenology in order to support a similar ideal of authenticity. The work of the Polish philosopher and sociologist Karól Wojtyła, for example, is of particular interest for the theological standpoint from which he reformulated the phenomenological position.[55] There are, however, at least two major difficulties presented by the eastern European attempt to attack totalitarianism from the phenomenological point of view.

The first difficulty is that the attack on totalitarianism becomes indistinguishable from an attack on western modernity at large. It then ceases to offer a politically constructive programme, being in danger of collapsing into a romantic (albeit very refined and intellectual) drop-out cult. This difficulty, noted earlier in Havel's case, is accompanied by a second that applies more especially to what has been termed Patočka's 'boredom theory of war'. It is that the retreat from public to private life which he bemoans has been more commonly associated with the rise of a peaceful democratic and consumer ideal than with a militant one. Perhaps the fairest assessment of Patočka's gloomy and one-sided assault on modernity, however, is that of Roger Scruton, who remarked that 'If we understand Patočka, not as a philosopher of the modern consciousness [in general], but as a critic of the communist order', then his pessimistic writings may be seen to shed light on the extent of the spiritual disorientation produced by totalitarianism in eastern Europe.[56]

In contrast to Patočka's version of the third way, the more optimistic one developed by István Bibó is open to the charge of replacing an exaggerated pessimism by an equally untenable optimism. For Bibó, the concept of a third way was defined in opposition to the polarized structure imposed on western European politics by the French Revolution, which he maintained had reduced all subsequent politics to a struggle between Left and Right – between, that is, revolutionaries and reactionaries prepared to sanction violence to promote radical change or to oppose it. In between these poles the West has as yet been unable to identify a viable 'third way', mainly because of the mistaken assumption that liberalism and socialism are radically opposed to each other. In reality, socialism is the logical extension of liberalism, out of which it should emerge by way of organic growth rather than violent revolution. Bibó's vision is of a world which no longer stumbles, as east-central Europe thus far has, from one despotism to another but instead conducts experiments which 'humanize and moralize power in a durable and institutionalized way ... control it with elements of freedom, and as the final goal ... eliminate it'.[57] Unfortunately, this optimistic view of modern history, in which power is gradually replaced by the recognition of human dignity, owed less to irresistible historical trends than to Bibó's faith in the inevitability of a gradual translation of the original Christian ideal of equality into secular political practice.[58] For those without that faith, his political vision was less convincing.

In terms of political influence, however, the most significant version of the third way was the ideal of civil society developed by Polish and Czech dissidents in particular. This differed in at least three important respects from the one developed by western European thinkers. In the first place, the western concept was integrated into a concept of the state, whereas the eastern conception was of a body organized parallel to the state and independent of it. Secondly, the eastern concept presupposed a natural, pre-political harmony within civil society which is achieved without the need for any institutional structures such as that of law. Thirdly, the eastern concept was more closely associated with an 'anti-politics' of personal authenticity than with establishing the constitutional structure of a limited state. As György Konrád (author of *Antipolitics*[59]) wrote, 'I would not want to be a minister in any government whatever ... We must push the state out of our nightmares, so as to be afraid of it less. That is antipolitics.'[60]

The main problem presented by this 'antipolitics' is well illustrated by Václav Havel, who wrote in *The Power of the Powerless* that the totalitarian lie referred to earlier completely dehumanizes man by preventing him from 'living in truth'.[61] Confronted by this spiritual disaster, Havel's primary concern was not with anything as restricted as the rule of law, which is the central theme of the western European concept of civil association, but with salvation – 'the salvation of us all, of myself and my interlocutor equally'.[62] Salvation takes the form of moral regeneration, and it is this at which 'antipolitics' aims. Such a goal, Havel explains, can only be achieved by turning away from the modern world of science to the piety of the pre-scientific medieval world, a world which 'knows the dividing line between all that is intimately familiar and appropriately a subject for our concern, and that which lies beyond its horizon, that before which we should bow down humbly because it partakes of a mystery'.[63]

Although this was an inspiring position to adopt in opposition, the apolitical ideal of 'living in truth', echoing as it did the phenomeno-logical tradition of thought, provoked Havel's fellow countryman, Pietr Fidelius, to note the irony by which 'many a sworn opponent of a totalitarian "establishment" may (perhaps unconsciously) share its "spiritual" perspective'.[64] What Fidelius had in mind is the fact that the 'spiritual' nature of Havel's 'antipolitical politics' left no firm place for such prosaic things as political parties, constitutionalism, compromise and the other political characteristics of a pluralist social order.[65] From the spiritual standpoint, such things could easily appear as irrelevant, or even as divisive.

Amongst dissidents who, like Fidelius, rejected the antipolitics of the third way as a flight into apolitical idealism was the future Czech Prime Minister Václav Klaus, who once described the third way as 'the fastest way to the third world'.[66] Klaus attempted to achieve greater realism by radically redefining the concept of civil society in a way which extricated it from the romantic cult of authenticity and connected it instead to the free market. On the evening of 26 November 1989, he read a short document to the Czech Civic Forum which was subsequently adopted by the Forum as its pro-gramme.[67] In it, Klaus revealed the influence of western European thinkers like Hayek on his thought when he called for 'a new Czechoslovakia with the rule of law guaranteed by an independent judiciary, free elections at all levels, a market economy, social justice, respect for the environment and independent academic and cul-tural life'.[68]

Klaus's attempt to get rid of Havel's 'organic' or spiritualist concept of civil society and replace it by one which gave priority to economic issues, however, merely opened the door to a new problem. This was that faith in the power of the market to solve all problems was no more realistic than faith in the power of 'living in truth' to do so. The limitations of what is termed 'the new Czech liberalism' were made explicit in 1996, when Klaus informed the Mont Pèlerin Society that he did not wish to 'succumb to the kind of statist, interventionist, paternalistic social democracy that we see in so many free societies to the west of us'.[69] He had acknowledged two years earlier, however, that it is necessary in the initial stage of economic transformation 'to grant a large "constructing" role to the economic centre'.[70] Whether the market would ever become independent of the state intervention needed to create it was arguable, as was the issue of whether the state would in fact be prepared to withdraw. There was, in addition, the question of whether the social resistance generated by the hardships of the market would prove politically acceptable.

Above all, however, what Klaus failed to take into account was the possibility that Ralf Dahrendorf was right to suggest, in his *Reflections on the Revolution in Europe* (1990), that a rigid faith in free market ideology did not mark a complete break with the totalitarian system Klaus rejected. All it did, Dahrendorf claimed, was replace one all-embracing system with another. 'It is', Dahrendorf remarked about faith in the market system, 'a passive system to be sure, but one complete in itself and intolerant of untidy realities.'[71]

Other factors, related in particular to Catholic teaching and communitarian sentiment, provoked resistance to implementing the free market concept of civil society in Poland even among those who appeared committed to it in theory. Miroslaw Dzielski, the leader of neo-liberal Association for Free Enterprise in Cracow, for example, rejected central planning, expressed deep admiration for Mrs Thatcher and the free market, but also rejected the consumerism he feared an unregulated market would encourage. In order to raise the moral tone of capitalism, Dzielski required that income redistribution should be brought about through the market itself, rather than by the state.[72] Since this requirement could only be met by more self-denying saintliness than most Poles were likely to manage, however, it never represented a viable option.

Although the free market interpretation of civil society was more popular in Hungary,[73] where it fitted in with the relatively liberal economic policy of Kadar after 1956, it never worked well in practice. This was because an essentially partial compromise with the market resulted in 'a hybrid which is no longer central planning but not yet the market, and often combines the worst of both worlds'.[74] The lesson to be learned from Hungarian experience was that New Right theorists were correct in asserting that economic freedom could not exist without the political freedom which the regime refused to grant. Just how difficult this lesson was to draw, however, was evident from the fact that the Hungarian philosopher Mihàly Vajda – an admirer of István Bibó – persisted in maintaining, shortly before the collapse of the Soviet Union, that the most viable form of government for east-central Europe was what he termed 'the Hungarian alternative'. This alternative 'may leave all political power in the hands of the rulers, and at the same time allow a fair measure of independence for society as a whole'.[75] The impossibility of making this neat separation between the economic and the political realms was still not clear.

What is clear, then, is that the concept of civil society which dissident thinkers in east-central Europe opposed to the totalitarian order was never a very coherent alternative to it. This became painfully apparent in 1989, when they were suddenly compelled to cope with the problems of transition.

The Velvet Revolutions of 1989 and the Problem of Transition

If the revolutions of 1989 brought liberation from Soviet rule, they also exposed what has been described as a 'theoretical vacuum' at the heart of dissident thinking about the future political order.[76] The problem, as Michnik observed, was that dissident political ideas had been inspired by moral absolutism and therefore could not be used to construct a democratic order, since 'a democratic world is a chronically imperfect one'.[77] This also explained, he believed, the surprising speed with which former dissidents were almost entirely swept to one side after 1989. Commenting ruefully on their fate, Michnik observed that 'We are the children of a past epoch, museum pieces ... '.[78] Instead of being drawn from the former democratic opposition, 'The post-1989 political elite either came from the "grey zone" of sympathizers who for prudential reasons never made any open protest against the communist system or ... from the lower and middle ranks of the former *nomenklatura*.'[79]

As the east European states struggled to develop western European institutions such as political parties and free market institutions which many dissident eastern intellectuals had despised, three things were noticeable about the democratization process. The first was that western Europe did very little to ease the transition: no equivalent of the Marshall Plan, for example, was forthcoming. On the contrary, the west even refused to write off the huge debts incurred by many of the eastern Europe states during the 1970s,[80] while the Common Market quickly imposed shackles on eastern European exports. The second thing noticeable, as Tismaneanu observed, was that 'It was only after the disintegration of Yugoslavia and the velvet divorce ... of [the Czech Republic and Slovakia] that scholars and policy-makers realized that the liberal promise of these revolutions should not be taken for granted and that the aftermath of communism is not necessarily liberal democracy.'[81] Last but not least, what was particularly noticeable, in line with the point just made, was the rapid emergence of a conflict between the democratization process, on the one hand, and the quest for membership of the EU, on the other. In 2003, the three east-central states were officially signed up as full members, starting from the following year. What was likely to be the result?

From a fatalistic point of view, the future seemed reasonably clear. 'Ever since the collapse of the Austro-Hungarian Empire in 1918', Robert Bideleux and Ian Jeffries remarked, 'Eastern Europe has been an economic and power vacuum waiting to be filled, formerly by Germany and/or Russia, but since 1989 by Germany and/or the EU...The most likely outcome is German domination under EU auspices.'[82] If EU membership compromised the democratization process, Bideleux observed elsewhere, that might be no bad thing, since the EU is a fundamentally liberal project, whereas democracy in its eastern European forms has been quite compatible with oppression of minorities. Tony Judt, by contrast, was more critical of the search for early membership in the European Union, on the ground that it was likely to prevent an education in freedom by occupying 'the space that in other circumstances would be taken up by liberal and democratic projects'.[83] No sooner had eastern European states achieved independence, it seemed, than they were anxious to get rid of it once more, this time by voluntarily surrendering it to the new European empire. A more optimistic view might seek a compromise between these two standpoints, on the ground that the need to satisfy the liberal and democratic conditions for entry into the European Union might itself involve an education in limited politics, in some degree at least.

Conclusion

Looking back on the decades since 1945, and avoiding speculation about what the future may hold for east-central states, the most difficult question posed by the course of eastern European politics during the second half of the twentieth century concerns the interpretation of what actually happened in 1989. More precisely, 'The crucial question to be addressed', Vladimir Tismaneanu writes, 'is: Were the events of 1989 genuine revolutions?'[84] It is said that when Mao-Tse Tung was asked what he thought was the meaning of the French Revolution, he replied that it was too early to say. Three views, nevertheless, are worth pondering.

According to the first, the revolutions of 1989 were genuine revolutions, in the sense of constituting the beginning of a moral and spiritual rebirth. This was the interpretation adopted by, for example, Misha Glenny, the BBC's central European correspondent, who describes how he wept quietly as he listened to Dubcek emerge from political obscurity to address the crowd.[85] An equally sweeping affirmation of the revolutionary nature of the events of 1989 was provided by Bruce Ackerman, for whom they marked 'the re-emergence of liberal revolution as a world-historical possibility'.[86] By 'liberal' revolution, Ackerman explained, he meant a moderate, constructive, essentially non-totalistic, non-utopian sort, unlike the radical kind favoured by communists and fascists. 'In spite of the tragic consequences of revolutionary mobilizations since 1917', he wrote,

> the century closes with a great affirmation: men and women *can* make a new beginning and build a better world – one that won't look anything like utopia but that still promises more diversity and freedom than the grim bureaucratic tyranny it has replaced.[87]

At the opposite extreme to these interpretations is the sceptical view of Tony Judt, for example, for whom the collapse of the Soviet Union was not a revolution of any kind but merely served to accentuate internal problems of east European states which had previously been contained by the imperial system. What happened, more precisely, was that the end of Soviet power 'left a vacuum into which ethnic particularism, nationalism, nostalgia, xenophobia, and ancient quarrels could flow ... Together with religious affiliation, ... they and the past they describe and represent have returned to haunt and distort postcommunist politics and memory.'[88] What was easily forgotten by those who admired the idealism of Havel and other dissidents, Judt observed, was that it had no significant impact on the masses. In Czechoslovakia, for example, 'just 1,864 persons in a population of 15 million signed Charter 77'.[89]

Judt's scepticism is bolstered by that of Vladimir Tismaneanu, who opposes to the somewhat simplistic reading of the revolutions offered by Ackerman and other liberal enthusiasts, a sober stress on their essentially complex and ambiguous nature. 'Very few analysts insisted', Tismaneanu remarked,

> on the less visible, but nonetheless persistent illiberal and neo-authoritarian components of the anticommunist upheaval in the East. Carried away by the exhilarating effects of the revolutionary turmoil, most observers preferred to gloss over the heterogeneous nature of the anticommunist movements: not all those who rejected Leninism did it because they were dreaming of an open society and liberal values. Among the revolutionaries were quite a few enragés, ill-disposed towards the logic of compromise and negotiation. There were also populist fundamentalists, religious dogmatics, nostalgics of the procommunist regimes, including those who admired pro-Nazi dictators like Romania's Ion Antonescu and Hungary's Miklos Horthy.[90]

There is, finally, a third view of the events of 1989 which occupies a viable halfway house between liberal optimism and Namierite scepticism. This is represented by, for example, Robert Bideleux and Ian Jeffries, according to whom 1989 was indeed a revolution in the sense that 'the collapse of communist rule in Eastern Europe marked the termination of one of the most extreme expressions of the various "modernist" projects set in motion by the Renaissance and the Enlightenment', but immediately add that it is still 'too soon to proclaim the end of the modernist project' in its entirety, since it may be unwittingly perpetuated by those who believe, for example, that the market can solve all life's problems. If there is a lesson to be learned from the events of 1989, they conclude, it is not a novel one, although it is none the worse for that. It is, they write, the need to beware 'of doctrines claiming to have found the universal cognitive keys and panaceas'.[91]

7

Towards a New
Post-Democratic Agenda?

What conclusion, then, emerges about the postwar western European democratic project? Few political thinkers would deny that it has achieved much in the way of rights, welfare provision and, to a lesser extent, an accommodation with cultural pluralism. To the optimistic eye of an American observer, indeed, the overall result has been nothing short of a triumphant success, culminating in the creation of a united Europe which 'really has emerged as a paradise', free from nationalist strife and blood feuds, as well as military competition and arms races.[1] To more sceptical commentators, however, this view was unduly optimistic. The reality was that by the end of the twentieth century the nationally based democratic project of earlier decades had run its course, while the implications of creating a supra-national European future remained deeply uncertain. As one sceptic put it, the project had ended with what 'the ancients would have called elective oligarchies',[2] with only qualified consolation to be found in the prospect of a supra-national political order which might ensure the survival of rights, welfare and cultural pluralism only at the cost of finally abandoning the ideal of democratic self-government. Before considering more closely what a supra-national European political order might involve, however, it is necessary to notice the considerations which had led, by the end of the twentieth century, to a widespread sense of disillusion with the democratic project in its national form.

It is true, a thoughtful historian remarked at the end of the century, that many Europeans remain committed to democracy. But that, Mark Mazower contends, is only because they associate it with an apolitical ideal of prosperity and consumer choice. It is for this reason, he adds, that there is no contradiction in the co-existence of 'both high levels of support for democracy in cross-national opinion polls and high rates of political apathy'.[3]

A further reason for disillusion was alienation from national institutions caused by the fact that 'National parliaments are increasingly marginal to the processes of government, and only a small fraction of the huge volume of government business is scrutinised by elected parliaments in most Western liberal democracies.'[4] As Chantal Mouffe noted, alienation was intensified by the fact that an increasing number of people simply 'feel that traditional parties have ceased to take their interests into account', with the result that 'extreme right-wing parties are making significant inroads in many European countries. Even among those who are resisting the call of the demagogues, moreover, there is a marked cynicism about politics and politicians, and this has a very corrosive effect on popular adhesion to democratic values.'[5]

For Jürgen Habermas, the principal source of concern was what he termed the 'abdication of politics' by European nation-states, by which he referred to an increasing willingness to accept 'a chronically high level of unemployment and the dismantling of the welfare state as the price to be paid for international competitiveness'. In an ominous passage, Habermas maintained that

the sources of social solidarity are drying up, with the result that social conditions of the former Third World are becoming commonplace in the urban centers of the First World. These trends are crystallizing in the phenomenon of a new 'underclass'... [comprising] those pauperized groups who are left to fend for themselves, although they are no longer in a position to improve their social lot through their own initiative.[6]

Habermas' concern about the rise of a new underclass and the more general decline of civil society was shared by other thinkers, who maintained that well-intentioned attempts to arrest the decline have been largely counterproductive, merely producing a bureaucratic system of benign service agencies which threatens to transform citizens into passive consumers.[7]

Last but not least, the postwar democratic project has been undermined by the process of globalization, which has called into question the sovereignty of the nation-state it originally took for granted. By the end of the twentieth century, as Habermas put it, globalization

> of commerce and communication, of economic production and finance, of the spread of technology and weapons, and above all of ecological and military risks, pose[d] problems that can no longer be solved within the framework of nation-states or by the traditional method of agreements between sovereign states.[8]

What, if must be asked, can be done to arrest the disintegration of the postwar democratic project? An initial answer is suggested by the prophetic vision of George Santayana. Only a few years after the Second World War, Santayana claimed that Europe's great need was for the creation of a post-national 'liberal empire' which would supersede parliamentary democracy. The latter, he believed, has ceased to be an appropriate form of government for the modern industrial age, in which ease of transport and communication means that men are 'positively crying out for a universal government, and almost creating it against all national will'.[9] Although this universal government will not be democratic, it will have the more important advantage of being rational. It will be rational, Santayana maintained, by virtue of three characteristics.

The first characteristic is that the liberal empire does not promote moral or religious beliefs but is primarily concerned with the economic order, in which it is committed to helping men achieve not only security and prosperity but also satisfaction in their work. It does this through a post-parliamentary form of limited government which is 'autocratic but not totalitarian'.[10] Although an independent judiciary is a desirable feature of the liberal empire, its independence would be at the discretion of the executive.[11] Secondly, the liberal empire will be enlightened and impartial, in the sense that it will 'speak for the material conditions imposed by nature on the realisation of an ideal without dictating to any person or society what its ideal should be'.[12] The liberal empire is tolerant, that is to say, of every manner of spiritual diversity. Thirdly, the rulers 'would be selected, not by popular elections, but by co-option among the members of each branch of the [state] service, as promotion normally ensues in armies, banking-houses, universities, or ecclesiastical hierarchies'.[13] Although parties and elected assemblies may exist, they are acceptable only when they reflect a moral consensus amongst broad sections of the populace. Given such a consensus, Santayana believed, the liberal empire can dispense with the classic ideal of negative liberty since that only made sense so long as unrepresentative forms of dynastic government survived.

Suggestive as Santayana's post-national vision may be, he failed to explain convincingly how the technocratic rulers of the liberal empire are to achieve legitimacy in the absence of any democratic basis for their power. Since it is this problem – that is, the notorious 'democratic deficit' – which continues to be the main difficulty encountered by European integration, it is necessary to consider whether a genuinely democratic concept of European political identity is possible, or whether claims by defenders of the European Union that it is moving in that direction merely transfer the early twenty-first century's problems of political apathy, social division, atomization and failed welfare provision from national to supra-national level.

The Nature of European Political Identity

Scepticism about the possibility of a democratic form of European political identity is particularly strong among thinkers who believe that a spontaneous, non-coercive political identity can only flourish in the basically homogeneous moral and cultural community which they believe that only the nation-state can provide. This sentiment, which earlier chapters explored in some detail in the case of contemporary French and German thinkers, is echoed by contemporary British Eurosceptics. Notable amongst them is Anthony Smith, who maintains that while it is possible to create a European political bond which transcends the limits of national unity, such a bond is inevitably synonymous with soulless bureaucratization.

Unlike Smith, Julius Evola maintains that a European form of nationalism is not only possible but is in fact inescapable. For him, 'Euronationalism' is indeed the very core of European political identity, the essence of which consists in a timeless European moral essence that lies hidden beneath the diverse surface of European cultures. The problem, as Evola himself admits, is that everyone has a different idea about what this moral essence actually is.[14] This does not, however, deter him from putting forward his own dogmatic definition of it as the manifestation of an eternal, organic and hierarchical Tradition based on aristocratic warrior values. In short, although

Evola's Euronationalism offers an alternative to the soulless bureacracy envisaged by Anthony Smith, it does so only by envisaging a European political order only likely to appeal to a tiny handful of Nietzschean romantics.

More appealing than the bureaucratic and Euronationalist models of European political identity is Jürgen Habermas' attempt to extend his 'discourse' theory of democracy to the European Union by a modified version of the ideal of constitutional patriotism. The most relevant aspect of this enterprise is Habermas' contention that any viable concept of European political identity must be a 'thin' or formal one. As he emphasizes, an important implication of this conclusion is that it excludes the possibility that European unity can be based upon an ideal of community, of the kind associated with nationalist doctrine. Talk of Europe as a community, Habermas remarks, is fostered partly by the misleading idea that western European states share a common origin in the Middle Ages, and partly by an equally misleading tendency to think of a united Europe as a sort of super version of the nation-states created during the nineteenth century. The mistake in both cases consists of thinking of European political identity as grounded in a pre-political or 'natural' kind of community. In fact, Habermas holds, any political identity achieved at the European level must necessarily be artificial, in the sense that it will be the outcome of political action rather than of nature or a shared history. It must be based, more precisely, on a common commitment to the political principles of democracy and the constitutional state, which together yield the thin ideal of European political identity which Habermas describes as 'European constitutional patriotism'. A political identity of this kind, he insists, must not, and indeed cannot, be imposed on the diverse peoples of Europe from above, but must be expressed through different national cultures and traditions.[15]

Even if the European-wide communicative dialogue required to make Habermas' extended concept of democracy a reality could be achieved, it is difficult to accept that his thin concept of European political identity would have the emotional power to override conflicting national and local allegiances and interests. In particular, as the American sociologist Edward Shils has observed, Habermas' assumption that European constitutional patriotism entails the rejection of territorial frontiers appears to be no more than a piece of utopian yearning.[16] Behind it lies an impossible ideal of universality which is more likely to provoke national conflict rather than create the supra-national harmony to which Habermas aspires.

What remains to be considered is the model of European political identity favoured by the European Union itself. This is the model of civil association invoked in its 2001 *White Paper on European Governance*. Originally developed by Hobbes at national level, transfer of the civil model to supra-national level appears to offer a particularly attractive conception of European political identity because of its ability to accommodate diversity of every kind. It can do this, as Hobbes made clear, because civil association is held together not by a common faith or purpose but solely by the mutual commitment of its members to an authoritative body of rules, in the form of laws, together with the conditions necessary for making those rules, adjudicating them and securing compliance with them. It is, in short, because civil association is integrated not by directives or orders or commands, but only by rules which specify formal conditions to be observed, that it permits maximum social and cultural diversity.

What makes the civil model even more attractive to the European Union, however, is that its formal, rule-based nature fits well with the juridical style of politics that has been fostered by the integration project – a style aptly termed by Alec Stone 'governing with judges'. This juridical dimension of the integration project, Stone has argued, means that what is emerging is a new kind of supra-national constitutionalism. According to contemporary European constitutional theory, he explains, 'legislation, in order to be considered legally valid, must conform to the dictates of the constitution *as interpreted by constitutional courts*'.[17] What happens in practice is that

> Constitutional judges...routinely intervene in policy-making processes, establishing limits on legislative behaviour, but also drafting the precise terms of legislation. Further, the development of European constitutionalism has not been limited to national political systems, but has instead infected the politics of the European Community. The European Court of Justice, the constitutional court of the EC, has fashioned a kind of supra-national constitution, and this constitution binds – again – governments and the parliaments they control. European politics is today, in part, constitutional politics.[18]

This development may be especially welcomed in the vastly expanded European Union now being created, Robert Bideleux has argued, in so far as it permits the protection of minorities by legal and constitutional safeguards that eastern European states, for example, might otherwise fail to provide.[19] What is disturbing, however, is the fact that conferring on judges the power of constitutional review risks politicizing them, thereby destroying the independence and impartiality which are the condition for the legitimacy of the judiciary.

The greatest attraction which the civil model possesses for the European Union has yet to be noticed. Above all, its 2001 *White Paper on European Governance* invoked the civil model in the hope that it solved the problem of the democratic deficit without any need to adopt such inconvenient characteristics of national democracy as parliamentary accountability.[20] Instead of restraints of this kind, the White Paper maintained, the civil model offers democratization through a new, pluralist concept of sovereignty that reflects the emergence of multi-level, cross-national forms of rule which it terms 'governance' – a complex kind of rule, that is, over which the state no longer enjoys the monopoly it possessed in the past.[21]

Critics have not been slow to question the EU's claim that it is moving in a democratic direction. Civil association, they rightly maintain, is a constitutional rather than a democratic ideal. As such, it does not require the European Union to abandon the fundamentally elitest style of government which, as Larry Siedentop has remarked, it has inherited from France. Indeed, Siedentop insists, 'The European Union is a French creation. The major initiatives – from Schuman's plan for a Coal and Steel Community, through the Common Agricultural Policy, to the single currency – have been French and have served French interests.'[22] What is particularly disturbing about the French executive style of rule, another critic has remarked, is that it subverts democratic control not only at EU level but also at national level, by enabling national elites to move issues out of the area of parliamentary scrutiny into the non-accountable executive area.[23]

On balance, then, EU claims that 'governance' measures will democratize EU citizenship seem unlikely to be fulfilled. The possibility that they might create more democracy at sub-national than at supra-national level, however, has still to be considered. The optimistic view is that they will certainly do so if the EU implements the new, pluralist theory of sovereignty by supplementing centralized and hierarchical ways of distributing power by encouraging such local, decentralizing developments as 'Workplace democracy and parent governors at schools...corporatist representation of unions, employer organizations and professional associations...[and] consociational representation for given ethnic, linguistic, religious and cultural groups'. In principle at least, Richard Bellamy maintains, such mechanisms help to create a republican form of democracy in which 'On the one hand, all groups (including those asking for special consideration) are obliged to consult the broader interests and concerns of society as a whole. On the other, these same mechanisms operate as checks and balances on the purely self-interested or partial exercise of power.'[24]

Against Bellamy's optimism may be set the scepticism of, for example, Paul Magnette, for whom the governance measures proposed by the Commission may actually create a disincentive to democratization by increasing the complexity of the decision procedures. Yet another disincentive is created by the fact that the EU traditionally presents key policy decisions as the outcome of a consensus about which any further political disagreement is considered inappropriate, with the result that political parties in their familiar national form have no place. In these complicated and depoliticized conditions, Magnette concludes, 'citizenship in the European Union is likely to remain an elitist practice'.[25]

Although powerful arguments can be made in favour of a 'civil' interpretation of the European integration project, then, the civil ideal cannot solve the problem of democratic legitimation, as the EU hopes it will. The integration project remains, at most, only an indirectly democratic one, through the constitutions of member states. It may be objected, however, that this sceptical conclusion has emerged only because the principal condition for a European democratic political identity has not yet been considered. According to the model of political identity associated with Carl Schmitt, political unity is impossible without the relation between Friend and Foe. Applied to the European Union, this means that a democratic European political identity is perfectly conceivable, but only when there is an enemy in opposition to whom it can be defined. From this standpoint, the disappearance of the Soviet Union as the constitutive European 'other' has made not only European democracy, but a European political identity of any kind, unattainable until a new enemy (or series of enemies) is found. How tenable, one must ask, is this sceptical theory of political identity?

Schmitt is misleading in so far as he conceives unity in such simple, intensely organic terms that it can only be achieved through war with an essentially antagonistic 'other'. For those content with the more complex, less intense form of unity that peacetime involves, a less militant form of European political identity becomes conceivable. One important implication of Schmitt's position, however, is clearly correct, which is that far from being an unmixed blessing, the end of the Cold War has created what is in effect a European identity crisis. As Mark Mazower observed, it is no longer clear, in particular, whether Europe is part of the 'West', or is a western outcrop of 'Eurasia', or both, or neither.[26]

What is particularly disturbing in this connection is the possibility raised by Anthony Smith, which is that 'the process of pan-European identity formation' may have built into it 'the logic of cultural exclusion'. In that case, the danger is that 'of an increasingly affluent, stable, conservative but democratic European federation, facing, and protecting itself from, the demands and needs of groupings of states in Africa, Asia and Latin America'. To some extent, Smith adds, this prospect 'is still mitigated by the remaining ex-colonial ties between certain European and certain African or Asian states', but if the European project achieves its political goals, it will 'also entail, not just economic exclusion, but also cultural differentiation and with it the possibility of cultural and racial exclusion'.[27] The only way of avoiding this unpleasant version of the Schmittian model of European political identity is to abandon any dream of creating a deeper cultural one. As has already been remarked in connection with Habermas' European constitutional patriotism, however, a 'thin' political identity may lack the emotional power required to provide effective integration.

The Schmittian model has a further important implication for European identity, which is that the end of the Cold War not only meant that Europe lost its 'signficant other' but was also confronted by a radical change in its relation to the USA. At one level, as an American commentator put it, the change simply meant that the 'free ride' which Europe had received under the American security umbrella after 1945 was over.[28] At a deeper level, however, what the end of the Cold War meant was that the USA no longer automatically shared a common identity with Europe as part of 'the West'. Indeed, the possibility arose that Europe and the USA may in future become bitter opponents, as US relations with France and Germany over the Iraq war of 2003 indicated. Schmitt's theory of political identity, then, is a sobering reminder of political realities which Europhile optimism may easily overlook. In so far as solidarity between the

Europe and the US can be preserved without a common enemy of the kind which Schmitt's analysis presupposes, its creation and maintenance require not only political self-restraint but great diplomatic skill. Whether either Europe or the US possesses these resources on the appropriate scale has still to be determined.

At the deepest level of all, however, there still remains an issue posed by European political and cultural identity alike which has not yet been explicitly confronted. This concerns the limitations of a secular culture. More precisely, the question is whether such a culture can command significant loyalty from those subject to it, or has only a superficial hold on them. The answer is unclear, although the suspicion must be that the predominant mixture of materialist and nationalist sentiment provides, by its very nature, little consolation for the three issues which disturbed Buddha, viz. suffering, age and death. Whether it provided any secure obstacle to the disastrous quest for personal salvation through political action which inspired the totalitarian ideologies of the twentieth century is also a matter for doubt. The danger, more precisely, is that although the old 'universalist' ideologies on which totalitarianism previously relied may be in terminal decline, there is no guarantee that a new 'particularist' one, inspired perhaps by various kinds of identity politics, may not take their place.

Complacency, in short, would be foolish. But suppose, to end on a speculative note, that the European Union adopts the constitution drafted by Giscard d'Estaing's committee and the existence of a federal state is confirmed: What kind of European political identity is in fact likely to be created? That it will be a genuine state identity is not in doubt, despite the insistence by the British government that the constitution does no more than tidy up an existing non-federal organization, since European political unity will no longer rest on treaties but will hinge instead on acknowledgement of a constitution. With this change, Noel Malcolm has observed, 'the EU crosses the Rubicon, from something that could not legally be called a state to something that most definitely can'. The consitution, it is true, 'will be brought into being by treaty – but that will be a final, self-denying treaty, one that will repeal the treaties of Rome, Maastricht and so on and that will ensure that the authority of the EU will, from that moment onwards, no longer be treaty based'. Thereafter, 'the authority of the EU will be located entirely within 'its own governing document', and any disputes about that document will have to be

dealt with, not under international law, 'but by the EU's own constitutional court – whose powers will themselves be derived from the
EU's own authority'. It is true, Malcolm adds, that many federal
constitutions 'have phrases stating or implying that the powers of the
provinces were somehow prior; that some powers have passed to the
federal government; and that the rest remain with the provinces'.
Even if these claims are valid, however, the crucial point is that 'their
validity flows from, and depends on, the – federal – constitution'.
The fact that the word 'federal' has been removed from the constitution
as a sop to British sensitivities does not alter these facts.[29]

With this in mind, it may reasonably be assumed that the kind of
political identity to be created will consist of a combination of civil
association (notably, the formal or juridical aspect), *dirigisme* and
concessions, at a variety of levels, to the requirements of democratic
legitimation. The crucial issue, however, concerns the interpretation
given to these different elements and to the kind of balance struck
between them. So far as the democratic element is concerned, a sug-
gestion made by Giscard d'Estaing in the course of defending the
draft constitution confirms that this is unlikely to receive significant
concessions. There might be, he was reported to have said, a 'new
"citizens' initiative" under which groups of more than one million
citizens would be able to press the European Commission to propose
new, pan-European legislation'.[30] Quite how a million citizens could
place themselves in this position – especially on a cross-national basis –
was too pedestrian an issue for him to pursue.

It is tempting to seek consolation for the lack of democracy in the
idea that, in terms of overall balance, the EU might nevertheless be
a limited state, committed to the ideal of civil association. Robert
Bideleux, for example, has argued that the EU budget is so small (it
has not been allowed to exceed 1.27 per cent of the combined GDP
of its member states) that it has in effect been '*forced*...to remain an
essentially regulatory "civil association"'.[31] This is a false source of
comfort, however, for two reasons. One is that making regulations is
cheap, and is therefore not restricted by a small budget. The other
reason is more fundamental. It is the predominance amongst the
European political elite at large of an instrumental mode of thought
identified by a thoughtful commentator as

a mix of neo-functionalism and occasional federalism. That is to
say, technical (and not overly political) co-operation in some fields,

leading to further co-operation and integration in others through the guidance of determined élites and in a process focused on élite politics (neo-functionalism). From time to time, the option of appealing directly to the people, asking them to transfer power to a European constitution and parliament in a grand federal gesture has been exercised (federalism). But in the mix of neo-functionalism and federalism, the former has dominated over the latter.[32]

The problem created by the functionalist perspective is that it does not permit intrinsic value to be attributed to the forms and procedures which were central to the European ideal of civil association from the time of Hobbes, through de Tocqueville, to Hayek, Oakeshott and, it may be added, to Habermas. Bluntly put, functionalism permits the use of only a single political vocabulary, which is that of power. Power may of course be used benignly, and words and institutions associated with constitutionality and legitimacy may well survive. In this situation, it is possible to enjoy prosperity, personal security, welfare provision and the toleration of diversity, but individual liberty, which rest on a non-functional commitment, will be in a precarious position.

In short, the emerging form of European political identity, far from being either democratic or 'civil', may perhaps best be brought out by recalling the situation which existed in ancient Rome after the battle of Actium, when Augustus effected a revolutionary shift from republic to empire with such subtlety that few noticed the dramatic change that had occurred. More precisely, Augustus left the outward shell of all the old republican institutions intact while simultaneously introducing a variety of more or less invisible measures that reserved all final decisions to himself, thereby ensuring the old institutions could no longer operate as instruments of self-government.[33] For two centuries thereafter, Romans enjoyed an imperial golden age. They enjoyed it, however, by sacrificing *libertas* to non-accountable *imperium*.

Notes

Chapter 1: The Postwar Agenda

1. M. Mazower, *Dark Continent: Europe's Twentieth Century* (London: Allen Lane, 1998), pp. 3–4.
2. *The Times*, 18 November 1940.
3. E. H. Carr, *Conditions of Peace* (London: Macmillan, 1942), p. 9.
4. M. Mazower, *Dark Continent: Europe's Twentieth Century* (London: Allen Lane, 1998), p. xi.
5. The quotation is from a 1959 address which is reprinted in *The Crooked Timber of Humanity: Chapters in the History of Ideas*, H. Hardy (ed.) (New York: Knopf, 1991), p. 202.
6. B. Russell, *A History of Western Philosophy* (London: Allen & Unwin, 1946), p. 834.
7. T. D. Weldon, *The Vocabulary of Politics* (Baltimore: Penguin Books, 1953), p. 192.
8. For an excellent exploration of possible ways of distinguishing between analytical and Continental philosophy, see S. Critchley, *A Very Short Introduction to Continental Philosophy* (Oxford: OUP, 2001).
9. A. Schütz, 'On Multiple Realities', *Philosophy and Phenomenological Research*, vol. 5, no. 4 (June 1945), pp. 533–74.
10. G. Santayana, 'The Intellectual Temper of the Age', in N. Henfrey (ed.) *Selected Critical Writings of George Santayana*, vol. 2 (Cambridge: CUP, 1968), p. 5.
11. Ibid., p. 4.
12. Ibid., pp.14–15.
13. E. Laclau (ed.) *The Making of Political Identities* (London: Verso, 1994), p. 1.
14. A. MacIntyre, *After Virtue* (London: Duckworth, 1981), p. 2.
15. R. Dahendorf , in M. Howard and W. Roger Louis (eds) *The Oxford History of the Twentieth Century* (Oxford: OUP, 1998), p. 342.
16. J. Lacan, *Écrits: A Selection* (London: Tavistock Publications, 1977). See also B. Benvenuto and R. Kennedy, *The Works of Jacques Lacan: An Introduction* (London: Free Association Books, 1986).
17. T. Eagleton, *Literary Theory: An Introduction* (Oxford: Blackwell, 1994), p. 104.
18. See A. Mason, 'Communitarianism and its Legacy', in *Political Theory in Transition* (ed.) N. O'Sullivan (London: Routledge, 2000), pp. 19–32.

19. What Derrida actually says is that: 'To deconstruct the subject does not mean to deny its existence. There are subjects, "operations" or "effects" (*effets*) of subjectivity. This is an incontrovertible fact. To acknowledge this does not mean, however, that the subject is what it *says* it is. The subject is not some meta-linguistic substance or identity, some pure *cogito* of self-presence; it is always inscribed in language. My work does not, therefore, destroy the subject; it simply tries to resituate it.' J. Derrida, in Kearney, R. (ed.) *Dialogues With Contemporary Continental Thinkers* (Manchester: Manchester University Press, 1968), p. 125. Original italics.

20. G. Barraclough, *An Introduction to Contemporary History* (Harmondsworth: Penguin Books, 1964), p. 152.

21. Quoted in M. Mazower, *Dark Continent: Europe's Twentieth Century* (London: Allen Lane, 1998), p. 326.

22. M. Mazower, *Dark Continent: Europe's Twentieth Century* (London: Allen Lane, 1998), pp. 330–1.

23. Ibid., p. 330. On the French and German concepts of citizenship, see R. Brubaker, *Citizenship and Nationhood in France and Germany* (Cambridge, Massachusetts: Harvard University Press, 1992).

24. M. Mazower, *Dark Continent: Europe's Twentieth Century* (London: Allen Lane, 1998), p. 330.

25. Ibid., p. 325.

26. See John Gray, 'The Politics of Cultural Diversity', *Salisbury Review*, vol. 7, no. 1 (1988).

27. Editorial commentary, the *Political Quarterly*, special issue on 'Being British', vol. 71, no. 1, January–March 2000, p. 2.

28. Ibid.

29. J. C. D. Clark (ed.) *Ideas and Politics in Modern Britain* (London: Macmillan, 1990), p. 32.

30. On the French and German concepts of citizenship, see R. Brubaker, *Citizenship and Nationhood in France and Germany* (Cambridge, Massachusetts: Harvard University Press, 1992).

31. G. Lichtheim, *Europe in the Twentieth Century* (London: Sphere Books, 1974), p. 417.

32. Ibid., p. 418.

33. P. Valéry, *Reflections on the World Today* (trans.) F. Scarfe (London: Thames and Hudson, 1951), p. 22.

34. Ibid., pp. 21–2. Italics in the original text.

35. Ibid., p. 22.

36. P. F. Drucker, *The Age of Discontinuity* (NY: Harper and Row, 1978, first published 1968), p. 81.

37. Ibid.

38. J. Maritain, *Man and the State* (Chicago: University of Chicago Press, 1951), p. 190.

39. A. S. Milward, *The European Rescue of the Nation-State* (London: Routledge, 1992), p. 4.

40. Ibid., p. 4.

41. Ibid., p. 45.

42. Ibid., p. 19.

43. For a powerful critique of Milward and a defence of the federalist case, see M. Burgess, *Federalism and European Union: The Building of Europe, 1950–2000* (London: Routledge, 2000), pp. 56–76.

44. R. Bideleux, '"Europeanisation" and the Limits to Democratisation in East-Central Europe', in G. Pridham and A. Ágh (eds) *Prospects for Democratic Consolidation in East-Central Europe* (Manchester: Manchester University Press, 2001), p. 29.

45. J. Laughland, *The Tainted Source: The Undemocratic Origins of the European Idea* (London: Warner Books, 1998), p. 12.

46. J. Laughland, *The Tainted Source: The Undemocratic Origins of the European Idea* (London: Warner Books, 1998), pp. 14–15.

47. Ibid., p. 15.

48. Ibid., p. 19.

49. Ibid., p. 36.

50. Ibid., p. 27.

51. See I. Deák, J. T. Gross and T. Judt (eds) *The Politics of Retribution in Europe* (NJ: Princeton University Press, 2000).

52. Ibid., p. 297.

53. Ibid., p. 297.

54. Ibid., p. 298.

55. Ibid., p. 304.

56. T. Judt, review of J. Semprun, *Literature or Life* (USA: Penguin, 1998), *TLS*, 27 February 1998.

57. See A. Milward, *TLS*, 14 April 2000, p. 7.

58. In R. Burns (ed.) *German Cultural Studies* (Oxford: OUP, 1995), p. 213.

Chapter 2: British Political Thought since 1945: The Limitations of Pragmatism

1. E. Voegelin, 'The Oxford Political Philosophers', *The Philosophical Quarterly*, vol. 3, no. 11 (April 1953), p. 101.

2. Ibid., p. 101.

3. T. D. Weldon, *States and Morals: A Study in Political Conflict* (London: Murray, 1946), p. 39.

4. E. Voegelin, 'The Oxford Political Philosophers', *The Philosophical Quarterly*, vol. 3, no. 11 (April 1953), p. 113.

5. A. Quinton, *Political Philosophy* (Oxford: OUP, 1967), p. 1.

6. E. Gellner, *Thought and Change* (London: Weidenfeld and Nicolson, 1964), p. 35.

7. Ibid., p. 35.

8. Ibid., p. 39.

9. P. Laslett, *Philosophy, Politics and Society* (ed.) (Oxford: Blackwell, 1956), pp. vii–ix.

10. J. Plamenatz, 'The Use of Political Theory', in A. Quinton, *Political Philosophy* (Oxford: OUP, 1967), p. 25.

11. Ibid., p. 29.
12. H. Laski, *Reflections on the Constitution* (Manchester: Manchester University Press 1951), p. 9.
13. J. Strachey, *Contemporary Capitalism* (London: Gollancz, 1956), p. 276.
14. R. H. S. Crossman (ed.) *New Fabian Essays* (London: Dent, 1952; ref. is to the 1970 edn), p. 26.
15. On the British dream of the New Jerusalem, see C. Barnett, *The Audit of War* (London: MacMillan, 1986).
16. R. Barker, *Political Ideas in Modern Britain* (London: Methuen, 1978), p. 185. Barker is referring in particular to Titmuss' *Essays on the Welfare State* (2nd edn, 1963), p. 231.
17. T. H. Marshall, *Citizenship and Social Class* (Cambridge: CUP, 1950), pp. 56–7.
18. B. Wootton, *Political Quarterly*, vol. XXIV, 1953, p. 66.
19. R. Williams, *The Long Revolution* (The ref. is to the 1965 Penguin edn. The first edn was in 1961), p. 330.
20. C. A. R. Crosland, *The Future of Socialism* (London: Cape, 1964. First published, 1956), p. 346. Italics in the original.
21. E. Roberts, *Workers' Control* (London: Allen & Unwin, 1973), p. 210.
22. N. Poulantzas, in an exchange with Ralph Miliband in R. Blackburn (ed.) *Ideology in Social Science* (London: Fontana, 1975), p. 250. See also ch. 8, 'The New Capitalism', by R. Blackburn.
23. E. P. Thompson *et al.*, *Out of Apathy* (London: Stevens, 1960), p. 194.
24. D. Miller, *Market, State and Community: Theoretical Foundations of Market Socialism* (Oxford: Clarendon Press, 1989).
25. For an introduction, see J. Shearmur, *The Political Thought of Karl Popper* (London: Routledge, 1996).
26. G. R. G. Mure, 'The Organic State', *Philosophy*, vol. 24 (1949), p. 206.
27. K. Popper, *The Poverty of Historicism* (London: Routledge, 1961), p. 68.
28. I. Berlin, 'The Originality of Machiavelli', *Against the Current* (London: OUP, 1981), p. 68.
29. Ibid., pp. 74–5.
30. I. Berlin, *Four Essays on Liberty* (London: OUP, 1969), p. 166.
31. M. Ignatieff, 'Understanding Fascism?', in E. and A. Margalit (eds) *Isaiah Berlin: A Celebration* (London: Hogarth Press, 1991), pp. 135–45.
32. Q. Skinner, 'A Third Concept of Liberty', *London Review of Books* (4 April 2002), pp. 16–18.
33. K. Haakonssen, 'Republicanism', in *A Companion to Political Philosophy* (Oxford: Blackwell, 1999), p. 572.
34. M. Cranston, 'Postscriptum', in G. Feaver and F. Rosen (eds) *Lives, Liberties and the Public Good* (London: MacMillan, 1987), p. 254.
35. B. Parekh, *Contemporary Political Thinkers* (Oxford: Martin Robertson, 1982), p. 46.
36. I. Berlin, *Four Essays on Liberty* (London: OUP, 1969), p. xlix, fn. 1. Italics in the original.
37. H. L. Hart, *The Concept of Law* (London: OUP, 1961).
38. I. Berlin, *Four Essays on Liberty* (London: OUP, 1969), p. 164.

194

Notes

39. 'It would not, I think, be an exaggeration to say that no political movement today, *at any rate outside the western world*, seems likely to succeed unless it allies itself to national sentiment.' Berlin, *Against the Current* (London: OUP, 1981), p. 355. (Italics added).

40. For a useful bibliography, see C. Kukathas, *Hayek and Modern Liberalism* (Oxford: OUP, 1990). See also A. Gamble, *Hayek* (Oxford: Polity, 1996).

41. F. Hayek, *New Studies in Philosophy, Politics, Economics and the History of Ideas* (London: Routledge and Kegan Paul, 1978), p. 253.

42. See, for example, J. Shklar, *After Utopia* (Princeton: Princeton University Press, 1957).

43. See, for example, C. Kukathas, *Hayek and Modern Liberalism* (Oxford: OUP, 1990), esp. ch. 6.

44. See M. Forsyth, 'Hayek's Bizarre Liberalism', *Political Studies*, vol. XXXVI (1988), pp. 235–50, 246–7.

45. F. A. Hayek, *The Constitution of Liberty* (London: Routledge and Kegan Paul, 1960), p. 62.

46. I. Kristol, 'Capitalism, Socialism and Nihilism', *The Public Interest*, vol. 31 (1973), p. 12.

47. F. A. Hayek, *The Constitution of Liberty* (London: Routledge and Kegan Paul, 1960), p. 21.

48. R. N. Berki, *On Political Realism* (London: Dent, 1981), pp. 216–17.

49. M. Oakeshott, *Rationalism in Politics* (Indianapolis: Liberty Press, 1991), p. 399.

50. Ibid., pp. 41–2.

51. Ibid., p. 41.

52. Ibid., p. 388 ('conversation') and p. 433 ('referee').

53. M. Oakeshott, *On Human Conduct* (Oxford: Clarendon Press, 1975), pp. 146–7.

54. M. Oakeshott, *On History* (Oxford: Blackwell, 1983), p. 160. Italics in the original.

55. Ibid.

56. B. Crick, *In Defence of Politics*, revised edn (Harmondsworth: Penguin, 1964), p. 15.

57. On British leftwing intellectuals after Stalin, see M. Kenny, *The First New Left* (London: Lawrence and Wishart, 1995). On R. D. Laing, see D. Martin's essay in M. Cranston (ed.) *The New Left* (London: The Bodley Head, 1970), pp. 179–208.

58. R. D. Laing, *The Politics of Experience and the Bird of Paradise* (Harmondsworth: Penguin Books, 1967), p. 31. The answer to Laing's rhetorical question is of course that nothing would separate us – but only because we had ceased to exist as separate beings, *and hence to exist at all*. So far as Laing ever succeeded in envisaging any viable approximation to this impossible ideal, he did so not in his theorizing but in his life, when he retreated to an oriental monastery for several years.

59. B. Barry's *Political Argument* (London: Routledge, 1965) has as its objective the creation of 'a detailed casuistry of political principles', p. xviii.

60. Ibid., p. 290, fn. 1.

61. Ibid., p. 290.
62. Ibid., p. xviii.
63. B. Barry, *Justice as Impartiality* (Oxford: OUP, 1996), p. 3.
64. Ibid., p. 152.
65. D. Miller, 'Recent Theories of Social Justice', *British Journal of Political Science,* vol. 21 (1991), p. 376.
66. G. Newey, *After Politics: The Rejection of Politics in Contemporary Liberal Philosophy* (London: Palgrave, 2001), p. 155. Italics in the original.
67. For this criticism of liberalism, see in particular C. Mouffe, *The Return of the Political* (London: Verso, 1993).
68. G. Newey, 'The Political Form of the Constitution: The Separation of Powers, Rights and Representative Democracy', in R. Bellamy and D. Castiglione (eds) *Political Studies,* vol. 44, no. 3 (Special Issue on 'Constitutionalism in Transformation'), p. 436.
69. R. Scruton, 'In Defence of the Nation', in J. C. Clark (ed.) *Ideas and Politics in Modern Britain* (London: Macmillan, 1990), p. 55.
70. Ibid., p. 59.
71. R. Scruton, *The Meaning of Conservatism* (Harmondsworth: Penguin Books, 1980), p. 25.
72. Ibid., p. 120.
73. D. Miller, *On Nationality* (Oxford: OUP, 1995).
74. M. Canovan, *Nationhood and Political Theory* (Cheltenham: Edward Elgar, 1996), p. 14.
75. J. Gray, *Post-liberalism* (London: Routledge, 1993), p. 288.
76. J. Gray, *Enlightenment's Wake* (London: Routledge, 1995), p. 67.
77. Ibid., p. 125.
78. Ibid., p. 279.
79. J. Gray, *Two Faces of Liberalism* (Cambridge: Polity Press, 2000), pp. 6–7.
80. A. Phillips, 'Dealing with Difference: A Politics of Ideas or a Politics of Presence?' *Constellations,* vol. 1, no. 1 (April 1994), pp. 74–91.
81. Ibid., p. 75.
82. Ibid., p. 77.
83. Ibid., pp. 75–6.
84. C. Mouffe, *The Return of the Political* (London: Verso, 1993), p. 88.
85. Ibid., p. 83.
86. Ibid., p. 84.
87. Ibid., pp. 84–5.
88. M. Ignatieff, 'Identity Parades', *Prospect* (April 1998), p. 19.
89. Raz, J. (1994) 'Multiculturalism: A Liberal Perspective', *Dissent,* Winter, p. 68.
90. Ibid., p. 68.
91. Ibid., p. 69.
92. Ibid., p. 69.
93. Ibid., p. 77.
94. Ibid., p. 74.
95. Raz, J. (ed.) (1990) *Authority* (Oxford: Blackwell), p. 13.
96. Raz, J. (1979) *The Authority of Law* (Oxford: Clarendon Press), pp. 10–11.

97.   B. Parekh, *Rethinking Multiculturalism* (Basingstoke: Macmillan, 2000), p. 3.
98.   Ibid., p. 3.
99.   Ibid., p. 167.
100. B. Parekh, 'The Cultural Particularity of Liberal Democracy', *Political Studies*, vol. XL, 1992 (Special Issue on *Prospects for Democracy* D. Held (ed.)), p. 175.
101. B. Parekh, *Rethinking Multiculturalism* (Basingstoke: Macmillan, 2000), p. 195.
102. Ibid., p. 262.
103. Ibid., p. 263.
104. Ibid., p. 263.
105. B. Parekh, 'The Cultural Particularity of Liberal Democracy', *Political Studies*, vol. XL, 1992 (Special Issue on *Prospects for Democracy* D. Held (ed.)), p. 171.
106. Ibid., p. 175.
107. Ibid., p. 174.
108. S. Žižek, *Did Somebody Say Totalitarianism?* (London: Verso, 2001), p. 238.
109. D. Miller, 'Citizenship and Pluralism', *Political Studies*, vol. 43, no. 3 (September 1995) p. 449.
110. R. Bellamy, 'The Political Form of the Constitution: The Separation of Powers, Rights and Representative Democracy', in R. Bellamy and D. Castiglione (eds) *Political Studies*, vol. 44, no. 3, 1996 (Special Issue on 'Constitutionalism in Transformation'), p. 456.
111. Q. Skinner, *Liberty Before Liberalism* (Cambridge: Cambridge University Press, 1998). See also P. Pettit, *Republicanism: A Theory of Freedom and Government* (Oxford: Clarendon Press, 1997).
112. Q. Skinner, 'The Republican Ideal of Political Liberty', in M. Rosen and J. Wolff (eds) *Political Thought* (Oxford: OUP, 1999), p. 171.
113. G. Brown, *The Times*, 11 January 2001, p. 22.
114. Ibid., p. 22.
115. Ibid., p. 22.
116. D. Held, 'Democracy and the Global System', in D. Held (ed.) *Political Theory Today* (Cambridge: Polity Press, 1991), p. 234.
117. *Daily Telegraph* (19 April 2002). What incurred the special ire of the conservative press was that a child tax credit for six million families, the biggest new benefit introduced by the budget, was so structured that even couples on a combined income of £66,000 a year would be eligible to receive nearly £550 a year if they had children under one year old.
118. J. Bartholomew, 'Gordon Brown, the Man who Means-tested a Nation', in *Daily Telegraph*, 19 April 2002.
119. The outcome on this view, it is said, is not a form of civil association but a new medievalism: see for example the French thinker, Mink, quoted in A. Giddens' *Third Way*, and also A. Giddens' quote from J. Gray, in the same book.
120. Interview with Blair, *Prospect*, no. 77 (August 2002), p. 19.

121. M. Phillips, *Sunday Times*, 9 July 2000.
122. J. Dunn, *The Cunning of Unreason* (London: Harper Collins, 2000), pp. 362–3.
123. R. Dworkin, 'Constitutionalism and Democracy', *European Journal of Philosophy*, vol. 3 (1995), p. 2.
124. R. Bellamy, 'The Political Form of the Constitution: The Separation of Powers, Rights and Representative Democracy', *Political Studies*, vol. 44, no. 3, Special Issue 1996, p. 436.
125. Sir John Baker, in *Daily Telegraph*, 10 December 2003.
126. T. Prosser, 'Understanding the British Constitution', in *Political Studies*, vol. 44, no. 3, Special Issue 1996, p. 474.
127. Ibid.
128. Ibid., p. 480.
129. *Political Quarterly*, vol. 71, no. 1, January–March 2000, p. 1.
130. R. Bellamy, 'The Political Form of the Constitution: The Separation of Powers, Rights and Representative Democracy', *Political Studies*, vol. 44, no. 3, Special Issue 1996, p. 436.
131. K. Kumar, *The Making of English National Identity* (Cambridge: CUP, 2003), p. 273.
132. D. Marquand, *Prospect* (June, 1999). Reprinted in *The National Interest* (Fall 1999), p. 40.
133. K. Minogue, *Citizenship and Monarchy: A Hidden Fault Line in Our Civilisation* (University of London: Institute of United States Studies, 1998), p. 27.
134. R. Scruton, *England: An Elegy* (London: Pimlico, 2001), pp. 254–5.
135. Noel Malcolm, 'A Federal Constitution with the Heart of a Manifesto', *Daily Telegraph*, 28 July 2003.

Chapter 3: From Revolutionary Idealism to Political Moderation: The French Search for an Accommodation with Liberal Democracy since 1945

1. S. Khilnani, *Arguing Revolution: The Intellectual Left in Postwar France* (New Haven and London: Yale University Press, 1993), p. 180. I have learned a great deal from this excellent book.
2. M. Merleau-Ponty, *Sens et non-sens* (Paris: Nagel, 1948), trans. as *Sense and Non-Sense* by H. L. and P. A. Dreyfus (Evanston: Northwestern University Press, 1964), pp. 149–50.
3. J.-P. Sartre, 'The Responsibility of the Writer', in D. Hardman (ed.) *Reflections on Our Age* (London: Allan Wingate, 1948), p. 76.
4. M. Merleau-Ponty, *Sens et non-sens* (Paris: Nagel, 1948), trans. as *Sense and Non-Sense* by H. L. and P. A. Dreyfus (Evanston: Northwestern University Press, 1964), p. 140.
5. N. Bobbio, *The Philosophy of Decadentism: A Study in Existentialism* (Oxford: Blackwell, 1948), p. 59.

6. J.-P. Sartre, *Being and Nothingness* (Eng. trans., London: Methuen, 1958. First published 1943, Gallimard), p. 617.
7. Ibid., p. 615.
8. G. Marcel, *The Philosophy of Existence* (London: Harvill Press, 1948), pp. 52–4.
9. Ibid., p. 41.
10. Ibid., p. 74.
11. Quoted by G. Marcel, *The Philosophy of Existence* (London: Harvill Press, 1948), p. 75.
12. J.-P. Sartre, *Critique of Dialectical Reason* (London: Verso, 1976), pp. 52–3.
13. Ibid., p. 637.
14. P. Rosanvallon, 'Le socialisme francais et la peur de la social-démocratie', in *Faire*, Qu'est-ce que c'est la Social-Démocratie?, Paris (1979), p. 8.
15. E. Mounier, 'Reflections on an Apocalyptic Age', in D. Hardman (ed.) *Reflections on Our Age* (London: Allan Wingate, 1948), p. 28.
16. Ibid., p. 33.
17. Ibid., p. 32.
18. Ibid., p. 31.
19. Quoted by R. W. Rauch, Jr, in his foreword to E. Mounier, *Personalism* (London: Routledge, 1952), p. xii (First published in France in 1950, as *Le Personnalisme*).
20. For Mounier's influence on Delors and Schuman, see J. Laughland, *The Tainted Source* (London: Warner, 1998), pp. 62–6.
21. See, for example, L. Colletti's critique of Althusser in *New Left Review*, no. 86 (July–August 1974), esp. p. 17.
22. L. Althusser, *Lenin and Philosophy and Other Essays* (London: NLB, 1971), p. 13.
23. Ibid., p. 21.
24. J. Pasqualini, *Prisonnier de Mao* (Paris: Gallimard, 1975). See also C. and J. Broyelle and E. Tschirhart, *Deuxième Retour de Chine* (Paris: Seuil, 1977).
25. For G. Lipovetsky's interpretation of 1968, see for example his essay 'May '68, or the Rise of Transpolitical Individualism', in Mark Lilla (ed.) *New French Thought: Political Philosophy* (NJ: Princeton University Press, 1994), pp. 212–19.
26. G. Lipovetsky, *The Empire of Fashion: Dressing Modern Democracy* (NJ: Princeton University Press, 1994), p. 243.
27. Ibid., p. 226.
28. Ibid., p. 238.
29. B.-H. Lévy, *Adventures on the Freedom Road: The French Intellectuals in the Twentieth Century* (London: Harvill Press, 1995). Originally published as *Les Aventures de la Liberté* (Paris: Grasset, 1991), p. 49.
30. J. L. Talmon, *The Rise of Totalitarian Democracy* (Boston: Beacon Press, 1952).
31. M. Foucault, *Discipline and Punish* (Harmondsworth: Penguin, 1977). Originally published in France as *Surveiller et punir: Naissance de la prison* (Paris: Gallimard, 1975), p. 222.

32. G. Deleuze, *The Deleuze Reader*, C. V. Boundas (ed.) (New York: Columbia University Press, 1993), pp. 242–3.

33. J. Baudrillard, *The Ecstasy of Communication*, pp. 36–7.

34. See the section on 'Seduction, or The Superficial Depths', in J. Baudrillard, *The Ecstasy of Communication* (NY: Autonomedia, 1988. First published as *L'Autre par lui-même*, Paris: Editions Galilee, 1987), pp. 57–76.

35. A good introduction to Irigaray is provided by T. Moi, *Sexual/Textual Politics* (London: Routledge, 1985), pp. 127–50.

36. *The Independent on Sunday*, 9 February 1992.

37. See for example M. Patrick, *Derrida, Responsibility and Politics* (Aldershot: Ashgate, 1997); and S. K. White, *Political Theory and Postmodernism* (Cambridge: CUP, 1991).

38. T. Eagleton, 'Marxism without Marx', *Radical Philosophy*, vol. 73 (September–October 1995), p. 37.

39. M. Foucault, *Power/Knowledge. Selected Interviews and Other Writings, 1972–1977* (ed.) C. Gordon (Brighton: Harvester Press, 1980), p. 16.

40. For Foucault's views on Iran, see D. Macey, *The Lives of Michel Foucault* (London: Vintage, 1994), pp. 410–11.

41. The opinions referred to are those of C. and J. Broyelle, reported in *Le Matin* and quoted in D. Macey, *The Lives of Michel Foucault* (London: Vintage, 1994), p. 410.

42. J.-F. Lyotard, *Tombeau de l'intellectuel et autres papiers* (Paris: Editions Galilée, 1984).

43. C. Lefort, 'The Contradiction of Trotsky', in J. B. Thompson (ed.) *The Political Forms of Modern Society: Bureaucracy, Democracy, Totalitarianism* (Cambridge: Polity Press, 1986), pp. 21–31.

44. C. Lefort, 'The Logic of Totalitarianism', in J. B. Thompson (ed.) *The Political Forms of Modern Society: Bureaucracy, Democracy, Totalitarianism* (Cambridge: Polity Press, 1986), p. 277.

45. Ibid., p. 277.

46. Ibid., p. 281.

47. See 'Pushing Back the Limits of the Possible', C. Lefort, in J. B. Thompson (ed.) *The Political Forms of Modern Society: Bureaucracy, Democracy, Totalitarianism* (Cambridge: Polity Press, 1986), pp. 313–17.

48. The best biography of Camus is *Albert Camus: A Life*, by O. Todd (n. p.: Alfred A. Knopf, 1997; Eng. edn published by Chatto and Windus, 1997). See also T. Judt, *The Burden of Responsibility: Blum, Camus, Aron and the French Twentieth Century* (London: University of Chicago Press, 1998).

49. A. Camus, *Caligula and Cross Purpose* (London: Penguin, 1968).

50. A. Camus, *The Rebel: An Essay on Man in Revolt* (New York: Knopf, 1956. Original French edn, 1951), p. 167.

51. Ibid., p. 169.

52. Ibid., p. 169.

53. Ibid., p. 169.

54. T. Judt, *The Burden of Responsibility: Blum, Camus, Aron and the French Twentieth Century* (London: University of Chicago Press, 1998), p. 127.

55. J. Maritain, *Man and the State* (Chicago: University of Chicago Press, 1963), p. 146.

56. Ibid., p. 146.
57. R. Aron, *An Essay on Freedom* (NY: World Publishing, 1970), p. 48. Italics in the original.
58. T. Judt, *The Burden of Responsibility: Blum, Camus, Aron and the French Twentieth Century* (London: University of Chicago Press, 1998), pp. 163–4.
59. Ibid., p. 182.
60. M. Weber, *German Sociology* (NY: Glencoe, 1964. Originally published in France, 1936, as *La Sociologie Allemande Contemporaine*), pp. 85–6.
61. F. Furet, *Penser la Révolution Française* (Paris: Editions Gallimard, 1978. Translated into English as *Interpreting the French Revolution*, Cambridge: CUP, 1981). My page refs. are to the English translation.
62. S. Khilnani, *Arguing Revolution: The Intellectual Left in Postwar France* (New Haven and London: Yale University Press, 1993), p. 156.
63. On French muliticulturalism, see C. Laborder, 'The Culture(s) of the Republic: Nationalism and Republicanism in French Republican Thought', *Political Theory*, vol. 29, no. 5 (October 2001), pp. 716–35.
64. R. Debray, 'Etes-vous démocrate ou républicain?', *Le Nouvel Observateur* (30 Novembre–6 Decembre 1989), pp. 49–55. See also the open letter, 'Profs, ne capitulons pas!' by E. Badinter, R. Debray, A. Finkielkraut, E. de Fontenay and C. Kintzler in *Le Nouvel Observateur* (2–8 Novembre 1989), pp. 30–31.
65. J. Roman, 'Un multiculturalisme à la française?', *Esprit*, vol. 212 (1995), pp. 157–8. Quoted by J. Jennings in 'From "Imperial State" to "l'Etat de Droit": Benjamin Constant, Blandine Kriegel and the Reform of the French Constitution', in *Political Studies*, vol. 44, no. 3, Special Issue (1996) on Constitutionalism in Transformation, p. 504.
66. J. Rawls' *A Theory of Justice* was first translated into French in 1987.
67. Quoted by C. Audard, in 'Rawls in France' in *European Journal of Political Theory*, vol. 1, no. 2 (October 2002), pp. 215–27.
68. See B. Manin, 'On Legitimacy and Political Deliberation', in Mark Lilla (ed.) *New French Thought: Political Philosophy* (NJ: Princeton University Press, 1994), pp. 186–200.
69. B. Constant, *De la liberté chez des Modernes* (ed.) M. Gauchet (Paris: Hachette, 1980).
70. M. Gauchet, 'Tocqueville', in M. Lilla (ed.) *New French Thought: Political Philosophy* (NJ: Princeton University Press, 1994), p. 106.
71. M. Gauchet. *The Disenchantment of the World: A Political History of Religion* (NJ: Princeton, 1997. Originally published as *Le désenchantement du monde*, Paris: Gallimard, 1985), p. 23.
72. Ibid., p. 121.
73. Quoted by M. Lilla, in M. Lilla (ed.) *New French Thought: Political Philosophy* (NJ: Princeton University Press, 1994), p. 23.
74. See C. Taylor's Foreword to M. Gauchet. *The Disenchantment of the World: A Political History of Religion* (NJ: Princeton University Press, 1997. Originally published as *Le désenchantement du monde*, Paris: Gallimard, 1985).

75. P. Manent, 'The Modern State', in M. Lilla (ed.) *New French Thought: Political Philosophy* (NJ: Princeton University Press, 1994), p. 124.

76. B. Barret-Kriegel, *L'Etat et la democratie: Rapport à François Mitterrand, président de la République française* (Paris: La Documentation française, 1985).

77. Ibid., p. 79.

78. Ibid., p. 85.

79. Quoted by J. Jennings in 'From "Imperial State" to "l'Etat de Droit": Benjamin Constant, Blandine Kriegel and the Reform of the French Constitution', in *Political Studies*, vol. 44, no. 3, Special Issue (1996) on Constitutionalism in Transformation, p. 503.

80. Ibid., p. 504.

81. D. Schnapper, *Community of Citizens: On the Modern Idea of Nationality* (London: Transaction Publishers, 1998. Originally published as *Communauté des Citoyens* (Paris: Editions Gallimard, 1994).

82. Ibid., p. 165.

83. Ibid., p. 80.

84. Ibid., p. 80.

85. Ibid., p. 1.

86. P. Manent, 'The Modern State', in M. Lilla (ed.) *New French Thought: Political Philosophy* (NJ: Princeton University Press, 1994), p. 127.

87. A. Madelin (ed.) *Aux sources du modèle libéral français* (Librairie Académique: Perrin/Association d'Histoire de l'Enterprise, 1997), p. II.

88. See L. Ferry and A. Renaut, *French Philosophy of the Sixties* (1985). See also L. Ferry and A. Renaut, *Political Philosophy: From the Rights of Man to the Republican Idea* (London: University of Chicago Press, 1992. Originally published in 1985, as *Philosophie politique, vol. 3: Des droits de l'homme à l'idée républicaine*, Presses Universitaires de France). See also A. Renaut's *The Era of the Individual: A Contribution to a History of Subjectivity* (NJ: Princeton University Press, 1997. Originally published as *L'ère de l'individu: Contribution à une histoire de la subjectivité*, Paris: Gallimard, 1989).

89. A. Nehamas, in his foreword to A. Renaut, *The Era of the Individual: A Contribution to a History of Subjectivity* (NJ: Princeton University Press, 1997. Originally published as *L'ère de l'individu: Contribution à une histoire de la subjectivité*, Paris: Gallimard, 1989), p. xvi.

90. See V. Wright, 'The Fifth Republic: From the Droit de L'Etat to the Etat de Droit?, in R. Elgie (ed.) *The Changing French Political System* (London: Cass, 2000), pp. 92–119.

91. J. Hayward, 'L'Individu Effacé ou le paradoxe du libéralisme française', *History of European Ideas* (Paris: Fayard, 1997, vol. 24, no. 3) pp. 239–42, 241–2.

92. M. Lilla (ed.) *New French Thought: Political Philosophy* (NJ: Princeton University Press, 1994), pp. 15–16. Italics in the original.

93. F. Furet, J. Juillard and Pierre Rosanvallon, *La République au centre. La fin de l'exception francaise* (Paris: Odile Jacob, 1989).

94. E. Cohen, *La tentation héxagonal. La souverainté a l' épreuve de la mondialisation* (Paris: Fayard, 1996).

95. J. Lovecy, 'The End of French Exceptionalism?', in R. Elgie (ed.) *The Changing French Political System* (London: Cass, 2000), p. 221.

Chapter 4: Nationalism, Democracy and Unification in Postwar German Political Thought

1. Quoted in C. FitzGibbon, *Denazification* (London: Michael Joseph, 1969), p. 120.
2. See the *Report on the tripartite Conference of Berlin*, in I. von Münch (ed.) *Dokumente des geteilten Deutschland*, 2nd edn (Stuttgart: Kröher, 1976), p. 35f.
3. General Clay, the commander of the US occupying forces, took the decision in August 1947, giving 31 March 1948 as the date by which the denazification process was to end. See *German Cultural Studies*, R. Burns (ed.) (London: OUP, 1995), p. 213.
4. For a succinct account of the Allied change of attitude, see W. Laqueur, *Europe Since Hitler* (Harmondsworth: Penguin Books, 1982), pp. 94–8.
5. See R. Wolin's instructive comments on the lectures in his edited volume, *The Heidegger Controversy* (Cambridge, MA: MIT, 1998), pp. 186–97. Habermas' instructive review is reprinted in the same volume.
6. M. Heidegger, *An Introduction to Metaphysics* (New York: Anchor Books edn, 1961. First published in German in 1953 by Max Niemeyer Verlag), p. 30.
7. Ibid., p. 37.
8. Ibid., pp. 30, 47.
9. Ibid., p. 41.
10. For an account of Heidegger's postwar attitude to Nazism, see R. Fine, 'Crimes against Humanity: Hannah Arendt and the Nuremberg Debates', *European Journal of Social Theory*, vol. 3, no. 3 (August 2000), pp. 293–311.
11. The interview is reprinted in English trans. in R. Wolin (ed.) *The Heidegger Controversy: A Critical Reader* (Cambridge, MA: MIT, 1998), pp. 91–116.
12. F. Meinecke, *The German Catastrophe* (Massachusetts: Harvard University Press, 1950), p. 108.
13. Ibid., p. 110.
14. Ibid., p. 112.
15. Ibid., p. 110.
16. See F. Meinecke, *Machiavellism* (New Haven: Yale University Press, 1957).
17. F. Meinecke, *The German Catastrophe* (Massachusetts: Harvard University Press, 1950), p. 113.
18. Ibid., p. 121.
19. F. Meinecke, *Machiavellism* (New Haven: Yale University Press, 1957), p. 433.
20. L. Strauss, *Liberalism Ancient and Modern* (Chicago: University of Chicago Press, 1989), p. 24.
21. E. Voegelin, *The New Science of Politics* (Chicago: University of Chicago Press, 1952), p. 38.
22. H. Kelsen, 'Foundations of Democracy', *Political Thought since World War I*, W. J. Stankiewicz (ed.) (New York: Free Press of Glencoe, 1964),

p. 73. Voegelin completed his doctorate with Hans Kelsen and Othmar Spann in 1922. On Voegelin's subsequent relationship to the former, see B. Cooper's introduction to E. Voegelin, *Political Religions* (New York: Edwin Mellen Press, 1996), pp. vi–viii.

23. A. and M. Mitscherlich, *Die Unfahigkeit zu trauern* (Munich: n.p., 1967).

24. K. Jaspers, *Wohin treibt die Bundesrepublik? Tatsachen-Gefahren-Chancen* (Munich: R. Piper & Co., 1966).

25. K. Jaspers, *The Future of Mankind* (Chicago: University of Chicago Press, 1963. Originally published in Munich, by R. Piper, 1958, as *Die Atombombe und die Zukunft des Menschen*), p. 202.

26. K. Jaspers, 'Philosophical Memoir', in *Philosophy and the World* (Chicago: Gateway, 1963), pp. 296–7.

27. K. Jaspers, *The Future of Mankind* (Chicago: University of Chicago Press, 1963. Originally published in Munich, by R. Piper, 1958, as *Die Atombombe und die Zukunft des Menschen*), p. 310.

28. Quoted in E. Ehrlich, L. H. Erhlich and G. B. Pepper, *Karl Jaspers: Basic Philosophical Writings* (Ohio: Humanities Press, 1994), p. 398.

29. Ibid., p. 398.

30. K. Jaspers, *The Future of Mankind* (Chicago: University of Chicago Press, 1963. Originally published in Munich, by R. Piper, 1958, as *Die Atombombe und die Zukunft des Menschen*), p. 310.

31. Quoted in E. Ehrlich, L. H. Erhlich and G. B. Pepper, *Karl Jaspers: Basic Philosophical Writings* (Ohio: Humanities Press, 1994), p. 399.

32. L. Kohler and H. Saner (eds) *Correspondence of Hannah Arendt and Karl Jaspers, 1926–1969*, trans. R. Kimber and R. Kimber (New York: Harcourt Brace Jovanich, 1992), p. 62.

33. Quoted in E. Ehrlich, L. H. Erhlich and G. B. Pepper, *Karl Jaspers: Basic Philosophical Writings* (Ohio: Humanities Press, 1994), p. 407.

34. Ibid., p. 410.

35. T. W. Adorno and M. Horkheimer, *The Dialectic of Enlightenment* (London: Verso, 1979), p. x.

36. J.-W. Müller, 'Portrait of Jürgen Habermas', in *Prospect* (March 2001), p. 46.

37. Quoted by M. Cranston in 'Herbert Marcuse', M. Cranston (ed.) *The New Left* (London: The Bodley Head, 1970), p. 88.

38. H. Marcuse, *One Dimensional Man* (London: Sphere, 1964), p. 70. Italics in the original.

39. Essays by R. P. Wolff, B. Moore, Jr and H. Marcuse *A Critique of Pure Tolerance* (Boston, MA: Beacon Press, 1966), pp. 109 and 110. Italics in the original.

40. P. Dews (ed.) *Autonomy and Solidarity: Interviews with Jürgen Habermas* (London: Verso, 1986), p. 193.

41. E.-W. Böckenförde, *State, Society and Liberty: Studies in Political Theory and Constitutional Law* (Oxford: Berg, 1991), p. 48.

42. Ibid., p. 49.

43. H. Kelsen, 'Foundations of Democracy', in W. J. Stanciewcz (ed.) *Political Thought since World War II* (London: Collier-Macmillan, 1964), p. 66. Italics in the original.

44. Quoted in A. Peacock and H. Willgerodt (eds) *German Neo-Liberals and the Social Market Economy* (London: Macmillan, 1989), p. 27. Italics in the original.

45. Ibid., p. 27.

46. Chancellor Ludwig Erhardt acknowledged his personal indebtedness to Röpke in generous terms. 'My own services towards the attainment of a free society', he wrote, 'are scarcely enough to express my gratitude to him [viz. Röpke] who, to such a high degree, influenced my position and conduct.' Quoted in the editorial introduction to W. Röpke, 'Liberalism and Christianity', in G. A. Panichas (ed.) *Modern Age: The First Twenty-five Years* (Indianopolis: Liberty Press, 1988), p. 513.

47. W. Röpke, *A Humane Economy* (London: Oswald Wolff, 1960), p. 12.

48. 'Liberalism and Christianity', in G. A. Panichas (ed.) *Modern Age: The First Twenty-five Years* (Indianopolis: Liberty Press, 1988), pp. 515–16.

49. Ibid., pp. 513–19.

50. 'Liberalism and Christianity', in G. A. Panichas (ed.) *Modern Age: The First Twenty-five Years* (Indianopolis: Liberty Press, 1988), p. 516.

51. R. Dahrendorf, *Reflections on the Revolution in Europe* (London: Chatto and Windus, 1990), p. 90.

52. G. Almond and S. Verba, *The Civic Culture* (Princeton: Princeton University Press, 1963). Referred to in K. Sontheimer, *The Government and Politics of West Germany* (London: Hutchinson, 1972), p. 71.

53. K. Sontheimer, *The Government and Politics of West Germany* (London: Hutchinson, 1972), p. 195.

54. P. Dews (ed.) *Autonomy and Solidarity: Interviews with Jürgen Habermas* (London: Verso, 1986), p. 155.

55. J. Habermas, 'The European Nation-State: On the Past and Future of Sovereignty and Citizenship', *Public Culture*, vol. 2, no. 2 (1998), pp. 397–416, 409.

56. P. Dews (ed.) *Autonomy and Solidarity: Interviews with Jürgen Habermas* (London: Verso, 1986), p. 53.

57. Ibid., p. 206.

58. Ibid., p. 170. Italics in the original.

59. J.-W. Müller, *Another Country: German Intellectuals, Unification and National Identity* (New Haven: Yale University Press, 2000), p. 97.

60. Dolf Sternberger, 'Verfassungspatriotismus', *Frankfurter Allgemeine Zeitung*, 23 May 1979.

61. Ibid., p. 97.

62. J. Habermas, 'Yet Again: German Identity – A Unified Nation of Angry GM-Burghers', in H. James and M. Stone (eds) *When the Wall Came Down* (London: Routledge, 1992), p. 99.

63. Ibid., p. 99.

64. N. Luhmann, *Social Systems* (Stanford: Stanford University Press, 1995. First published in German, 1984), p. li.

65. N. Luhmann, *Erkenntis als Konstruktion* (Bern: n.p., 1988), p. 24. Quoted by E. M. Knodt in her Foreword to N. Luhmann, *Social Systems* (Stanford: Stanford University Press, 1995), pp. xxxv–xxxvi.

66. N. Luhmann, *Political Theory in the Welfare State* (Berlin: Walter de Gruyer & Co., 1990. First published in German in 1981. The English edn is a revised version), p. 238.
67. C. Offe, *Contradictions of the Welfare State*, J. Keane (ed.) (London: Hutchinson, 1984), p. 255.
68. H.-G. Gadamer, *Truth and Method* (London: Sheed and Ward, 1988), especially Second Part, Section II. For a discussion of Habermas' reply to Gadamer, and his relation to Gadamer's thought as a whole, see P. Gorner, *Twentieth Century German Philosophy* (Oxford: OUP, 2000), chs. 5 and 6.
69. P. Dews (ed.) *Autonomy and Solidarity: Interviews with Jürgen Habermas* (London: Verso, 1986), pp. 160–1.
70. U. Beck, *Risk Society: Towards a New Modernity* (London: Sage Publications, 1992. First published in German in 1986), p. 183. Italics in the original.
71. Ibid., p. 49.
72. M. Steuer, 'A Little too Risky?', *LSE Magazine*, vol. 10, no. 1 (Summer 1998), p. 16.
73. Ibid.
74. R. Dahrendorf, 'Blind to the Greater Liberty', *The Times* (Friday, 9 November 1990. This article was an abridged version of Dahrendorf's Toynbee Lecture delivered earlier at Oxford University).
75. J.-W. Müller, *Another Country: German Intellectuals, Unification and National Identity* (New Haven: Yale University Press, 2000), p. 283.
76. A. Gehlen, *Man in the Age of Technology* (New York: Columbia University Press, 1980), p. 81.
77. Ibid.
78. Ibid.
79. J. Fest, 'Schweigende Wortführer: Uberlegungen zu einer Revolution ohne Vorbild', *Frankfurter Allgemeine Zeitung* (30 December, 1989). Reprinted in H. James and M. Stone (eds) *When the Wall Came Down* (London: Routledge, 1992), pp. 53–4.
80. Ibid., pp. 53–4.
81. D. Goldhagen, *Hitler's Willing Executioners: Ordinary Germans and the Holocaust* (New York: Knopf, 1996).
82. Grass, G. 'Don't Reunify Germany', in H. James and M. Stone (eds) *When the Wall Came Down* (London: Routledge, 1992), p. 59.
83. H. M. Enzensberger, 'Rigmarole', *Time* magazine (9 July 1990). Reprinted in H. James and M. Stone (eds) *When the Wall Came Down* (London: Routledge, 1992), p. 85.
84. Quoted by S. Howe, in *New Statesman and Society* (17 February 1989), p. 30.
85. Especially Andreas Hillgruber, Michael Stürmer, Klaus Hildebrand, Joachim Fest and Erich Gänschalz.
86. On the German New Right during the 1970s and 1980s, see P. Moreau, 'Revolution Conservatrice et Nouvelles Droites Allemandes', in *Les Temps Modernes*, 39 Année, no. 436 (Novembre 1982), pp. 893–959.

87. M. Walser, R. Zitelmann and B. Strauss were amongst those who originally had leftwing sympathies.

88. R. Zitelmann *et al*. (eds) *Westbindung: Risiken und Chancen für Deutschland* (Berlin: Propyläen-Verlag, 1993), p. 16.

89. Quoted in J. Heilbrunn, 'Germany's New Right', *Foreign Affairs*, vol. 75, no. 6 (1996), pp. 80–98. Here, p. 92.

90. R. Zitelmann, K. Weissmann and M. Grossheim (eds), op. cit.

91. J. Heilbrunn, 'Germany's New Right', *Foreign Affairs*, vol. 75, no. 6 (1996), pp. 80–98. Here, p. 93.

92. Ibid., p. 89.

93. Quoted by Heilbrunn, ibid., p. 82.

94. On Schmitt, see R. Cristi, *Carl Schmitt and Authoritarian Liberalism* (Cardiff: University of Wales Press, 1998).

95. On E. Jünger, see J. Herf, *Reactionary Modernism: Technology, Culture, and Politics in Weimar and the Third Reich* (Cambridge: CUP, 1984).

96. *Another Country: German Intellectuals, Unification and National Identity* (New Haven: Yale University Press, 2000), p. 168. I have relied heavily on Müller's excellent account of Walser's thought.

97. See S. Brockmann, *Literature and German Reunification* (Cambridge: Cambridge University Press, 1999).

98. J.-W. Müller, *Another Country: German Intellectuals, Unification and National Identity* (New Haven: Yale University Press, 2000), p. 163.

99. K. H. Bohrer, *Suddenness: On the Moment of Aesthetic Appearance* (New York: Columbia University Press, 1994), p. 83. My reference is to Bohrer's sympathetic comments about Paul Feyerabend.

100. Ibid., p. ix (on Derrida) and pp. 81–2 (on Kleist).

101. J.-W. Müller, *Another Country: German Intellectuals, Unification and National Identity* (New Haven: Yale University Press, 2000).

102. J. Heilbrunn, 'Germany's New Right', *Foreign Affairs*, vol. 75, no. 6 (1996), pp. 80–98. Here, p. 98. For critical responses to Heibrunn's article, arguing that it exaggerated the importance of the New Right, see the letters to the editor, *Foreign Affairs*, vol. 76, no. 2 (1997), pp. 152–61.

103. J.-W. Müller, *Another Country: German Intellectuals, Unification and National Identity* (New Haven: Yale University Press, 2000), p. 245.

104. J. Heilbrunn, 'Germany's New Right', *Foreign Affairs*, vol. 75, no. 6 (1996), pp. 80–98. Here, p. 98.

105. Ibid., p. 88.

106. R. Dahrendorf, *Reflections on the Revolution in Europe* (London: Chatto and Windus, 1990), p. 93.

107. J.-W. Müller, *Another Country: German Intellectuals, Unification and National Identity* (New Haven: Yale University Press, 2000), p. 276.

108. M. Fulbrook, *German National Identity after the Holocaust* (Cambridge: Polity Press, 1999), p. 231.

109. J. Gross, *Begründung der Berliner Republik: Deutschland am Ende des 20. Jahrhundert* (Stuttgart: Deutsche Verlags-Anstalt, 1995).

110. J. Breuilly, 'Commentary on Bernd Weisbrod: "German Unification and the National Paradigm"', in *German History*, vol. 14. no. 2 (1996), pp. 204–7. Here, p. 206.

111. R. Brubaker, *Citizenship and Nationhood in France and Germany* (Cambridge, Mass: Harvard University Press, 1996), p. x.
112. Ibid., p. 176.
113. See P. Stirk (ed.) *Mitteleuropa: History and Prospects* (Edinburgh: Edinburgh University Press, 1994).

Chapter 5: In the Shadow of *The Prince*: Italian Political Thought since Liberation

1. The reference is to Machiavelli's work of that name.
2. G. Warner, 'Italy and the Powers, 1943–49', in S. J. Woolf (ed.) *Italy and the Powers* (London: Longman, 1972), p. 39.
3. Ibid., pp. 47–8.
4. The Resistance movement developed mainly in the north during 1943. Despite their desire to promote democracy, the Allies viewed the revolutionary committees of the Resistance with profound suspicion, fearing that they might easily become (in Harold Macmillan's words) 'mere instruments of communism'. See G. Warner, 'Italy and the Powers, 1943–49', in S. J. Woolf (ed.) *Italy and the Powers* (London: Longman, 1972), p. 43.
5. P. McCarthy (ed.) *Italy since 1945* (Oxford: Oxford University Press, 2000), p. 7.
6. The most useful general introduction to Croce's philosophy is the anthology of his essays translated by C. Sprigge: see C. Sprigge, *Philosophy, Poetry, History* (London: OUP, 1966). An illuminating analysis of his political philosophy is provided by R. Bellamy, *Modern Italian Social Theory: Ideology and Politics from Pareto to the Present* (Oxford: Polity Press, 1987), ch. 5. The most comprehensive study of his thought as a whole is D. D. Roberts, *Benedetto Croce and the Uses of Historicism* (Berkeley and Los Angeles: University of California Press, 1987).
7. B. Croce, *History of Europe in the Nineteenth Century* (London: Kimble and Bradford, 1934), pp. 353–4.
8. D. D. Roberts, *Benedetto Croce and the Uses of Historicism* (Berkeley and Los Angeles: University of California Press, 1987), p. 235.
9. Ibid., p. 226.
10. B. Croce, 'The Principle, the Ideal and the Theory of Liberty' (1939), in C. Sprigge, *Philosophy, Poetry, History* (London: OUP, 1966), p. 720.
11. Ibid., p. 720.
12. Ibid., p. 713.
13. Croce was President of the Italian Liberal Party (PLI) from 1943 to 1947. On Croce and the PLI, see D. D. Roberts, *Benedetto Croce and the Uses of Historicism* (Berkeley and Los Angeles: University of California Press, 1987), pp. 229–31, p. 230.
14. Ibid., p. 263.

15. B. Croce, *La Storia come Pensiero e come Azione* (Bari: n.p., 1978), p. 238. Quoted by R. Bellamy, *Modern Italian Social Theory: Ideology and Politics from Pareto to the Present* (Oxford: Polity Press, 1987), p. 96.

16. Ibid., p. 96.

17. Quoted in J. Gatt-Rutter, *Writers and Politics in Modern Italy* (Sevenoaks: Hodder and Stoughton, 1978), p. 24.

18. C. Levi, *Christ Stopped at Eboli* (Harmondsworth: Penguin, 1982).

19. Ibid., p. 238.

20. On modern fragmentation, and Levi's belief that it was the source of Nazism in particular, see his *The Two-Fold Night: A Narrative of Travel in Germany* (London: Cresset Press, 1962), p. x.

21. G. Spadolini, *L'Italia della ragione: Lotta politica e cultura nel Novecento* (Florence: Le Monnier, 1978).

22. Quoted by N. Bobbio, *Ideological Profile of Twentieth-Century Italy* (New Jersey: Princeton University Press, 1995. Originally published in Italian, 1990), p. 185.

23. A. Gramsci, *Selections from the Prison Notebooks* and trans. Q. Hoare and G. Nowell Smith (eds) (London: Lawrence and Wishart, 1972), p. 12.

24. On 'traditional' and 'organic' intellectuals, see *Selections from the Prison Notebooks*, ibid., pp. 3–23.

25. G. Quazza, 'The Politics of the Italian Resistance', in S. J. Woolf (ed.) *Italy and the Powers* (London: Longman, 1972), p. 25.

26. See R. Bellamy, *Modern Italian Social Theory: Ideology and Politics from Pareto to the Present* (Cambridge: Polity, 1987), pp. 146–50.

27. I. Calvino, *Six Memos for the Next Millennium* (London: Cape, 1992), p. 3.

28. Quoted in J. Gatt-Rutter, *Writers and Politics in Modern Italy* (Sevenoaks: Hodder and Stoughton, 1978), p. 46.

29. Quoted in J. Gatt-Rutter, *Writers and Politics in Modern Italy* (Sevenoaks: Hodder and Stoughton, 1978), p. 43.

30. I. Silone, in R. Crossman, *The God that Failed: Six Studies in Communism* (London: Hamish Hamilton, 1950).

31. I. Silone, *The Story of a Humble Christian* (London: Victor Gollancz, 1970), p. 33.

32. On Eco, see M. Caesar, *Umberto Eco: Philosophy, Semiotics and the Work of Fiction* (Cambridge: Polity Press, 1999).

33. R. Lumley, Introduction to U. Eco's *Apocalypse Postponed* (Bloomington: Indiana University Press, 1994), p. 5.

34. U. Eco, 'Ur-Fascism', in *Five Moral Pieces* (London: Vintage, 2002), p. 87.

35. See P. Ginsborg, *A History of Contemporary Italy: Society and Politics 1943–1988* (London: Penguin, 1990), pp. 354–8.

36. A. Negri, *The Savage Anomaly* (Minneapolis: University of Minnesota Press, 1991. Original Italian edn 1981).

37. Ibid., p. xxi.

38. Interview with Negri by Danilo Zolo, in *Radical Philosophy* (July–August 2003, no. 120), p. 24.

39. On immaterial and affective labour, see the comments of J. Kraniauskas, 'Empire, or Multitude?', *Radical Philosophy*, no. 103 (September/October 2000), p. 34.

40. Ibid., p. 33.
41. A. Negri 'Constituent Republic', in P. Virnoand and M. Hardt (eds) *Radical Thought in Italy* (University of Minnesota Press: Minneapolis, 1996), pp. 215–16.
42. M. Hardt and A. Negri, *Empire* (Cambridge MA and London: Harvard University Press, 2000), p. xii. See also the earlier work by A. Negri, *Insurgencies: Constituent Power and the Modern State* (Minneapolis and Oxford: University of Minnesota Press, 1992).
43. A. Negri *et al.*, 'Do You Remember Revolution?', in P. Virno and M. Hardt (eds) *Radical Thought in Italy* (Minneapolis: University of Minnesota Press, 1996), pp. 215–16.
44. M. Hardt and A. Negri, *Empire* (Cambridge MA and London: Harvard University Press, 2000), pp. 212–13.
45. P. Virno and M. Hardt (eds) *Radical Thought in Italy* (Minneapolis: University of Minnesota Press, 1996), p. 221.
46. See M. Hyland, 'Continuous Crisis: Historical Action and Passion in Antonio Negri's Insurgencies', *Radical Philosophy*, no. 112 (March/April 2002), p. 31.
47. M. Tronti, *Con le spalle al futuro* (1992). Quoted by N. Bobbio, *Ideological Profile of Twentieth-Century Italy* (New Jersey: Princeton University Press, 1995. Originally published in Italian, 1990), p. 199.
48. On Del Noce, see N. Bobbio, *Ideological Profile of Twentieth-Century Italy* (New Jersey: Princeton University Press, 1995. Originally published in Italian, 1990), pp. 165, 177–8, 200–1.
49. J. Gatt-Rutter, *Writers and Politics in Modern Italy* (Sevenoaks: Hodder and Stoughton, 1978), p. 29.
50. For an introduction to De Felice's work, see his *Fascism: An Informal Introduction to its Theory and Practice* (New Brunswick: Transaction Books, 1976). See also B. W. Parker, 'Renzo De Felice and the History of Italian Fascism', in *American Historical Review* (1990).
51. M. Ledeen, 'Renzo De Felice and the Controversy over Italian Fascism', in *Journal of Contemporary History*, vol. 11, no. 4 (October, 1976. Special Issue on Theories of Fascism), p. 279.
52. In fact, G. Quazza, of Turin University, had already made this point before De Felice sprung to national attention. See 'The Politics of the Italian Resistance', in S. J. Woolf (ed.) *The Rebirth of Italy, 1943–50* (London: Longman, 1972), pp. 1–29.
53. N. Bobbio, *Ideological Profile of Twentieth-Century Italy* (New Jersey: Princeton University Press, 1995. Originally published in Italian, 1990), p. 195.
54. N. Bobbio, *A Political Life* (Cambridge: Polity Press, 2002), p. 71 and p. 109 on Kelsen; pp. 74–5 on Popper; p. 109 on Schumpeter.
55. N. Bobbio, *The Philosophy of Decadentism: A Study in Existentialism* (Oxford: Blackwell, 1948), p. 1.
56. Ibid., pp. 44–5.
57. N. Bobbio, *A Political Life* (Cambridge: Polity Press, 2002), p. 69.
58. See R. Bellamy's illuminating introduction to N. Bobbio, *The Future of Democracy: A Defence of the Rules of the Game* (Cambridge: Polity Press, 1987. Original Italian edn, Einaudi, 1984), p. 3.

59. R. Bellamy summarizes Bobbio's critique of participatory democracy in his introduction to N. Bobbio, *The Future of Democracy: A Defence of the Rules of the Game* (Cambridge: Polity Press, 1987. Original Italian edn, Einaudi, 1984), pp. 8–9.
60. Ibid., p. 70.
61. D. Zolo, *Democracy and Complexity: A Realist Approach* (Cambridge: Polity Press, 1992), p. 105.
62. Ibid., p. 180.
63. Ibid., p. 38. Italics in the original.
64. Ibid., p. 180.
65. Ibid., p. 109.
66. Ibid., p. 182.
67. Ibid., p. 181.
68. *The Sunday Telegraph*, 29 January 1995, p. 21.
69. Quoted by P. Ginsborg, *Italy and Its Discontents: Family, Civil Society, State 1980–2001* (London: Allen Lane, Penguin Press, 2001) p. 297.
70. M. Ricciardi, 'Rawls in Italy', *European Journal of Political Theory*, vol. 1, no. 2 (October 2002), p. 234.
71. *The Sunday Telegraph*, 29 January 1995, p. 21.
72. For de Felice's view of J. Evola, see H. T. Hansen's introduction to J. Evola, *Revolt against the Modern World* (Vermont: Inner Traditions International, 1969), p. xviii. The following three articles provide a useful introduction to Evola's political thought: F. Ferraresi, 'Julius Evola: Tradition, Reaction and the Radical Right', *European Journal of Sociology*, vol. 1 (1987); F. Ferraresi, 'The Radical Right in Postwar Italy', *Politics and Society*, vol. 1 (1988); R. Griffin, 'Revolts against the Modern World', *Literature and History*, vol. 1 (1985). See also T. Sheehan, 'Myth and Violence: The Fascism of Julius Evola and Alain de Benoist', *Social Research*, vol. 48 (Spring 1981); and R. Drake, 'Julius Evola and the Ideological Origins of the Radical Right in Contemporary Italy', in P. H. Merkl (ed.) *Political Violence and Terror* (California: Berkeley, 1986).
73. J. Evola, *The Doctrine of Awakening* (London: Luzac, 1951. First published, 1943), pp. 3–15.
74. On Evola and race, see T. Sheehan, 'Myth and Violence: The Fascism of Julius Evola and Alain de Benoist', *Social Research*, vol. 48 (Spring 1981).
75. Ibid., p. 61.
76. Evola claimed that his 'integral' concept of Tradition is the same that Vico speaks of in connection with 'heroic' ages: J. Evola, *Essais Politiques: Idée Impériale et Nouvel Ordre Européen Économie et Critique Sociale Gemanisme et Nazisme* (Puiseaux: Pardès, 1988), p. 167.
77. J. Evola, *Revolt against the Modern World* (Vermont: Inner Traditions International, 1995), p. xxxiv.
78. J. Evola, *Les Hommes au Milieu des Ruines* (Puiseaux and Paris: Edns Pardès: Guy Trédaniel/Editions de la Maisnie, 1984, for the French translation; published in Italy in 1972), p. 19.
79. Ibid., p. 20.

80. J. Evola, *Revolt against the Modern World* (Vermont: Inner Traditions International, 1995), p. 364.

81. G. Vattimo, *Beyond Interpretation: The Meaning of Interpretation for Philosophy* (Cambridge: Polity Press, 1997; original Italian edn, 1994), p. 6.

82. G. Vattimo, *The Transparent Society* (Cambridge: Polity Press, 1992. Original Italian edn, 1989), pp. 42–3. Italics in the original.

83. J. Derrida and G. Vattimo (eds) *Religion* (Cambridge: Polity Press, 1998. Original French edn, 1996), p. 92.

84. G. Vattimo, 'The Trace of the Trace', in J. Derrida and G. Vattimo (eds) *Religion* (Cambridge: Polity Press, 1998. Original French edn, 1996), p. 88.

85. Ibid., p. 88.

86. Ibid., p. 92.

87. G. Vattimo, *Beyond Interpretation: The Meaning of Interpretation for Philosophy* (Cambridge: Polity Press, 1997. Original Italian edn, 1994), p. 40.

88. G. Vattimo, *The Transparent Society* (Cambridge: Polity Press, 1992. Original Italian edn, 1989), p. 5.

89. G. Vattimo, *Beyond Interpretation: The Meaning of Interpretation for Philosophy* (Cambridge: Polity Press, 1997. Original Italian edn, 1994), pp. 39–40.

90. Ibid., p. 46.

91. G. Vattimo, *The Transparent Society* (Cambridge: Polity Press, 1992. Original Italian edn, 1989), p. 6.

92. S. Gundle and S. Parker (eds) *The New Italian Republic: From the Fall of the Berlin Wall to Berlusconi* (London: Routledge, 1997), p. 1. See also P. Ginsborg, *Italy and Its Discontents: Family, Civil Society, State 1980–2001* (London: Allen Lane, Penguin Press, 2001).

93. S. Gundle and S. Parker (eds) *The New Italian Republic: From the Fall of the Berlin Wall to Berlusconi* (London: Routledge, 1997), p. 311.

94. P. Ginsborg, *Italy and Its Discontents: Family, Civil Society, State 1980–2001* (London: Allen Lane, Penguin Press, 2001), p. 319.

95. Reported in *The Independent*, Wednesday, 27 November 2002.

96. E. Semino and M. Masci, 'Politics is Football: Metaphor in the Discourse of Silvio Berlusconi', *Discourse and Society*, vol. VII, no. 2 (1996), p. 248.

97. Ibid., p. 197.

98. On the influence of Rawls in Italy, see M. Ricciardi, 'Rawls in Italy', *European Journal of Political Theory*, vol. 1, no. 2 (October 2002), pp. 229–41. Ricciardi notes that Rawls' influence on Italian political philosophy has been wider among leftwing authors than among liberals, attributing this to 'some peculiarities of the liberal tradition in Italian philosophy', on which see p. 233 *et seq.* of his essay.

99. See S. Veca, *Le mosse della ragione* (Milan: Il Saggiatore, 1980). See also his *La società giusta: Argomenti per il contrattualism* (Milan: Il Saggiatore, 1982); *Questioni di giustizia* (Parma: Pratiche, 1985); *Una filosofia pubblica* (Milan: Feltrinelli, 1986).

100. P. Ginsborg, *Italy and Its Discontents: Family, Civil Society, State 1980–2001* (London: Allen Lane, Penguin Press, 2001), p. 324.

101. N. Bobbio, *Ideological Profile of Twentieth-Century Italy* (New Jersey: Princeton University Press, 1995. Originally published in Italian, 1990), p. 198.

102. Ibid., p. 197.

103. P. Ginsborg, *Italy and Its Discontents: Family, Civil Society, State 1980–2001* (London: Allen Lane, Penguin Press, 2001), p. 323.

104. P. Anderson, 'Land without Prejudice', *London Review of Books* (21 March 2002), p. 11.

105. P. Ginsborg, *Italy and Its Discontents: Family, Civil Society, State 1980–2001* (London: Allen Lane, Penguin Press, 2001), p. 243.

106. Ibid., p. 239.

107. Ibid., p. 240.

108. Ibid., p. 245.

109. Quoted by P. Anderson, 'Land without Prejudice', *London Review of Books* (21 March 2002), p. 6.

Chapter 6: Political Thought in East-Central Europe: From Empires to the European Union

1. G. Schöpflin, 'The Political Traditions of Eastern Europe', *Daedalus*, vol. 119, no. 1 (Winter 1990), pp. 55–90.

2. T. G. Masaryk, *The Making of a State* (London: Allen and Unwin, 1927), p. 371.

3. M. Mazower, *Dark Continent* (London: Penguin, 1998), See Table 1 of the appendices.

4. G. Schöpflin, *Politics in Eastern Europe* (Oxford: Blackwell, 1993), p. 11.

5. C. Miłosz, *The Captive Mind* (Harmondsworth: Penguin, 2001 [1953]), pp. 8–16.

6. Ibid., p. 217.

7. Ibid., p. xv.

8. J. Rupnik, 'Totalitarianism Revisited', in J. Keane (ed.) *Civil Society and the State* (London: Verso, 1988), p. 265.

9. Ibid., p. 267.

10. On Wiatr and Staniszkis, see J. Rupnik, 'Totalitarianism Revisited', in J. Keane (ed.) *Civil Society and the State* (London: Verso, 1988), p. 267.

11. Z. Mlynář, *Nightfrost in Prague* (London: n.p., 1980).

12. Quoted by J. Rupnik, *The Other Europe* (New York: Pantheon Books, 1989), p. 237.

13. M. Šimečka, *The Restoration of Order* (London: n.p., 1987).

14. J. Rupnik, *The Other Europe* (New York: Pantheon Books, 1989), p. 238.

15. Quoted by J. Rupnik, *The Other Europe* (New York: Pantheon Books, 1989), p. 237.

16. J. Rupnik, *The Other Europe* (New York: Pantheon Books, 1989), p. 238.

17. A. Michnik, *Letters from Freedom* (Berkeley: University of California, 1998), p. 104.

18. A. Kolnai, *The Utopian Mind and Other Papers*, F. Dunlop (ed.) (London: Athlone Press, 1995), p. 154.

19. Ibid., p. 155.

20. Quoted by J. Rupnik, 'Totalitarianism Revisited', in J. Keane (ed.) *Civil Society and the State* (London: Verso, 1988), p. 270.

21. V. Havel, 'The Power of the Powerless', in *Living in Truth* (London: Faber and Faber, 1987), p. 116.

22. *The Salisbury Review*, no. 6 (Winter 1984), p. 33.

23. L. Kolakowski, 'Totalitarianism and the Virtue of the Lie', I. Howe (ed.) *1984 Revisited* (New York: Harper and Rowe, 1983), p. 128.

24. Ibid., p. 130.

25. T. Judt, 'The Past is Another Country: Myth and Memory in Postwar Europe', in I. Deák, T. Gross and T. Judt (eds) *The Politics of Retribution in Europe* (Princeton: Princeton University Press, 2000), pp. 316–17.

26. L. Kolakowki, *Marxism and Beyond* (London: Paladin, 1971), p. 58.

27. M. Polanyi, *The Logic of Liberty* (London: Routledge and Kegan Paul, 1951), p. 124.

28. Ibid., p. 136.

29. Ibid., p. 35.

30. Ibid., p. 148.

31. Ibid., p. vii.

32. For a documentation of these different historical approaches, see J. Rupnik, 'Totalitarianism Revisited', in J. Keane (ed.) *Civil Society and the State* (London: Verso, 1988), pp. 281–3.

33. See I. Bibó, 'The Meaning of the Social Evolution of Europe', in G. Schöpflin and N. Wood (eds) *In Search of Central Europe* (Oxford: Polity, 1989), pp. 30–46. For historical interpretations of central European identity inspired by Bibó's work, see J. Szücs, 'Three Historical Regions of Europe', J. Keane (ed.) *Civil Society and the State* (London: Verso, 1988), pp. 291–332, and also P. Hanák, 'Central Europe: A Historical Region in Modern Times', in G. Schöpflin and N. Wood (eds) *In Search of Central Europe*, pp. 57–69. For a critical assessment of István Bibó as a political theorist, see R. N. Berki, 'The Realism of Moralism: The Political Philosophy of István Bibó', *History of Political Thought*, vol. XIII, no. 3 (1992), pp. 513–34.

34. R. N. Berki, 'The Realism of Moralism: The Political Philosophy of István Bibó', *History of Political Thought*, vol. XIII, no. 3 (1992), p. 515.

35. Ibid., 516.

36. *The Salisbury Review*, no. 3 (Spring 1983), p. 30.

37. *The Salisbury Review*, vol. 5, no. 3 (April 1987), p. 20.

38. M. Kundera, 'A Kidnapped West or Culture Bows Out', *Granta*, no. 11 (1984), p. 114.

39. T. Garton Ash, 'Does Central Europe Exist?', in G. Schöpflin and N. Wood (eds) *In Search of Central Europe* (Oxford: Polity, 1989), p. 197.

40. J. Hradec, in *Střední Evropa*, January 1985. The essay is translated in *The Salisbury Review*, vol. 4, no. 2 (January 1986), pp. 35–9. The quotation is from p. 37 of the translation.

41. M. Šimečka, 'Another Civilization? An Other Civilization?', in G. Schöpflin and N. Wood (eds) *In Search of Central Europe* (Oxford: Polity, 1989), p. 159.

42. Ibid., p. 160. For an outraged response to Šimečka which insists on Lenin's genuinely Russian credentials, see J. Mellor, 'Is the Russian Intelligentsia European?', G. Schöpflin and N. Wood (eds) *In Search of Central Europe* (Oxford: Polity, 1989), pp. 163–7.

43. M. Kundera, 'A Kidnapped West or Culture Bows Out', *Granta*, no. 11 (1984), pp. 113–14.

44. V. Bělohradský, 'The Loss of Politics', *The Salisbury Review*, vol. 4, no. 2 (January 1986), p. 46.

45. J. Rupnik, 'Totalitarianism Revisited', J. Keane (ed.) *Civil Society and the State* (London: Verso, 1988), p. 287.

46. A. Michnik, *Letters from Prison and Other Essays* (Berkeley: University of California Press, 1985), p. 144.

47. Ibid., p. 146.

48. Ibid., p. 147.

49. Ibid., p. 147.

50. Z. A. Pelczynski, 'Solidarity and the "Rebirth of Civil Society" in Poland', in J. Keane (ed.) *Civil Society and the State* (London: Verso, 1988), p. 365.

51. See R. Scruton, 'Masaryk, Patočka and the Care of the Soul', in *The Philosopher on Dover Beach* (Manchester: Carcanet, 1990), pp. 74–88. See also J. Patočka's *Heretical Essays in the Philosophy of History* (Chicago: Open Court, 1996).

52. See J. Rupnik, *The Other Europe* (New York: Pantheon Books, 1989), p. 222.

53. J. Patočka, *Platon et l'Europe*, trans. by E. Abrams (Paris: Verdier, 1983). See also J. Patočka's *Heretical Essays in the Philosophy of History* (Chicago: Open Court, 1996).

54. J. Patočka, *Heretical Essays in the Philosophy of History* (Chicago: Open Court, 1996), pp. 124–5.

55. R. Scruton, 'The New Right in Central Europe ll: Poland and Hungary', *Political Studies*, vol. XXXVI (1988), p. 642.

56. See R. Scruton, 'Masaryk, Patočka and the Care of the Soul', in *The Philosopher on Dover Beach* (Manchester: Carcanet, 1990), p. 87.

57. Quoted by R. N. Berki, 'The Realism of Moralism: The Political Philosophy of István Bibó', *History of Political Thought*, vol. XIII, no. 3 (1992), p. 520.

58. See I. Bibó, 'The Meaning of the Social Evolution of Europe', in G. Schöpflin and N. Wood (eds) *In Search of Central Europe* (Oxford: Polity, 1989), pp. 30–46.

59. G. Konrád, *Antipolitics* (London: Quartet, 1984).

60. Quoted by C. Tempest, 'Myths from Eastern Europe and the Legend of the West', R. Fine and S. Rai (eds) *Civil Society: Democratic Perspectives* (London: Cass, 1997), p. 132.

61. V. Havel, 'The Power of the Powerless', V. Havel *et al.*, *The Power of the Powerless* (London: Verso, 1985).

62. R. Scruton (ed.) 'Politics and Conscience', in *Conservative Thoughts* (London: Claridge Press, 1988), p. 194.
63. Ibid., p. 182.
64. *The Salisbury Review*, no. 6 (Winter 1984), p. 35.
65. For two lucid critical essays on the eastern European concept of civil society, see P. Hirst, 'The State, Civil Society and the Collapse of Soviet Communism', in *From Statism to Pluralism* (London: UCL, 1997), pp. 156–81; also C. Tempest, 'Myths from Eastern Europe and the Legend of the West', in R. Fine and S. Rai (eds) *Civil Society: Democratic Perspectives* (London: Cass, 1997), pp. 132–44.
66. V. Klaus, *Renaissance: The Rebirth of Liberty in the Heart of Europe* (Washington: Cato Institute, 1997), p. 25.
67. For essays by V. Klaus, see his *Renaissance: The Rebirth of Liberty in the Heart of Europe* (Washington: Cato Institute, 1997).
68. T. Garton Ash, *We the People* (Harmondsworth: Granta, 1990), p. 104.
69. V. Klaus, *Renaissance: The Rebirth of Liberty in the Heart of Europe* (Washington: Cato Institute, 1997), p. 40.
70. Quoted by K. Williams, in 'National Myths in the New Czech Liberalism', in G. Hosking and G. Schöpflin (eds) *Myths and Nationhood* (London: Hurst, 1997), p. 140.
71. R. Dahrendorf, *Reflections on the Revolution in Europe* (London: Chatto and Windus, 1990), p. 25.
72. J. Rupnik, *The Other Europe* (New York: Pantheon Books, 1989), p. 191.
73. On the influence of the New Right in Hungary, see R. Scruton, 'The New Right in Central Europe ll: Poland and Hungary', *Political Studies*, vol. XXXVI (1988), pp. 638–52. See also R. Scruton, 'The New Right in Central Europe l: Czechoslovakia', *Political Studies*, vol. XXXVI (1988), pp. 449–62.
74. J. Rupnik, *The Other Europe* (New York: Pantheon Books, 1989), p. 188.
75. M. Vajda, 'East-Central European Perspectives', in J. Keane (ed.) *Civil Society and the State* (London: Verso, 1988), p. 359.
76. P. Hirst, *From Statism to Pluralism* (London: UCL, 1997), p. 154.
77. A. Michnik, *Letters from Freedom* (California: University of California Press, 1998), p. 323.
78. Quoted by B. Fowkes, *The Post-Communist Era* (London: Macmillan, 1999), p. 187.
79. Ibid., p. 187.
80. M. Glenny, *The Rebirth of History* (London: Penguin, 1993), p. 194.
81. V. Tismaneanu (ed.) *The Revolutions of 1989* (London: Routledge, 1999), p. 4.
82. R. Bideleux and I. Jeffries, *A History of Eastern Europe: Crisis and Change* (London: Routledge, 1998), p. 639.
83. T. Judt, 'The Past is Another Country: Myth and Memory in Postwar Europe', in I. Deák, J. T. Gross and T. Judt (eds) *The Politics of Retribution in Europe* (NJ: Princeton, 2000), p. 317.
84. V. Tismaneanu (ed.) *The Revolutions of 1989* (London: Routledge, 1999), p. 6.
85. M. Glenny, *The Rebirth of History* (London: Penguin, 1993), p. 232.

86. B. Ackerman, 'The Future of Liberal Revolution', reprinted from his book of that title (Newhaven, CT: Yale University Press, 1992), pp. 113–23, in V. Tismaneanu (ed.) *The Revolutions of 1989* (London: Routledge, 1999), p. 207.
87. Ibid., p. 206.
88. T. Judt, 'The Past is Another Country: Myth and Memory in Postwar Europe', in I. Deák, J. T. Gross and T. Judt (eds) *The Politics of Retribution in Europe* (NJ: Princeton, 2000), p. 310.
89. Ibid., p. 308.
90. V. Tismaneanu (ed.) *The Revolutions of 1989* (London: Routledge, 1999), p. 4.
91. R. Bideleux and Ian Jeffries, *A History of Eastern Europe* (London: Routledge, 1998), p. 642.

Chapter 7: Towards a New Post-Democratic Agenda?

1. R. Kagan, *Paradise and Power: America and Europe in the New World Order* (London: Atlantic Books, 2003), pp. 97–8.
2. J. Burnheim, *Is Democracy Possible?* (Cambridge: Polity Press, 1985), p. 1.
3. M. Mazower, *Dark Continent: Europe's Twentieth Century* (London: Allen Lane, 1998), p. 404.
4. R. Bideleux, ' "Europeanisation" and the Limits to Democratisation in East-Central Europe', in G. Pridham and A. Ágh (eds) *Prospects for Democratic Consolidation in East-Central Europe* (Manchester: Manchester University Press, 2001), p. 28.
5. C. Mouffe, 'For an Agonistic Model of Democracy', in N. O'Sullivan (ed.) *Political Theory in Transition* (Routledge: London, 2000), p. 113.
6. J. Habermas, 'The European Nation-State: On the Past and Future of Sovereignty and Citizenship', *Public Culture*, vol. 10, nos 2, 3 (1998), pp. 97–416, 412.
7. P. Hirst, 'Globalization, the Nation State and Political Theory', in N. O'Sullivan (ed.) *Political Theory in Transition* (Routledge: London, 2000), p. 187.
8. J. Habermas, 'The European Nation-State: On the Past and Future of Sovereignty and Citizenship', *Public Culture*, vol. 10, no. 2 (1998), pp. 397–416, 398.
9. G. Santayana, *Dominations and Powers* (London: Constable, 1951), p. 453.
10. Ibid., p. 435.
11. Ibid., p. 423.
12. Ibid., p. 435.
13. Ibid., p. 382.
14. Evola in R. Griffin op. cit., p. 344.
15. J. Habermas (1992) 'Citizenship and National Identity: Some Reflections on the Future of Europe', *Praxis International*, vol. 12, no. 1, pp. 1–19.
16. E. Shils, op. cit., p. 222.

17. A. Stone, 'Governing with Judges: The New Constitutionalism', in J. Hayward and E. Page (eds) *Governing the New Europe* (Cambridge: Polity Press, 1995), p. 286. Italics in the original.

18. Ibid., p. 286. Italics in the original.

19. R. Bideleux, ' "Europeanisation" and the Limits to Democratisation in East-Central Europe', in G. Pridham and A. Ágh (eds) *Prospects for Democratic Consolidation in East-Central Europe* (Manchester: Manchester University Press, 2001), p. 26.

20. European Commission (2001), *European Governance: A White Paper*, COM (2001).

21. European Commission (2001), *European Governance: A White Paper*, COM (2001), pp. 4, 8.

22. L. Siedentop, *Democracy in Europe* (London: Penguin Press, 2000), p. 115.

23. D. Wincott, 'Does the European Union Pervert Democracy? Questions of Democracy in New Constitutionalist Thought on the Future of Europe', in Z. Bankowski and A. Scott (eds) *The European Union and Its Order* (Oxford: Blackwell, 2000), p. 123.

24. R. Bellamy, 'Citizenship Beyond the Nation State: The Case of Europe', in N. O'Sullivan (ed.) *Political Theory in Transition* (London: Routledge, 2000), p. 106.

25. P. Magnette, 'European Governance and Civic Participation: Beyond Elitist Citizenship?', *Political Studies*, vol. 51 (2003), pp. 144–160, 150.

26. M. Mazower, *Dark Continent: Europe's Twentieth Century* (London: Allen Lane, 1998), pp. xiv–xv.

27. A. D. Smith, 'National Identity and the Idea of European Unity', *International Affairs*, vol. 68, no. 1, 1992, p. 76.

28. R. Kagan, op cit., p. 54.

29. Noel Malcolm, 'A Federal Constitution with the Heart of a Manifesto', *Daily Telegraph*, 28 July 2003.

30. Report in *The Independent*, 13 June 2003.

31. R. Bideleux, ' "Europeanisation" and the Limits to Democratisation in East-Central Europe', in G. Pridham and A. Ágh (eds) *Prospects for Democratic Consolidation in East-Central Europe* (Manchester: Manchester University Press, 2001), p. 41. Italics added.

32. O. Waever, 'Europe since 1945: Crisis to Renewal', in Kevin Wilson and Jan van der Dusen (eds) *The History of the Idea of Europe* (London: Routledge, 1995), p. 174.

33. On Augustus' achievement, see F. E. Adcock, *Roman Political Ideas and Practice* (Michigan: Ann Arbor, 1964), ch. V.

Bibliography

Ackerman, B. 'The Future of Liberal Revolution', reprinted from his book of that title (Newhaven, CT: Yale University Press, 1992) in Tismaneanu, V. (ed.) *The Revolutions of 1989* (London: Routledge, 1999).

Adorno, T. W. and Horkheimer, M. *The Dialectic of Enlightenment* (Verso: London, 1979).

Ágh, A. and Pridham, G. (eds) *Prospects for Democratic Consolidation in East-Central Europe* (Manchester: Manchester University Press, 2000).

Almond, G. and Verba, S. *The Civic Culture* (Princeton: Princeton University Press, 1963).

Althusser, L. *Lenin and Philosophy and Other Essays* (London: NLB, 1971).

Anderson, P. 'Land without Prejudice', *London Review of Books* (21 March 2002), p. 11.

Aron, R. *An Essay on Freedom* (NY: World Publishing, 1970).

Audard, C. 'Rawls in France', *European Journal of Political Theory*, vol. 1, no. 2 (October 2002), pp. 215–27.

Badinter, E., Debray, R., Finkielkraut A., de Fontenay E. and Kintzler C. 'Profs, ne capitulons pas!' letter in *Le Nouvel Observateur* (2–8 November 1989), pp. 30–1.

Barraclough, G. *An Introduction to Contemporary History* (Penguin Books, Harmondsworth, 1964).

Barret-Kriegel, B. *L'Etat et la democratie: Rapport à François Mitterrand, président de la République française* (Paris: La Documentation française, 1985).

Barry, B. *Political Argument* (London: Routledge, 1965).

——*Justice as Impartiality* (Oxford: OUP, 1996).

Baudrillard, J. *The Ecstasy of Communication* (NY: Autonomedia, 1988. First published as *L'Autre par lui-même*, Paris: Editions Galilee, 1987).

Beck, U. *Risk Society: Towards a New Modernity* (London: Sage Publications, 1992. First published in German in 1986).

Bellamy, R. *Modern Italian Social Theory: Ideology and Politics from Pareto to the Present* (Oxford: Polity Press, 1987).

——'The Political Form of the Constitution: The Separation of Powers, Rights and Representative Democracy', Bellamy, R. and Castiglione, D. (eds) *Political Studies*, vol. 44, no. 3 (1996) (Special Issue on 'Constitutionalism in Transformation'), p. 456.

218

Bělohradský, V. 'The Loss of Politics', *The Salisbury Review*, vol. 4, no. 2 (January 1986), p. 46.

Benvenuto, B. and Kennedy, R. *The Works of Jacques Lacan: An Introduction* (London: Free Association Books, 1986).

Berki, R. N. *On Political Realism* (London: Dent, 1981).

——'The Realism of Moralism: The Political Philosophy of István Bibó', *History of Political Thought*, vol. XIII, no. 3 (1992), pp. 513–34.

Berlin, I. *Four Essays on Liberty* (London: OUP, 1969).

——'The Originality of Machiavelli', *Against the Current* (London: OUP, 1981).

——*The Crooked Timber of Humanity: Chapters in the History of Ideas*, in Hardy, H. (ed.) (New York: Knopf, 1991).

Bibó, I. 'The Meaning of the Social Evolution of Europe', in Schöpflin, G. and Wood, N. (eds) *In Search of Central Europe* (Oxford: Polity, 1989).

Bideleux, R. ' "Europeanisation" and the Limits to Democratisation in East-Central Europe', in Ágh, A. and Pridham, G. (eds) *Prospects for Democratic Consolidation in East-Central Europe* (Manchester: Manchester University Press, 2001).

Bideleux, R. and Jeffries, I. *A History of Eastern Europe: Crisis and Change* (London: Routledge, 1998).

Blair, T. Interview in *Prospect*, no. 77 (August 2002), p. 19.

Bobbio, N. *The Philosophy of Decadentism: A Study in Existentialism* (Blackwell: Oxford, 1948).

——*The Future of Democracy: A Defence of the Rules of the Game* (Cambridge: Polity Press, 1987. Original Italian edn, Einaudi, 1984).

——*Ideological Profile of Twentieth-Century Italy* (New Jersey: Princeton University Press, 1995. Original Italian edn 1990).

——*A Political Life* (Cambridge: Polity Press, 2002).

Böckenförde, E.-W. *State, Society and Liberty: Studies in Political Theory and Constitutional Law* (Oxford: Berg, 1991).

Bohrer, K. H. *Suddenness: On the Moment of Aesthetic Appearance* (New York: Columbia University Press, 1994).

Bosworth, R. J. B. *Explaining Auschwitz and Hiroshima* (London, 1993).

Breuilly, J. 'Commentary on Bernd Weisbrod: "German Unification and the National Paradigm" ', in *German History*, vol. 14, no. 2 (1996), pp. 204–7.

Brockmann, S. *Literature and German Reunification* (Cambridge: Cambridge University Press, 1999).

Brubaker, R. *Citizenship and Nationhood in France and Germany* (Cambridge, MA: Harvard University Press, 1996).

Burgess, M. *Federalism and European Union: The Building of Europe, 1950–2000* (London: Routledge, 2000).

Burnheim, J. *Is Democracy Possible?* (Cambridge: Polity Press, 1985).

Burns, R. (ed.) *German Cultural Studies* (London: OUP 1995).

Calvino, I. *Italian Folktales* (London: Penguin, 1980. Published in Italian by Einaudi, 1956).

Camus, A. *The Rebel: An Essay on Man in Revolt* (New York: Knopf, 1956. Original French edn 1951).

——*Caligula and Cross Purposes* (London: Penguin, 1968).

Canovan, M. *Nationhood and Political Theory* (Cheltenham: Edward Elgar, 1996).

Carr, E. H. *Conditions of Peace* (London: Macmillan, 1942).

Cerny, P. 'Neo Medievalism, Civil War and the New Security Dilemmas: Globalization as Durable Disorder', *Civil Wars*, vol. 1, no. 1 (1998).

Colletti, L. critique of Althusser in *New Left Review*, no. 86 (July–August 1974).

Constant, B. *De la liberté chez des Modernes*, Gauchet, M. (ed.) (Paris: Hachette, 1980).

Cooper, B. Introduction to E. Voegelin, *Political Religions* (New York: Edwin Mellen Press, 1996).

Cranston, M. (ed.) 'Herbert Marcuse', *The New Left* (London: The Bodley Head, 1970).

——'Postscriptum', in Feaver, G. and Rosen, F. (eds) *Lives, Liberties and the Public Good* (London: MacMillan, 1987).

Crick, B. *In Defence of Politics*, revised edn (Harmondsworth: Penguin, 1964).

Cristi, R. *Carl Schmitt and Authoritarian Liberalism* (Cardiff: University of Wales Press, 1998).

Croce, B. 'The Principle, the Ideal and the Theory of Liberty' (1939), in Sprigge, C. (ed.) *Philosophy, Poetry, History* (London: OUP, 1966).

——*La Storia come Pensiero e come Azione* (Bari: n.p., 1978).

Crossman, R. *The God that Failed: Six Studies in Communism* (London: Hamish Hamilton, 1950).

Dahrendorf, R. *Reflections on the Revolution in Europe* (London: Chatto and Windus, 1990).

Deák, I., Gross, J. T. and Judt, T. (eds) *The Politics of Retribution in Europe* (Princeton: Princeton University Press, 2000).

Debray, R. 'Etes-vous démocrate ou républicain?' in *Le Nouvel Observateur* (30 November–6 December 1989), pp. 49–55.

De Felice, R. *Fascism: An Informal Introduction to its Theory and Practice* (New Brunswick: Transaction Books 1976).

Deleuze, G. *The Deleuze Reader*, Boundas, C. V. (ed.) (New York: Columbia University Press, 1993).

Derrida, J. 'Choreographies'. Interview with Christie V. McDonald, *Diacritics*, vol. 12, no. 2, pp. 66–76, at 76.

Dews, P. (ed.) *Autonomy and Solidarity: Interviews with Jürgen Habermas* (London: Verso, 1986).

Dobson, A. 'Political Theory and the Environment: The Grey and the Green (and the In-between)', O'Sullivan, N. (ed.) *Political Theory in Transition* (London: Routledge, 2000).

Drake, R. 'Julius Evola and the Ideological Origins of the Radical Right in Contemporary Italy', in Merkl, P. H. (ed.) *Political Violence and Terror* (California: Berkeley, 1986).

Drucker, P. F. *The Age of Discontinuity* (NY: Harper and Row, 1978, first published 1968).

Drury, S. B. *Alexandre Kojève: The Roots of Postmodern Politics* (Basingstoke: Macmillan, 1994).

Dunn, J. *The Cunning of Unreason* (London: Harper Collins, 2000).

Eagleton, T. *Literary Theory: An Introduction* (Oxford: Blackwell, 1994).
——'Marxism without Marx', *Radical Philosophy*, vol. 73 (September–October 1995), p. 37.
Eatwell, R. *Fascism: A History* (London: Vintage Books, 1996).
Eco, U. *Apocalypse Postponed* (Bloomington: Indiana University Press, 1994).
Ehrlich, E., Erhlich, L. H. and Pepper, G. B. *Karl Jaspers: Basic Philosophical Writings* (Ohio: Humanities Press, 1994).
Enzensberger, H. M. 'Rigmarole', *Time* magazine (9 July 1990). Reprinted in James, H. and Stone, M. (eds) *When the Wall Came Down* (London: Routledge, 1992).
European Commission (2001), *European Governance: A White Paper*, COM (2001).
Evola, J. *The Doctrine of Awakening* (London: Luzac, 1951. First published, 1943).
——*Revolt against the Modern World* (Vermont: Inner Traditions International, 1969).
——*The Metaphysics of Sex* (London and The Hague: East-West Publications, 1983. Published in Italian in 1958).
——*Les Hommes au Milieu des Ruines* (Puiseaux and Paris: Edns Pardès: Guy Trédaniel/Editions de la Maisnie, 1984, for the French translation; published in Italy in 1972).
——*Essais Politiques: Idée Impériale et Nouvel Ordre Européen Économie et Critique Sociale Gemanisme et Nazisme* (Puiseaux: Pardès, 1988).

Ferraresi, F. 'Julius Evola: Tradition, Reaction and the Radical Right', *European Journal of Sociology*, vol. 1 (1987).
——'The Radical Right in Postwar Italy', *Politics and Society*, vol. 1 (1988).
Ferry, L. and Renaut, A. *Political Philosophy: From the Rights of Man to the Republican Idea* (London: University of Chicago Press, 1992. Originally published in 1985, as *Philosophie politique, vol. 3: Des droits de l'homme à l'idée républicaine*, Presses Universitaires de France).
Fest, J. 'Schweigende Wortführer: Uberlegungen zu einer Revolution ohne Vorbild', *Frankfurter Allgemeine Zeitung* (30 December 1989). Reprinted in James, H. and Stone, M. (eds) *When the Wall Came Down* (London: Routledge, 1992).
Fine, R. 'Crimes against Humanity: Hannah Arendt and the Nuremberg Debates', *European Journal of Social Theory*, vol. 3, no. 3 (August 2000), pp. 293–311.
Fine, R. and Rai, S. (eds) *Civil Society: Democratic Perspectives* (London: Cass, 1997).
FitzGibbon, C. *Denazification* (London: Michael Joseph, 1969).
Forsyth, M. 'Hayek's Bizarre Liberalism', *Political Studies*, vol. XXXVI (1988), pp. 235–50.
Foucault, M. *Discipline and Punish* (Harmondsworth: Penguin, 1977). Originally published in France as *Surveiller et punir: Naissance de la prison* (Gallimard: Lawrence & Wishart, 1975).
——*Power/Knowledge*. Selected interviews and other writings, 1972–1977, Gordon, C. (ed.) (Brighton: 1980).

Fowkes, B. *The Post-Communist Era* (London: Macmillan, 1999).

Fraser, J. *An Introduction to the Thought of Galvano della Volpe (1895–1969)* (London: 1977).

Fulbrook, M. *German National Identity after the Holocaust* (Cambridge: Polity Press, 1999).

Furet, F. *Penser la Révolution Française* (Paris: Editions Gallimard, 1978. Translated into English as *Interpreting the French Revolution*, Cambridge: CUP, 1981).

Gadamer, H.-G. *Truth and Method* (London: Sheed and Ward, 1988).

Gamble, A. *Hayek* (Oxford: Polity, 1996).

Garton Ash, T. 'Does Central Europe Exist?' Schöpflin, G. and Wood, N. (eds) *In Search of Central Europe* (Oxford: Polity, 1989).

——*We the People* (Harmondsworth: Granta, 1990).

Gatt-Rutter, J. *Writers and Politics in Modern Italy* (Sevenoaks: Hodder and Stoughton, 1978).

Gauchet, M. 'Tocqueville', in Lilla, M. (ed.) *New French Thought: Political Philosophy* (NJ: Princeton University Press, 1994).

——*The Disenchantment of the World: A Political History of Religion* (NJ: Princeton University Press, 1997. Originally published as *Le désenchantement du monde*, Paris: Gallimard, 1985).

Gehlen, A. *Man in the Age of Technology* (New York: Columbia University Press, 1980).

Gellner, E. *Thought and Change* (London: Weidenfeld and Nicolson, 1964).

Gentile, E. 'Fascism in Italian Historiography', *Journal of Contemporary History*, vol. 2 (1986).

Giddens, A. *The Third Way* (Oxford: Polity Press, 1998).

Ginsborg, P. *A History of Contemporary Italy: Society and Politics 1943–1988* (London: Penguin, 1990).

——*Italy and Its Discontents: Family, Civil Society, State 1980–2001* (London: Allen Lane, Penguin Press, 2001).

Glenny, M. *The Rebirth of History* (London: Penguin, 1993).

Goldhagen, D. *Hitler's Willing Executioners: Ordinary Germans and the Holocaust* (New York: KNOPF, 1996).

Gorner, P. *Twentieth Century German Philosophy* (Oxford: OUP, 2000).

Gramsci, A. *Selections from the Prison Notebooks* (London: Lawrence and Wishart, 1972).

Grass, G. 'Don't Reunify Germany', in James, H. and Stone, M. (eds) *When the Wall Came Down* (London:Routledge,1992).

Gray, J. *Post-liberalism* (London: Routledge, 1993).

——*Enlightenment's Wake* (London: Routledge, 1995).

——*Straw Dogs* (London: Granta, 2000).

——*Two Faces of Liberalism* (Cambridge: Polity Press, 2000).

Greider, W. *One World Ready or Not: The Manic Logic of Global Capitalism* (New York: Simon & Schuster, 1997).

Griffin, R. 'Revolts against the Modern World', *Literature and History*, vol. 1 (1985).

Gross, J. *Begründung der Berliner Republik: Deutschland am Ende des 20. Jahrhundert* (Stuttgart: Deutsche Verlags-Anstalt, 1995).
Gundle, S. and Parker, S. (eds) *The New Italian Republic: From the Fall of the Berlin Wall to Berlusconi* (London: Routledge, 1997).

Haakonssen, K. 'Republicanism', in *A Companion to Political Philosophy* (Oxford: Blackwell, 1999).
Habermas, J. 'Yet Again: German Identity – A Unified Nation of Angry DM-Burghers', in James, H. and Stone, M. (eds) *When the Wall Came Down* (London: Routledge, 1992).
——'The European Nation-State: On the Past and Future of Sovereignty and Citizenship', *Public Culture*, vol. 10, no. 2 (1998), pp. 397–416.
Hamilton, A. *The Appeal of Fascism* (London: Blond, 1971).
Hart, H. L. A. *The Concept of Law* (London: OUP, 1961).
Havel, V. 'The Power of the Powerless', in *Living in Truth* (London: Faber and Faber, 1987).
Hayek, F. A. *The Sensory Order* (London: Routledge and Kegan Paul, 1952).
——*The Constitution of Liberty* (London: Routledge and Kegan Paul, 1960).
——*New Studies in Philosophy, Politics, Economics and the History of Ideas* (London: Routledge and Kegan Paul, 1978).
Hayward, J. 'L'Individu Effacé ou le paradoxe du libéralisme française', *History of European Ideas*, vol. 24, no. 3 (Paris: Fayard, 1997), pp. 239–42.
Hayward, J. and Page, E. (eds) *Governing the New Europe* (Cambridge: Polity Press, 1995).
Heidegger, M. *An Introduction to Metaphysics* (New York: Anchor Books edn, 1961. First published in German in 1953 by Max Niemeyer Verlag).
Heilbrunn, J. 'Germany's New Right', *Foreign Affairs*, vol. 75, no. 6 (1996), pp. 80–98.
Held, D. 'Democracy and the Global System', in Held, D. (ed.) *Political Theory Today* (Cambridge: Polity Press, 1991).
Herf, J. *Reactionary Modernism: Technology, Culture, and Politics in Weimar and the Third Reich* (Cambridge: CUP, 1984).
Hirst, P. *From Statism to Pluralism* (London: UCL, 1997).
——'Globalization, the Nation State and Political Theory', in O'Sullivan, N. (ed.) *Political Theory in Transition* (Routledge: London, 2000).
Hosking, G. and Schöpflin, G. (eds) *Myths and Nationhood* (London: Hurst, 1997).
Hradec, J. in *Střední Evropa*, January 1985, translated in *The Salisbury Review*, vol. 4, no. 2 (January 1986), pp. 35–9.
Hyland, M. 'Continuous Crisis: Historical Action and Passion in Antonio Negri's Insurgencies', *Radical Philosophy*, no. 112 (March/April 2002), p. 31.

Ignatieff, M. 'Understanding Fascism?' in Margalit, A. and E. (eds), *Isaiah Berlin: A Celebration* (London: Hogarth Press, 1991).
——'Identity Parades', *Prospect* (April 1998), p. 19.

James, H. and Stone, M. (eds) *When the Wall Came Down* (London: Routledge, 1992).

Jaspers, K. 'Philosophical Memoir', in *Philosophy and the World* (Chicago: Gateway, 1963).

——*Wohin treibt die Bundesrepublik? Tatsachen-Gefahren-Chancen* (Munich: R. Piper & Co., 1966).

Jennings, J. 'From "Imperial State" to "l'Etat de Droit": Benjamin Constant, Blandine Kriegel and the Reform of the French Constitution', *Political Studies*, vol. 44, no. 3, Special Issue (1996) on Constitutionalism in Transformation, p. 503.

Judt, T. *The Burden of Responsibility: Blum, Camus, Aron and the French Twentieth Century* (London: University of Chicago Press, 1998).

Kagan, R. *Paradise and Power: America and Europe in the New World Order* (London: Atlantic Books, 2003).

Keane, J. (ed.) *Civil Society and the State* (London: Verso, 1988).

Kelly, P. 'Political Theory in Retreat? Contemporary Political Theory and the Historical Order', in O'Sullivan, N. (ed.) *Political Theory in Transition* (London: Routledge, 2000).

Kelsen, H. 'Foundations of Democracy', *Political Thought since World War I*, Stankiewicz, W. J. (ed.) (New York: Free Press of Glencoe, 1964).

Kennedy, R. and Benvenuto, B. *The Works of Jacques Lacan: An Introduction* (London: Free Association Books, 1986).

Kenny, M. *The First New Left* (London: Lawrence and Wishart, 1995).

Khilnani, S. *Arguing Revolution: The Intellectual Left in Postwar France* (New Haven and London: Yale University Press, 1993).

Klaus, V. *Renaissance: The Rebirth of Liberty in the Heart of Europe* (Washington: Cato Institute, 1997).

Kohler, L. and Saner, H. (eds) *Correspondence of Hannah Arendt and Karl Jaspers, 1926–1969*, trans. Kimber, R. and Kimber, R. (New York: Harcourt Brace Jovanich, 1992).

Kolakowki, L. *Marxism and Beyond* (London: Paladin, 1971).

——'Totalitarianism and the Virtue of the Lie', in Howe, I. (ed.) *1984 Revisited* (New York: Harper and Rowe, 1983).

Konrád, G. *Antipolitics* (London: Quartet, 1984).

Kraniauskas, J. 'Empire, or Multitude?' *Radical Philosophy*, no. 103 (September/October 2000) p. 33.

——'Capitalism, Socialism and Nihilism', *The Public Interest*, vol. 31 (1973), p. 12.

Kristol, I. ' "When Virtue Loses all Her Loveliness" – Some Reflections on Capitalism and "the Free Society" ', *The Public Interest*, vol. 21 (Fall 1970).

Kukathas, C. *Hayek and Modern Liberalism* (Oxford: OUP, 1990).

Kundera, M. 'A Kidnapped West or Culture Bows Out', *Granta*, no. 11 (1984), p. 114.

Kymlicka, W. *Ethnicities*, vol. 1, no. 1 (2001), p. 129.

Lacan, J. *Écrits: A Selection* (London: Tavistock Publications, 1977).

Laclau, E. (ed.) *The Making of Political Identities* (London: Verso, 1994).

Laing, R. D. *The Politics of Experience and the Bird of Paradise* (Harmondsworth: Penguin Books, 1967).

Laqueur, W. *Europe Since Hitler* (Harmondsworth: Penguin Books, 1982).

Laslett, P. *Philosophy, Politics and Society* (ed.) (Oxford: Blackwell, 1956).

Laughland, J. *The Tainted Source: The Undemocratic Origins of the European Idea* (London: Warner Books, 1998).

Ledeen, M. 'Renzo De Felice and the Controversy over Italian Fascism', *Journal of Contemporary History*, vol. 11, no. 4 (October 1976. Special Issue on Theories of Fascism), pp. 269–83.

Lefort, C. 'Pushing Back the Limits of the Possible', in Thompson, J. B. (ed.) *The Political Forms of Modern Society: Bureaucracy, Democracy, Totalitarianism* (Cambridge: Polity Press, 1986).

——'The Contradiction of Trotsky', in Thompson, J. B. (ed.) *The Political Forms of Modern Society: Bureaucracy, Democracy, Totalitarianism* (Cambridge: Polity Press, 1986).

——'The Logic of Totalitarianism', in Thompson, J. B. (ed.) *The Political Forms of Modern Society: Bureaucracy, Democracy, Totalitarianism*, (Cambridge: Polity Press, 1986).

Levi, C. *Of Fear and Freedom* (London: Cassell, 1950).

——*The Two-Fold Night: A Narrative of Travel in Germany* (London: Cresset Press, 1962).

——*Christ Stopped at Eboli* (Harmondsworth: Penguin, 1982).

Lévy, B.-H. *Adventures on the Freedom Road: French Intellectuals in the Twentieth Century* (London: Harvill Press, 1995). Originally published as *Les Aventures de la Liberté* (Paris: Grasset, 1991).

Lichtheim, G. *Europe in the Twentieth Century* (London: Sphere Books, 1974).

Lilla, M. (ed.) *New French Thought: Political Philosophy* (NJ: Princeton University Press, 1994).

Lipovetsky, G. *The Empire of Fashion: Dressing Modern Democracy* (NJ: Princeton University Press, 1994).

Lovejoy, A. O. *The Great Chain of Being* (NY: Harper Torch, 1960).

Luhmann, N. *Erkenntis als Konstruktion* (Bern: n.p., 1988).

——*Political Theory in the Welfare State* (Berlin: Walter de Gruyer & Co., 1990. First published in German in 1981).

——*Social Systems* (Stanford: Stanford University Press, 1995. First published in German in 1984).

Lumley, R. *States of Emergency: Cultures of Revolt in Italy from 1968 to 1978* (London: Verso, 1990).

Lyotard, J.-F. *Tombeau de l'intellectuel et autres papiers* (Paris: Editions Galilée, 1984).

Lyttelton, A. (ed.) *Italian Fascisms from Pareto to Gentile* (London: Cape, 1973).

McCarthy, P. (ed.) *Italy since 1945* (Oxford: OUP, 2000).

Macey, D. *The Lives of Michel Foucault* (London: Vintage, 1994).

MacIntyre, A. *After Virtue* (Duckworth: London, 1981).

Magnette, P. 'European Governance and Civic Participation: Beyond Elitist Citizenship?' *Political Studies*, vol. 51 (2003), pp. 144–60.

Malcolm, N. 'Conservative Realism and Christian Democracy', in Minogue, K. (ed.) *Conservative Realism* (London: HarperCollins, 1996).

Manent, P. 'The Modern State', in Lilla, M. (ed.) *New French Thought: Political Philosophy* (NJ: Princeton University Press, 1994).

Manin, B. 'On Legitimacy and Political Deliberation', in Lilla, M. (ed.) *New French Thought: Political Philosophy* (NJ: Princeton University Press, 1994).

Marcel, G. *The Philosophy of Existence* (London: Harvill Press, 1948).

Marcuse, H. *One Dimensional Man* (London: Sphere, 1964).

Marcuse, H., Wolff, R. P. and Moore, B. Jr *A Critique of Pure Tolerance* (Beacon Press, 1966).

Maritain, J. *Man and the State* (Chicago: University of Chicago Press, 1951).

Masaryk, T. G. *The Making of a State* (London: Allen and Unwin, 1927).

Mason, A. 'Communitarianism and its Legacy', in O'Sullivan, N. (ed.) *Political Theory in Transition* (London, Routledge, 2000), pp. 19–32.

Mazower, M. *Dark Continent: Europe's Twentieth Century* (London: Allen Lane, 1998).

Meinecke, F. *The German Catastrophe* (Massachusetts: Harvard University Press, 1950).

——*Machiavellism* (New Haven: Yale University Press, 1957).

Michnik, A. *Letters from Prison and Other Essays* (Berkeley: University of California Press, 1985).

Mellor, J. 'Is the Russian Intelligentsia European?', Schöpflin, G. and Wood, N. (eds) *In Search of Central Europe* (Oxford: Polity, 1989).

Merleau-Ponty, M. *Sens et non-sens* (Paris: Nagel, 1948); trans. as *Sense and Non-Sense* by H. L. and P. A. Dreyfus (Evanston: Northwestern University Press 1964).

Michnik, A. *Letters from Freedom* (California: University of California Press, 1998).

Milchman, A. and Roseberg, A. (eds) *Martin Heidegger and the Holocaust* (Atlantic Highlands, NJ: Humanities Press, 1997).

Miller, D. 'Recent Theories of Social Justice', *British Journal of Political Science*, vol. 21 (1991), p. 376.

——'Citizenship and Pluralism', *Political Studies*, vol. 43, no. 3 (September 1995), p. 449.

——*On Nationality* (Oxford: Clarendon Press, 1995).

Miłosz, C. *The Captive Mind* (Harmondsworth: Penguin, 2001 [1953]).

Milward, A. S. *The European Rescue of the Nation-State* (London: Routledge, 1992).

Minogue, K. *Citizenship and Monarchy: A Hidden Fault Line in Our Civilisation* (University of London: Institute of United States Studies, 1998), p. 27.

Mitscherlich, A. and M. *Die Unfähigkeit zu trauern* (Munich: n.p., 1967).

Mlynář, Z. *Nightfrost in Prague* (London, 1980).

Moi, T. *Sexual/Textual Politics* (London: Routledge, 1985).

Moreau, P. 'Revolution Conservatrice et Nouvelles Droites Allemandes', in *Les Temps Modernes*, 39 Année, no. 436 (Novembre 1982), pp. 893–959.

Mouffe, C. *The Return of the Political* (London: Verso, 1993).

——'For an Agonistic Model of Democracy', in O'Sullivan, N. (ed.) *Political Theory in Transition* (Routledge: London, 2000).

Mounier, E. 'Reflections on an Apocalyptic Age', in Hardman, D. (ed.) *Reflections on Our Age* (London: Allan Wingate, 1948).

——*Personalism* (London: Routledge, 1952. First published in France in 1950, as *Le Personnalisme*).

Müller, J.-W. *Another Country: German Intellectuals, Unification and National Identity* (New Haven: Yale University Press, 2000).
——'Portrait of Jürgen Habermas', *Prospect*, March 2001.
Mure, G. R. G. 'The Organic State', *Philosophy*, vol. 24 (1949), p. 206.

Negri, A. *The Savage Anomaly* (Minneapolis: University of Minnesota Press, 1991. Original Italian edn 1981).
——*The Politics of Subversion: A Manifesto for the Twenty-First Century* (Cambridge: Polity Press, 1989).
——'Twenty Theses on Marx', *Marx Beyond Marx: Lessons on the 'Grundrisse'*, trans. Cleaver, H., Ryan, M. and Viano, M., (ed.) Fleming, J. (New York and London: Autonomedia/Pluto, 1991).
——*Insurgencies: Constituent Power and the Modern State* (Minneapolis: University of Minnesota Press, 1992).
——'Constituent Republic', in Virno, P. and Hardt, M. (eds) *Radical Thought in Italy* (Minneapolis: University of Minnesota Press, 1996).
——and Hardt, M. *Empire* (Cambridge, MA and London: Harvard University Press, 2000).
Negri, A., Castellano, L., Cavallina, A., Cortiana, G., Dalmarira, M., Bravo, L. F., Funaro, C. *etal*. 'Do You Remember Revolution?' in Virno, P. and Hardt, M. (eds) *Radical Thought in Italy* (Minneapolis: University of Minnesota Press, 1996).
Newey, G. 'The Political Form of the Constitution: The Separation of Powers, Rights and Representative Democracy', *Political Studies*, vol. 44, no. 3 (1996).
——*After Politics: The Rejection of Politics in Contemporary Liberal Philosophy* (London: Palgrave, 2001).
Nolte, E. *Three Faces of Fascism* (New York: Mentor, 1969).

Oakeshott, M. *On Human Conduct* (Oxford: Clarendon Press, 1975).
——*On History* (Oxford: Blackwell, 1983).
——*Rationalism in Politics* (Indianapolis: Liberty Press, 1991).
Offe, C. *Contradictions of the Welfare State*, Keane, J. (ed.) (London: Hutchinson, 1984).
Ortegay Gasset, J. *The Revolt of the Masses* (London: Allen and Unwin, 1963).
O'Sullivan, N. (ed.) *Political Theory in Transition* (London: Routledge, 2000).

Parekh, B. *Contemporary Political Thinkers* (Oxford: Martin Robertson, 1982).
——'Theorizing Political Theory', in O'Sullivan, N. (ed.) *Political Theory in Transition* (London: Routledge, 2000).
——*Rethinking Multiculturalism* (Basingstoke: MacMillan, 2000).
Parker, B. W. 'Renzo De Felice and the History of Italian Fascism', in *American Historical Review* (1990).
Pasqualini, J. *Prisonnier de Mao* (Paris: Gallimard, 1975).
Patočka, J. *Platon et l'Europe*, trans. by E. Abrams (Paris: Verdier, 1983).
——*Heretical Essays in the Philosophy of History* (Chicago: Open Court, 1996).
Patrick, M. *Derrida, Responsibility and Politics* (Aldershot: Ashgate, 1997).
Peacock, A. and Willgerodt, H. (eds) *German Neo-Liberals and the Social Market Economy* (London: Macmillan, 1989).

Pelczynski, Z. A. 'Solidarity and the "Rebirth of Civil Society" in Poland', in Keane, J. (ed.) *Civil Society and the State* (London: Verso, 1988), p. 365.

Pettit, P. *Republicanism: A Theory of Freedom and Government* (Oxford: Clarendon Press, 1997).

Phillips, A. *Democracy and Difference* (Cambridge: Polity, 1993).

——'Dealing with Difference: A Politics of Ideas or a Politics of Presence?' *Constellations*, vol. 1, no. 1 (April 1994), pp. 74–91.

Plamenatz, J. 'The Use of Political Theory', in Quinton, A. *Political Philosophy* (Oxford: OUP, 1967).

Polanyi, M. *The Logic of Liberty* (London: Routledge and Kegan Paul, 1951).

Popper, K. *The Poverty of Historicism* (London: Routledge, 1961).

——*The Open Society and Its Enemies* (London: Routledge & Kegan Paul, 1962).

Pulzer, P. 'Model or Exception – Germany as a Normal State?' in Smith, G., Paterson, W. E. and Padgett, S. (eds) *Developments in German Politics 2* (Basingstoke: Macmillan, 1996).

Quazza, G. 'The Politics of the Italian Resistance', in Woolf, S. J. (ed.) *Italy and the Powers* (London: Longman, 1972).

Quinton, A. *Political Philosophy* (Oxford: OUP, 1967).

Rawls, J. *A Theory of Justice* (Cambridge, MA: Harvard University Press, 1971).

Raz, J. *The Authority of Law* (Oxford: Clarendon Press, 1979).

——(ed.) *Authority* (Oxford: Blackwell, 1990).

——'Multiculturalism: A Liberal Perspective', *Dissent* (Winter, 1994).

Renaut, A. *The Era of the Individual: A Contribution to a History of Subjectivity* (NJ: Princeton University Press, 1997. Originally published as *L'ère de l'individu: Contribution à une histoire de la subjectivité*, Paris: Gallimard, 1989).

Renaut, A. and Ferry, L. *Political Philosophy: From the Rights of Man to the Republican Idea* (London: University of Chicago Press, 1992. Originally published in 1985, as *Philosophie politique, vol. 3: Des droits de l'homme à l'idée républicaine*, Presses Universitaires de France).

Ricciardi, M. 'Rawls in Italy', *European Journal of Political Theory*, vol. 1, no. 2 (October 2002), pp. 229–41.

Roberts, D. D. *Benedetto Croce and the Uses of Historicism* (Berkeley: University of California Press, 1987).

Roman, J. 'Un multiculturalisme à la française?' *Esprit*, vol. 212 (1995), pp. 157–8.

Röpke, W. *A Humane Economy* (London: Oswald Wolff, 1960).

——'Liberalism and Christianity', in Panichas, G. A. (ed.) *Modern Age: The First Twenty-five Years* (Indianopolis: Liberty Press, 1988).

Rosanvallon, P. 'Le socialisme francais et la peur de la social-démocratie', in *Faire*, Qu'est-ce que c'est la Social-Démocratie?, Paris (1979), p. 8.

Rumford, C. 'Civil Society or Transnational Social Space?' *European Journal of Social Theory*, vol. 6, no. 1 (February 2003), pp. 25–43.

Rupnik, J. 'Totalitarianism Revisited', in Keane, J. (ed.) *Civil Society and the State* (London: Verso, 1988).

——*The Other Europe* (New York: Pantheon Books, 1989).

Russell, B. *A History of Western Philosophy* (London: Allen & Unwin 1946).

Santayana, G. *Dominations and Powers* (London: Constable, 1951).
——'The Intellectual Temper of the Age', in Henfrey, N. (ed.) *Selected Critical Writings of George Santayana*, vol. 2 (Cambridge: CUP, 1968).
Sartre, J.-P. *Being and Nothingness* (Eng. trans., London: Methuen, 1958. First published 1943, Gallimard).
——*Critique of Dialectical Reason* (London: Verso, 1976).
Sartori, G. 'Video-Power', *Government and Opposition*, vol. 24 (1989), pp. 39–53.
Schnapper, D. *Community of Citizens: On the Modern Idea of Nationality* (London: Transaction Publishers, 1998. Originally published as *Communauté des Citoyens* Paris: Editions Gallimard, 1994).
Schöpflin, G. 'The Political Traditions of Eastern Europe', *Daedalus*, vol. 119, no. 1 (Winter 1990), pp. 55–90.
——*Politics in Eastern Europe* (Oxford: Blackwell, 1993).
Schütz, A. 'On Multiple Realities', *Philosophy and Phenomenological Research*, vol. 5, no. 4 (June 1945), pp. 533–74.
Scruton, R. *The Meaning of Conservatism* (Harmondsworth: Penguin Books, 1980), p. 25.
——(ed.) 'Politics and Conscience', in *Conservative Thoughts* (London: Claridge Press, 1988).
——'The New Right in Central Europe l: Czechoslovakia', *Political Studies*, vol. XXXVI (1988), pp. 449–62.
——'The New Right in Central Europe ll: Poland and Hungary', *Political Studies*, vol. XXXVI (1988), p. 642.
——'In Defence of the Nation', in Clark, J. C. (ed.) *Ideas and Politics in Modern Britain* (London: Macmillan, 1990).
——'Masaryk, Patočka and the Care of the Soul', in *The Philosopher on Dover Beach* (Manchester: Carcanet, 1990).
Semino, E. and Masci, M. 'Politics is Football: Metaphor in the Discourse of Silvio Berlusconi', *Discourse and Society*, vol. VII, no. 2 (1996), p. 248.
Semprun, J. *Literature or Life* (USA: Penguin, 1998).
Shearmur, J. *The Political Thought of Karl Popper* (London: Routledge, 1996).
Sheehan, T. 'Myth and Violence: The Fascism of Julius Evola and Alain de Benoist', *Social Research*, vol. 48 (Spring 1981).
Shklar, J. *After Utopia* (Princeton: Princeton University Press, 1957).
Siedentop, L. *Democracy in Europe* (London: Penguin Press, 2000).
Silone, I. *The Story of a Humble Christian* (London: Victor Gollancz, 1970).
Šimečka, M. *The Restoration of Order* (London: n.p., 1987).
——'Another Civilization? An Other Civilization?' Schöpflin, G. and Wood, N. (eds) *In Search of Central Europe* (Oxford: Polity, 1989).
Skinner, Q. 'The Idea of Negative Liberty', in Rorty, R., Schneewind, J. B. and Skinner, Q. (eds) *Philosophy in History* (Cambridge: CUP, 1984).
——*Liberty Before Liberalism* (Cambridge: Cambridge University Press, 1998).
——'The Republican Ideal of Political Liberty', in Rosen, M. and Wolff, J. (eds) *Political Thought* (Oxford: OUP, 1999), p. 171.
——'A Third Concept of Liberty', *London Review of Books* (4 April 2002), pp. 16–18.
Sontheimer, K. *The Government and Politics of West Germany* (London: Hutchinson, 1972).

Stirk, P. (ed.) *Mitteleuropa: History and Prospects* (Edinburgh: Edinburgh University Press, 1994).

Stone, A. 'Governing with Judges: The New Constitutionalism', in Hayward, J. and Page, E. (eds) *Governing the New Europe* (Cambridge: Polity Press, 1995).

Strauss, L. *Liberalism Ancient and Modern* (Chicago: University of Chicago Press, 1989).

Szücs, J. 'Three Historical Regions of Europe', in Keane, J. (ed.) *Civil Society and the State* (London: Verso, 1988).

Talmon, J. L. *The Rise of Totalitarian Democracy* (Boston: Beacon Press, 1952).

Taylor, C. Foreword to M. Gauchet. *The Disenchantment of the World: A Political History of Religion* (NJ: Princeton University Press, 1997. Originally published as *Le désenchantement du monde*, Paris: Gallimard, 1985).

Tismaneanu, V. (ed.) *The Revolutions of 1989* (London: Routledge, 1999).

Todd, O. *Albert Camus: A Life* (n.p.: Alfred A. Knopf, 1997; Eng. edn published by Chatto and Windus, 1997).

Togliatti, P. *Lectures on Fascism* (London: Lawrence & Wishart, 1976).

Valéry, P. *Reflections on the World Today* (London: Thames and Hudson, 1951).

Vattimo, G. *The Transparent Society* (Cambridge: Polity Press, 1992; original Italian edn, 1989).

——*Beyond Interpretation: The Meaning of Interpretation for Philosophy* (Cambridge: Polity Press, 1997; original Italian edn 1994).

——'The Trace of the Trace', in Derrida, J. and Vattimo, G. (eds) *Religion* (Cambridge: Polity Press, 1998; original French edn, 1996).

——*Nietzsche: An Introduction* (California: Stanford University Press, 2002. Original Italian edn, 1985).

Veca, S. *La società giusta*: *Argomenti per il contrattualism* (Milan: Il Saggiatore, 1982).

——*Questioni di giustizia* (Parma: Pratiche, 1985).

Voegelin, E. *The New Science of Politics* (Chicago: University of Chicago Press, 1952).

——'The Oxford Political Philosophers', *The Philosophical Quarterly*, vol. 3, no. 11 (April 1953), p. 101.

Waever, O. 'Europe since 1945: Crisis to Renewal', in Wilson, K. and van der Dusen, J. (eds) *The History of the Idea of Europe* (London: Routledge, 1995).

Warner, G. 'Italy and the Powers, 1943–49', in Woolf, S. J. (ed.) *Italy and the Powers* (London: Longman, 1972).

Weber, M. *German Sociology* (NY: Glencoe, 1964. Originally published in France, 1936, as *La Sociologie Allemande Contemporaine*).

Weldon, T. D. *States and Morals: A Study in Political Conflict* (London: 1946).

——*The Vocabulary of Politics* (Baltimore: Penguin Books, 1953).

White, S. K. *Political Theory and Postmodernism* (Cambridge: CUP, 1991).

Wilson, K. and van der Dusen, J. (eds) *The History of the Idea of Europe* (London: Routledge, 1995).

Wincott, D. 'Does the European Union Pervert Democracy? Questions of Democracy in New Constitutionalist Thought on the Future of Europe', in Bankowski, Z. and Scott, A. (eds) *The European Union and Its Order* (Oxford: Blackwell, 2000).

Wolin, R. (ed.) *The Heidegger Controversy: A Critical Reader* (Cambridge, MA: MIT, 1998).

Woolf, S. J. (ed.) 'The Politics of the Italian Resistance', *The Rebirth of Italy, 1943–50* (London: Longman, 1972).

Yack, B. 'Multiculturalism and Political Theory', *European Journal of Political Theory*, vol. 1, no. 1 (July 2002), p. 109.

Zapponi, N. 'Fascism in Italian Historiography, 1986–1933: A Fading National Identity', *Journal of Contemporary History*, vol. 4 (1994).

Zitelmann, R. *et al.* (eds) *Westbindung: Risiken und Chancen für Deutschland* (Berlin: Propyläen-Verlag, 1993).

Žižek, S. *Did Somebody Say Totalitarianism?* (London: Verso, 2001).

Zolo, D. *Democracy and Complexity: A Realist Approach* (Cambridge: Polity Press, 1992).

Index

1949 constitution, 108, 120

Ackerman, B., 176, 177
Action Française, 86
Action Party, 129
Adenauer, K., 118
Adorno, T. W., 105
Almond, G., 110
Althusser, L., 70, 71, 73
amnesia, 16–19
Anderson, P., 152
Andreotti, G. 153
Aragon, L., 139
Arendt, H., 38, 104, 105, 158
Aristotle, 21, 35
Aron, R., 79, 83–4, 85
askesis, 145
Attlee, C., 24
Auschwitz, 113, 117, 119

Baader-Meinhof Gang, 68
Barraclough, G., 9
Barry, B., 41, 42, 43
Basic Law, 2, 8, 97, 104, 123, 124
Baudrillard, J., 75, 76
Beck, U., 115
Belgium, 110
Bellamy, R., 54, 58, 185
Belohradský, V., 166, 167
Benn, S. I., 22
Berlin republic, 116, 123–5
Berlin, I., 3, 27, 29, 30, 31, 32, 40, 45
Berlinguer, L., 134
Berlusconi, S., 137, 144, 149, 150, 151
Betti, U., 138, 139

Beveridge Report, 8, 24
Beveridge, W., 24
Bibó, I., 164, 170, 171, 173
Bideleux, R., 175, 177, 183, 188
Bismarck, O., 8
Bitburg cemetery, 117
Blair, T., 57
Bobbio, N., 66, 68, 133, 140–2, 143, 151, 152
Böckenförde, E-W., 107
Bohemia, 156
Bohrer, K. H., 120, 121–2
Bolshevik party, 79
Bossi, U., 151
Bousquet, R., 18
Brandenburg Gate, 123
Britain, 3, 8, 10, 11, 19, 20–62, 91, 94, 98, 103, 122, 126, 138
    analytical school of philosophy, 3
    citizenship, 10, 11
    complacency of, 20–1
    Conservative Party, 24
    constitutionalism, 58
    empire, 39
    European Union, 58–62
    Fabianism, 24
    global perspective, 56–7
    identity crisis, 58–62
    identity politics, 45–8
    immigration in, 10
    Labour Party, 23, 25
    Left, 23–8
    Marxism, 26
    middle way, 21, 29, 32
    multiculturalism, 11, 47, 48–54

232

New Labour, 27, 56
New Left, 41
New Right, 27, 35
pragmatism, 20–54
republican theory, 54–6
Royal Commission on Population, 10
rule of law, 34, 54
social democracy, 25–7, 29, 32, 40, 68
third way, 56–8
welfare state, 8, 25
Brown, G., 56, 57
Brubaker, R., 125
Byron, Lord 153

Calogero, G., 129
Calvino, I., 133
Camus, A., 79, 80–2
Canovan, M., 44
capitalism, 21, 23, 26, 32, 34, 45, 96, 97,
    106, 107, 110, 138
Carr, E. H., 1
Cartesianism, 66, 92, 147
Cassirer, E., 6
Castoriadis, C., 79
Catholic theology, 137, 138
Charter 77, 168, 176
Chiaromonte, N., 131
China, 13, 72
Chirac, J., 92
Christian Democracy
    in Germany, 8–9, 108, 109
    in Italy, 126, 131, 132, 133, 134, 137,
        144, 150
Christian Socialists, 108
Christianity, 68, 69, 78, 83, 85, 97, 100,
    109, 134, 148, 171
Churchill, W., 24, 126
citizenship, 10–12, 19, 37
    in Britain, 10, 11
    in France, 11–12
    in Germany, 11
Civic Forum (Czech), 173
civil association, 35, 36, 37–40, 45, 47, 62,
    156, 183–4, 189
    absence in East-Central Europe, 156
    and European Union, 183–4, 189
Cixous, H., 76
Clark, J. C. D., 11

Clay, L., 96
Cohen, E., 93
Cold War, 2, 32, 186
Coleridge, S. T., 40
Colley, L., 61
Common Market, 174
communism, 11, 33, 63, 69, 72, 138
Communist Party
    in Italy, 126, 131, 132, 133, 134,
        144, 150
    in Poland, 168
Confalonieri, F., 150
Conservative Party (Britain), 24
Constant, B., 31, 55, 64, 85, 88
constitutional patriotism, 112, 113,
    115–16, 117, 122, 125
constitutionalism, 20, 27, 58, 62, 64, 77,
    83, 84, 85, 93, 101–2, 135, 140–4
    in Britain, 20, 27, 58, 62
    in France, 64, 83, 84, 85, 93
    in Italy, 140–4
    in West Germany, 101–2
        (see also constitutional
        patriotism; Rechsstaat)
Cranston, M., 131
Crick, B., 41
Croce, B., 4, 128–31, 144, 150
Crosland, A., 25, 26
Crossman, R., 23, 13
Czechoslovakia, 117, 155, 156, 165, 166,
    172, 174, 176

Dahrendorf, R., 6, 110, 115, 123, 125, 173
Davies, N., 61
de Benoist, A., 85–6, 14
De Felice, R., 139
de Gasperi, A., 17
de Gaulle, C., 17, 64
de Jouvenel, B., 79, 82–3
de Ruggiero, G., 128
de Tocqueville, A. de, 40, 55, 64, 73, 84,
    85, 130, 136, 189
de Tracy, D., 91
Débray, R., 86, 87
Declaration of Human Rights, 53
Del Noce, A., 137, 138
Deleuze, G., 75
della Volpe, G., 133

Delors, J., 70
democratic deficit, 181, 184
Der Spiegel, 99, 123
Derrida, J., 7, 77, 92, 121, 147, 149
Descartes, R., 111
d'Estaing, G., 187, 188
di Lampedusa, T., 139
Dicey, A. V., 58
Die Zeit, 112
Dostoevsky, F., 40
Drucker, P., 13, 14
Dubcek, A., 176
Dumont, L., 72
Dunn, J., 58
Dworkin, R., 58
Dzielski, M., 173

East Berlin, occupation of, 96, 96, 100
East-Central Europe, 155–77
    absence of civil association, 156
    alternatives to totalitarianism, 167–74
    authoritarian political tradition, 155
    critique of totalitarianism, 157–67
    Czechoslovakia, 117, 155, 156, 165,
        166, 172, 174, 176
        Charter 77, 168, 176
        Czech Civic Forum, 173
        free market in, 172–3
    European Union, 157, 175
    Hungary, 156, 173–4
        free market in, 173–4
        nationalism, 156
    Poland, 117, 156, 157, 167, 168, 173
        Association for Free Enterprise, 173
        Communist Party, 168
        free market in, 173
        political thought since 1945, 155–77
        Solidarity movement, 158, 167
    post-war democratic project,
        155–77
    problems of transition, 174–5
    religious divisions, 155
    rule of law, 157, 171
    social divisions, 155
    totalitarian lie, 160–2, 168
    Velvet Revolutions, 155, 156, 174–5,
        175–7
Eco, U., 134

Eichmann, A., 104
Eléments, 85
Eliot, T. S., 60
England, 21, 60, 61, 62, 89, 142
Enlightenment, 11, 51, 53, 78
Enzensberger, H. M., 117
Erhard, L., 9
Esprit, 87
Euronationalism, 181, 182
European Convention on Human
    Rights, 61
European political identity
    nature of, 178–89
    search for, 12–16
European Union, 19, 58–62, 94, 95,
        181–9
    and Britain, 58–62
    civil association, 183–4, 189
    constitution, 187–8
    democratic deficit, 184
    and East-Central Europe, 157, 175
    European constitutional patriotism, 186
    European political identity, 12–16,
        181–9
    and Germany, 125
    integration, 15–16
    and Italy, 152–4
    juridical dimension, 183–9
    sovereignty, 184
    White Paper on European Governance, 184
Evola, J., 144, 145, 146, 181, 182
    askesis, 145
existentialism, 4, 67, 68, 8

Fanon, F., 68
fascism, 15–16, 30, 32, 70, 127,
        128, 129, 130, 131, 139, 140,
        144, 145
    in Italy, 128, 129, 130, 131, 139,
        140, 144
Federal Republic, 96, 97–105
feminism, 45, 46, 47, 76, 110
Ferry, L., 92
Fest, J., 116, 117
Fidelius, P., 160, 172
Fini, G., 144, 151
First World War, 97, 127, 155, 169
Forza Italia, 144, 149, 150

Foucault, M., 74, 75, 77, 92, 135
France, 2, 8, 10, 11, 12, 17, 18, 19, 61,
     63–94, 122, 181, 184
  Action Française, 86
  Cartesian tradition, 66
  citizenship, 11–12
  constitution of, 2–3
  Constitutional Council, 93
  exceptionalism, 93
  Fifth Republic, 85, 89, 143
  human rights, 2–3
  immigration, 10
  individualism, 72–3
  Jacobins, 65
  Left, The, 63, 64, 65, 79, 80, 86
  liberalism, 86–92
  Liberation, 63
  Marxism, 70–2
  May 1968, 68, 72, 73
  multiculturalism, 11–12
  National Front, 86
  national identity, 63
  nationalism, 65
  political moderation, 79–85
  postmodern philosophy, 74–8
  radical politics, 64–72
  republican tradition, 86–92, 93–4
  Resistance, 63, 65, 66
  Revolution, 63, 64, 65, 70, 84, 85,
     93, 170, 176
  rule of law, 75, 89
  Socialist Party, 63
  Third Republic, 8, 63
  Trotskyist Party (PCI), 79
  Vichy, 18, 63, 64, 65
  welfare state, 8
Frankfurt School, 105, 106
free market,
  in Britain, 32–5
  in Czechoslovakia, 172–3
  in France, 91
  in Hungary, 173–4
  in Italy, 150
  in Poland, 173
  in West Germany, 96, 110
  see also capitalism
French Revolution, 63, 64, 65, 70, 84,
     85, 93, 170, 176

Freud, S., 6
Furet, F., 84–5, 91, 93

Gadamer, H-G., 114
Garton Ash, T., 165
Gatt-Rutter, J., 139
Gauchet, M., 72, 88, 89, 91
Gehlen, A., 116
Gellner, E., 22
Germany, 2, 8, 9, 10, 11, 12, 17, 18, 19,
     68, 95–125, 126, 175, 181, 186
  1949 constitution, 108, 120
  Act to Promote the Preparedness of
     Foreign Workers to Return, 10
  Allied plans for, 95–7
  Basic Law, 2, 8, 97, 104, 123, 124
  Berlin republic, 116, 123–5
  Christian Democrats, 8–9, 108, 109
  Christian Socialists, 108
  Christian tradition, 8–9, 97
  citizenship, 11
  commitment to European Union, 125
  constitution of, 2
  constitutional patriotism, 112, 113,
     115–16, 117, 122, 125
  Federal Republic, 96, 97–105
    conservative critics of, 97–105
  Foreigners Act, 10
  Frankfurt school, 105, 106
  Green movement, 110, 115
  Historikerstreit, 118, 163
  Holocaust, The, 104, 113, 116, 119,
     123
  human rights, 2
  immigration in, 10
  Lander, 96
  Left, The, 117, 118, 119, 122, 123, 125
  multiculturalism, 11–12
  national identity, 95–7, 117, 118, 119,
     120–3, 123–5
  nationalism, 95–125
  New Right, 118, 119, 120, 121, 122,
     123, 125
  occupation of East Berlin, 95, 96, 105
  radical critique of post-war
     democracy, 105–7
  Rechsstaat, 97, 107, 108, 109, 110, 111,
     112, 113

Germany (*Continued*)
   responses to unification, 116–23
   rule of law, 99, 104, 106, 107, 112
   social democracy, 68
   Sozialstaat, 107, 108, 109, 110, 111,
      112, 113
   Weimar Republic, 33, 83, 96,
      104, 122
   welfare state, 8
Giddens, A., 56
Ginsborg, P., 151, 152, 153
Glenny, M., 176
globalization, 179–80
Gnosticism, 102, 103
Goebbels, J., 16
Goethe, J. W. von, 100
Goldhagen, D., 11
Göring, H., 16
Gramsci, A., 86, 129, 131, 132, 133, 134,
   146, 150, 168
Grass, G., 117
Gray, J., 43, 44, 45
Green movement, 110, 115
Gross, J., 124
Gruppo 63, 134
Gulf War, 117

Habermas, J., 107, 108, 110–16, 117,
   118, 119, 122, 123, 124, 125, 149,
   179, 180, 182, 183, 186, 189
Hain, P., 61
Hart, H. L. A., 31
Havel, V., 159, 160, 161, 170, 171,
   172, 176
Hayek, F. A., 7, 27, 32–5, 36, 40, 162,
   172, 189
Hegel, G. W. F., 28, 88
Heidegger, M., 45, 92, 98–9, 106, 117,
   147, 169
Held, D., 57
historicity, 4
Historikerstreit, 118, 163
Hitler, A., 1, 16, 18, 21, 28, 96, 123, 166
Hobbes, T., 32, 37, 101, 183, 189
Hoffmann, J., 123
Holocaust, The, 104, 113, 116, 119, 123
Horkheimer, 105
Hradec, J., 165, 166

human rights, 2, 3, 7, 19, 178
   in France, 2–3
   in Germany, 2
   in Italy, 2
Hungary, 156, 173–4
Husserl, E., 169

Il Mondo, 131
Immigration Act 1971, 10
immigration, 10–11
   in Britain, 10
   in Germany, 10
India, 50
international economy, 13, 14
Iran, 77
Iraq War, 186
Irigaray, L., 76
Italian Social Movement, 144
Italy, 2, 8, 17, 18, 19, 109, 125–54
   abolition of monarchy, 126
   Action Party, 129
   Christian Democrat Party, 126, 131,
      132, 133, 134, 137, 144, 150
   Church, the, 106, 131, 132
   Communist Party, 126, 131, 132,
      133, 134, 144, 150
   constitution of, 2
   constitutionalism, 140–4
   Crocean liberalism, 128–31
   democratic realism, 140–4
   explosion at Bologna railway
      station, 135
   extreme right, 144–6
   fascism, 128, 129, 130, 131, 139,
      140, 144
   Forza Italia, 144, 149, 150
   Gruppo 63, 134
   human rights in, 2
   Il Mondo, 131
   Italian Social Movement, 144
   judicial system, 152–3
   Liberal Party, 129
   liberalsocialismo, 129
   Liberation, 128, 132
   Marxism, 131
   membership of European Union,
      152–4
   National Alliance, 144, 150, 151

national divisions, 127
New Italian Republic, 149–52
New Left, 134, 135–7
Northern League, 150, 151
post-modern pluralism, 146–9
post-war democratic project in, 126–54
    conservative response, 137–40
radical left, 131–5
Resistance, 126, 127, 131, 140, 151
rule of law, 112, 135, 142, 143
social democracy, 140–4
Socialist Party, 144, 150
Tempo presente, 131
Third Force, 130, 131
trasformismo politics, 127, 128

Japan, 13
Jaspers, K., 98, 103, 104, 105
Jefferson, T., 91
Jeffries, I., 175, 177
Judt, T., 17, 18, 82, 83, 161, 175, 176
Jünger, E., 120, 169

Kadar, J., 173
Kant, I. 37, 103, 104, 105, 125
Kelsen, H., 102, 107–8, 110, 111, 141
Keynes, J. M., 24
Khilnani, S., 64
Khomeini, A., 77
Kierkegaard, S., 69, 70
Kiesinger, K-G, 103
Klaus, V., 172, 173
Kohl, H., 120
Kolakowski, L., 161
Kolnai, A, 159, 160
Konrád, G., 171
Koran, M., 164
Kosovo War, 117
Kriegel, B., 89–90, 91, 94
Krisis, 85
Kristeva, J., 76, 77
Kumar, K., 60
Kundera, M., 164, 165, 166

Labour Party (Britain), 23, 25
Lacan, J., 92
Laclau, E., 5
Laing, R. D., 41

Lander, 96
Laski, H., 23
Laslett, P., 22
Laughland, J., 16
League of Nations, 14
Lee Kuan Yew, 143
Lefort, C., 79–80
Left, The,
    in Britain, 23–8
    in France, 63, 64, 65, 79, 80, 86
    in Germany, 117, 118, 119, 122,
        123, 125
    in Italy, 131–7
Lenin, V. I. U., , 71, 166
Levi, C., 130
Lévy, B-H., 73
liberal empire, 180–1
Liberal Party (Italy), 129
liberalsocialismo, 129
Lichtheim, G., 12
Lipovetsky, G., 72, 73
Locke, J., 31
Lübke, H., 103
Luhmann, N., 113, 114, 142
Lyotard, J-F., 78

Mabbott, J. D., 20, 21
Machiavelli, N., 55, 100, 150, 154
MacIntyre, A., 6
Madelin, A., 91
Magnette, P., 185
Malcolm, N., 61, 62, 187, 188
Malfatti, F. M., 153
Manent, P., 87, 88, 91
Maoism, 72
Marcel, G., 67
Marcuse, H., 106–7, 134
Maritain, J., 14, 79, 83
Marquand, D., 60
Marshall Plan, 174
Marshall, T. H., 8, 24
Marx, K., 28, 34, 71, 132, 136
Marxism, 26–7, 33, 34, 66, 67, 70–2, 75,
        78, 79, 85, 111, 131–2, 133, 134,
        135, 136, 139, 140, 161
    in Britain, 26
    in France, 70–2

Marxism (*Continued*)
in Germany, 105–7
in Italy, 131–4, 136
Masaryk, T., 156
May 1968, 68, 72, 73
Mazower, M, 10, 178, 186
Meinecke, F., 99–101
Merleau-Ponty, M., 65, 66
Michnik, A., 159, 167, 168, 174
Mill, J. S., 28, 31, 38, 40, 51
Miller, D., 27, 42, 44, 54
Milosz, C., 157, 160
Milward, A., 14, 15
Minogue, K., 60
Mitscherlich, A., 103
Mitscherlich, M., 103
Mitterand, F., 89
Mlynár, Z., 158, 159
monism, 29, 136
Mont Pèlerin Society, 172
Montaigne, M. de, 77
Montale, E., 130
Moro, A., 135
Morris, W., 27
Mosca, G., 139, 141
Mouffe, C., 45, 47, 54, 179
Mounier, E., 68, 69, 70, 141
Müller-Armack, A., 109
Muller, J-W., 112, 116, 124
multiculturalism, 11, 47, 48–54, 86, 87, 90, 110
in Britain, 11, 47, 48–54
in France, 11–12
in Germany, 11–12
Mure, G. R., 28
Mussolini, B., 8, 16, 21, 128, 140, 144

nation-state, 14–15, 19
National Alliance, 144, 150, 151
National Front, 86
national identity
in Britain, 58–62
in France, 63
in Germany, 95–7, 117, 118, 119, 120–3, 123–5
nationalism, 34, 43, 44, 59–60, 65, 90, 99–100, 107, 112, 113, 115–16, 178–9

Nazism, 8, 11, 17, 33, 65, 96, 97, 98, 99, 100, 102, 103, 104, 105, 108, 116, 117, 118, 119, 123, 127, 144, 145, 155, 163
negative liberty, 30, 31, 32
Negri, A., 135–7
Nehamas, A., 92
neo-Roman school, 54, 55
New Deal, 123
New European Order, 16
New Labour, 27, 56
New Left Review, 26
New Left, 41
New Right, 9, 27, 35, 85–6, 115, 118, 119, 120, 121, 122, 123, 125, 145, 146, 173
in Britain, 27, 35
in France, 85–6
in Germany, 118, 119, 120, 121, 122, 123, 125
Newey, G., 42
Nietzsche, 69, 70, 85, 86, 138, 145, 187
nihilism, 81, 98, 169
Nolte, E., 117, 118
Northern Ireland, 60
Northern League, 150, 151
Nouvelle Droite, 85–6
Nouvelle Ecole, 85

Oakeshott, M., 27, 35–40, 45, 47, 62, 189
Offe, C., 114

Pannunzio, M., 131
Parekh, B., 31, 45, 48–54
Pareto, V., 139, 141
Pascal, B., 69
Pasolini, P. P., 133
Pasqualini, J., 72
Patocka, J., 168, 169, 170
Péguy, C., 69
Pelczynski, Z. A., 168
personalism, 69–70
Pétain, H. P., 63
Peters, R. S., 22
Pettit, P., 30
phenomenology, 4, 169, 170

Phillips, A., 45, 46–7, 54
philosophy
  analytical, 3–4, 20, 21, 22, 23, 42
  Continental, 3–4
  existentialist, 4, 67, 68, 81
  hermeneutic, 3–4, 147, 149
  sceptical, 4–5
Plamenatz, J., 22, 23
Plato, 21, 28, 35, 37, 49
pluralism, radical, 10–12
Poland, 117, 156, 157, 167,
    168, 173
  Association for Free Enterprise, 173
  Communist Party, 168
  free market in, 173
  Solidarity movement, 158, 167
Polanyi, M., 161–2
Popper, K., 27, 28–9, 32, 40, 41
positive liberty, 30
Potsdam conference, 96
Poulantzas, N., 26
pragmatism, 20–62
Prague uprising, 158
Prosser, T., 59

Quadragesimo Anno, 109, 110
Quinton, A., 22

Racek, V., 164
rational choice theory, 42
Rawls, J., 42, 52, 87, 151
Raz, J., 48, 49
Reagan, R., 117
Rechsstaat, 97, 107, 108, 109, 110,
    111, 112, 113
Red Brigades, 134, 135
relativism, 3, 4, 6, 7, 49, 52,
    147, 148
religion, 100, 132, 147–8
Renault, A., 92
Resistance movement
  in France, 63, 65, 66
  in Italy, 126, 127, 131, 140, 151
Revel, J-F., 73
Rights of Man, 73
Roman, J., 87
Röpke, W., 109, 110
Rosanvallon, P., 68

Rousseau, J. J., 46, 129
rule of law
  in Britain, 34, 54
  in East-Central Europe, 157, 171
  in France, 75, 89
  in Germany, 99, 104, 106, 107, 112
  in Italy, 112, 135, 142, 143
Rumania, 117
Rupnik, J., 158, 159, 167
Russell, B., 3
Russia, 11, 156, 163, 164, 165, 166, 175
  Revolution, 65
  see also Soviet Union

Sandel, M., 87
Santayana, G., 4, 5, 180–1
Sartre, J-P., 66–7, 68, 69, 82, 92
Saussure, F. de, 7
Schleyer, H-M., 18
Schmitt, C., 115, 120, 122, 124, 185,
    186, 187
Schnapper, D., 90, 91
Schuman, R., 70
Schumpeter, J. A., 141
Schütz, A., 4
Scotland, 60
Scruton, R., 43, 44, 60, 170
Second World War, 1, 4, 13, 70, 78, 119,
    123, 155, 156, 165, 180
Shils, E., 182
Siedentop, L., 184
Silone, I., 134
Šimecka, M., 166
Singapore, 143
Skinner, Q., 30, 31, 55
Slovakia, 156, 174
Smith, A., 91, 181, 182, 186
social democracy
  in Britain, 25–7, 29, 32, 40
  in Germany, 68
  in Italy, 140–4
social homogeneity, 10–12
social market, 109–10
socialism, 21, 110, 111, 112
Socialisme ou Barbarie, 79
Socialist Party
  in France, 63
  in Italy, 144, 150

Solidarity movement, 158, 167
Sollers, P., 72
Solzhenitsyn, A., 72
Sontheimer, K., 110
Soviet Union, 1, 7, 13, 18, 19, 65, 71, 72,
    73, 79, 86, 96, 97, 98, 103, 105, 118,
    120, 125, 146, 157, 161, 167, 173,
    174, 176, 185
  communism, 70, 72
  occupation of East Berlin, 95, 96
  see also Russia
Sozialstaat, 107, 108, 109, 110, 111,
    112, 113
Spadolini, G., 131
Spinoza, B. de, 135, 136
Stalin, J., 28, 79, 123
Stalinism, 19, 26, 71, 80
Staniszkis, J., 158
Stein, D., 118
Sternberger, D., 112, 113
Stone, A., 183
Storace, F., 144
Strachey, J., 23
Strauss, B., 119
Strauss, L., 101, 102
syndicalism, 70

Talmon, J. L., 73
Taylor, C., 87, 88
Tel Quel, 72
Tempo presente, 131
terrorism, 68, 135
Thatcher, M., 173
Thatcherism, 9
Third Force, 130, 131
Third Republic, 8, 63
third way, 170, 171, 172
Thompson, E. P., 27
Tismaneanu, V., 174, 175, 176, 177
Titmuss, R.M., 24
Togliatti, P., 126, 131, 132, 134
totalitarianism, 2, 7, 9, 17, 18, 28, 29,
    32, 33, 70, 73, 74, 79, 84, 106,
    109, 118, 126, 129, 156, 157–67,
    167–74
  alternatives to, 167–74
  critique of, 157–67
  lie, 160–2, 168

trasformismo politics, 127, 128
Treitschke, H. von, 125
Tronti, M., 137
Trotskyism, 79, 80
Truman, H. S., 126
Tung, Mao-Tse, 176
Turgot, A-R-J., 91

United Kingdom (UK)
  see Britain
United Nations (UN), 14, 53
  Declaration of Human Rights, 53
United States of America (USA),
    14, 18, 42, 72, 86, 90, 91,
    98, 103, 105, 106, 118,
    119, 120, 126, 131, 142,
    146, 186, 187
  New Deal, 123

Vajda, M., 173
Valéry, P., 13, 69
Vattimo, G., 146–9
Veca, S., 151
Velvet Revolutions, 155, 156, 174–5,
    175–7
Verba, S., 110
Verfassungspatriotismus, 112
Vichy, 18, 63, 64, 65
Voegelin, E., 20, 21, 98, 101,
    102, 103

Wales, 60
Walser, M., 120, 121
Walzer, M., 87
Weber, M., 84
Weimar Republic, 33, 83, 96,
    104, 122
Weissmann, K., 119
Weldon, T. D., 3, 20, 21
welfare state, 7–10, 19,
    178, 179
  in Britain, 8, 25
  Continental model, 8–9
  in France, 8
  in Germany, 8
Werfel, F., 166
White Paper on European
    Governance, 184

Wiatr, J., 158
Williams, R., 25
Wittgenstein, L. 3
Wojtyla, K., 170
Wootton, B., 24
world economy, 13, 14
world government, 14

Yalta, 163, 165
Young Freedom, 118
Yugoslavia, 156, 174

Zitelmann, R., 118, 119, 123
Žižek, S., 53
Zolo, D., 140, 142–3